LEGENDS
OF THE TOUR

JAN CLEIJNE

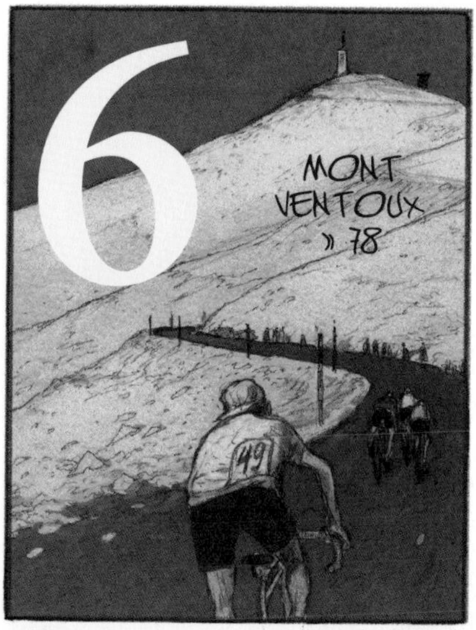
6
MONT VENTOUX » 78

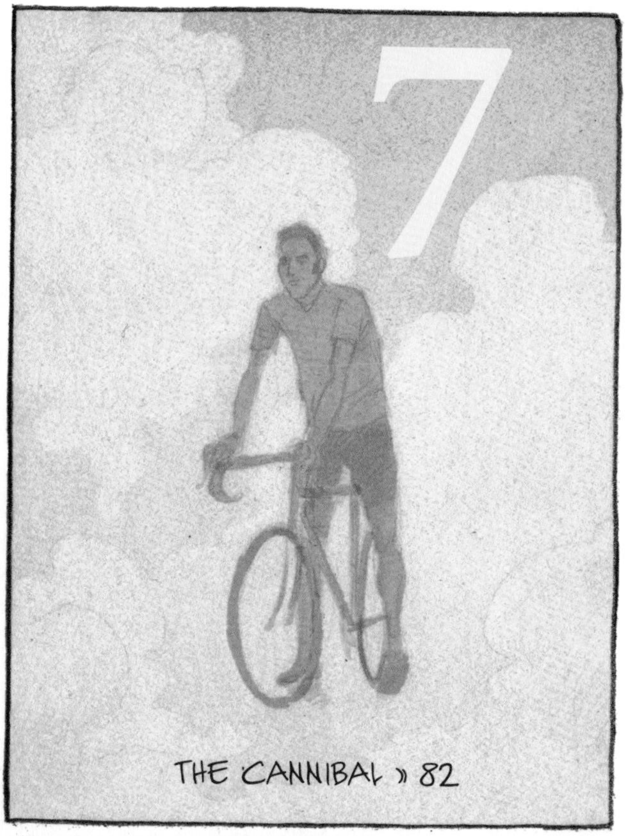
7
THE CANNIBAL » 82

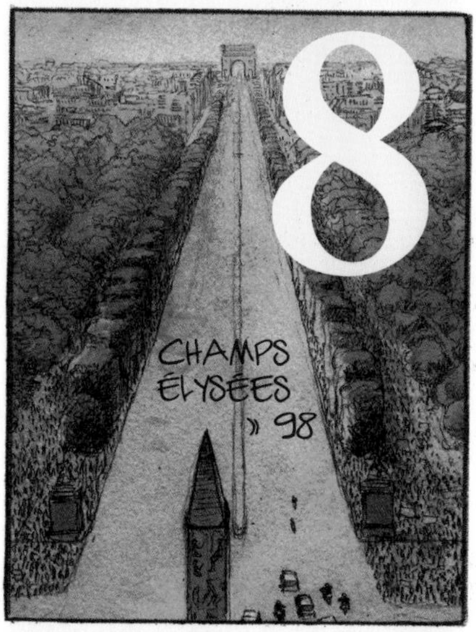
8
CHAMPS ÉLYSÉES » 98

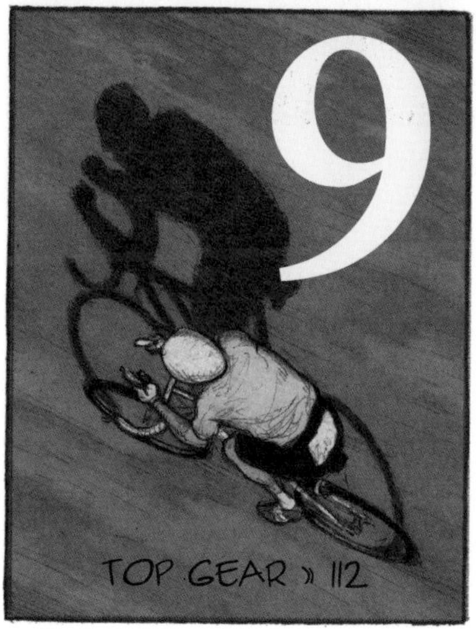
9
TOP GEAR » 112

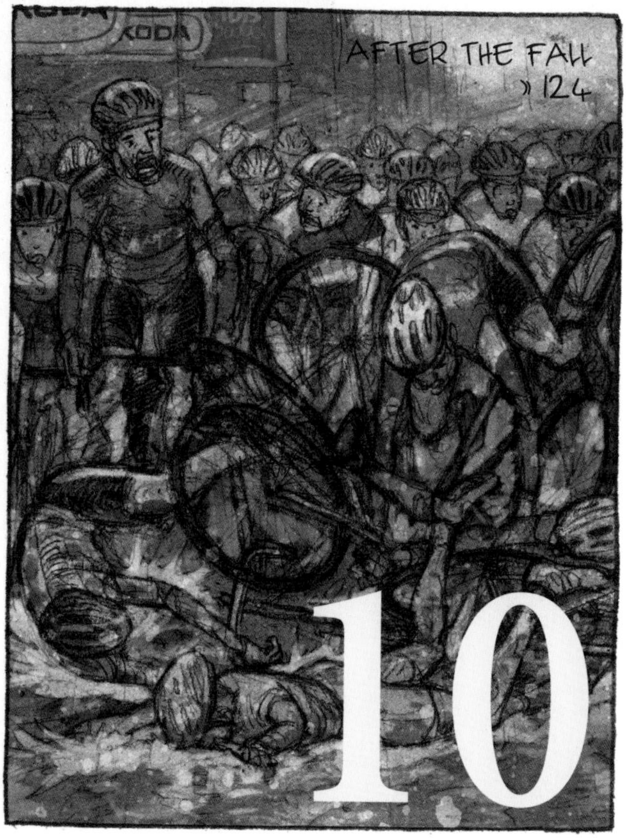
AFTER THE FALL » 124
10

IN THE BEGINNING

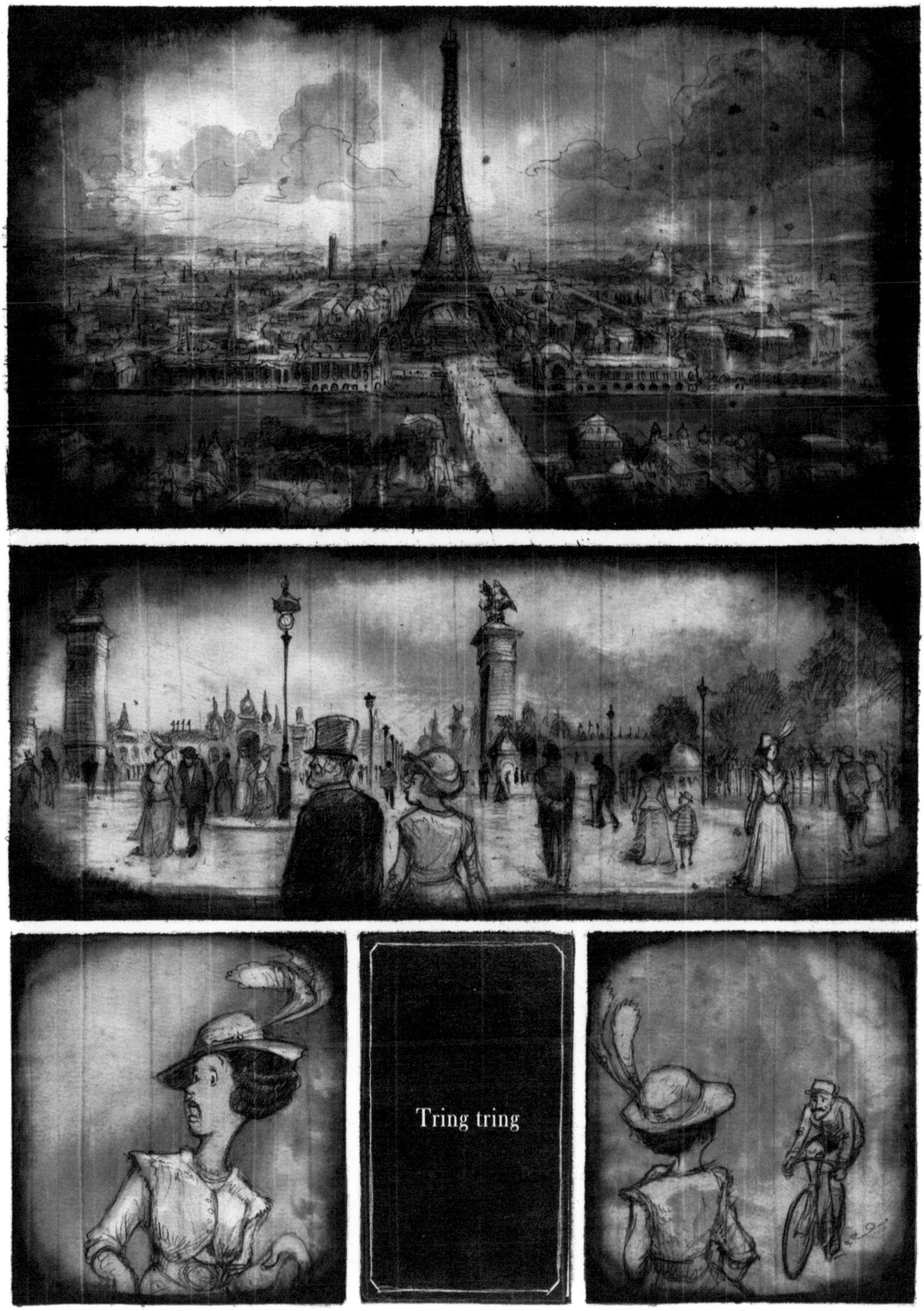
Tring tring

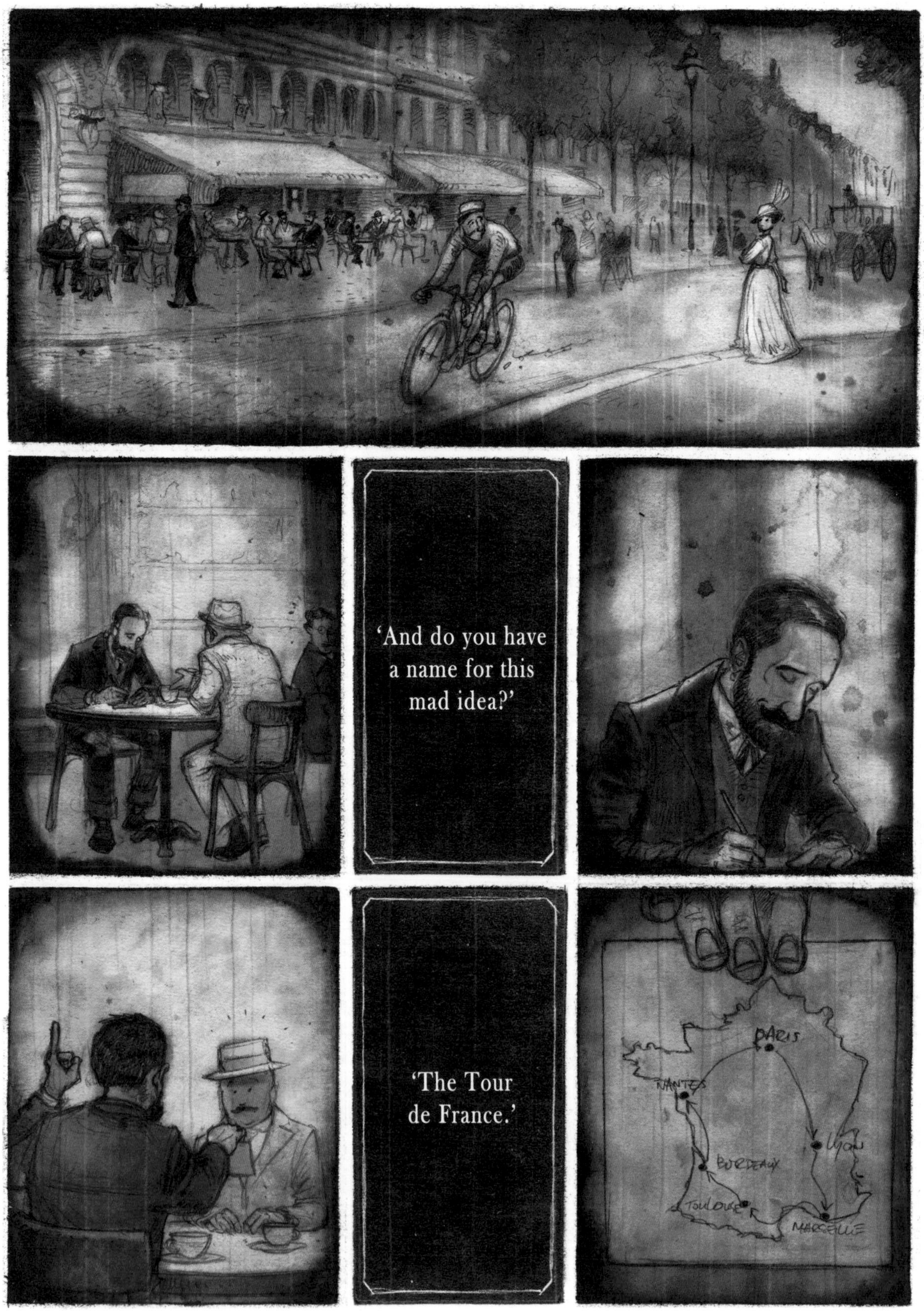
'And do you have a name for this mad idea?'
'The Tour de France.'
PARIS
NANTES
LYON
BORDEAUX
TOULOUSE
MARSEILLE

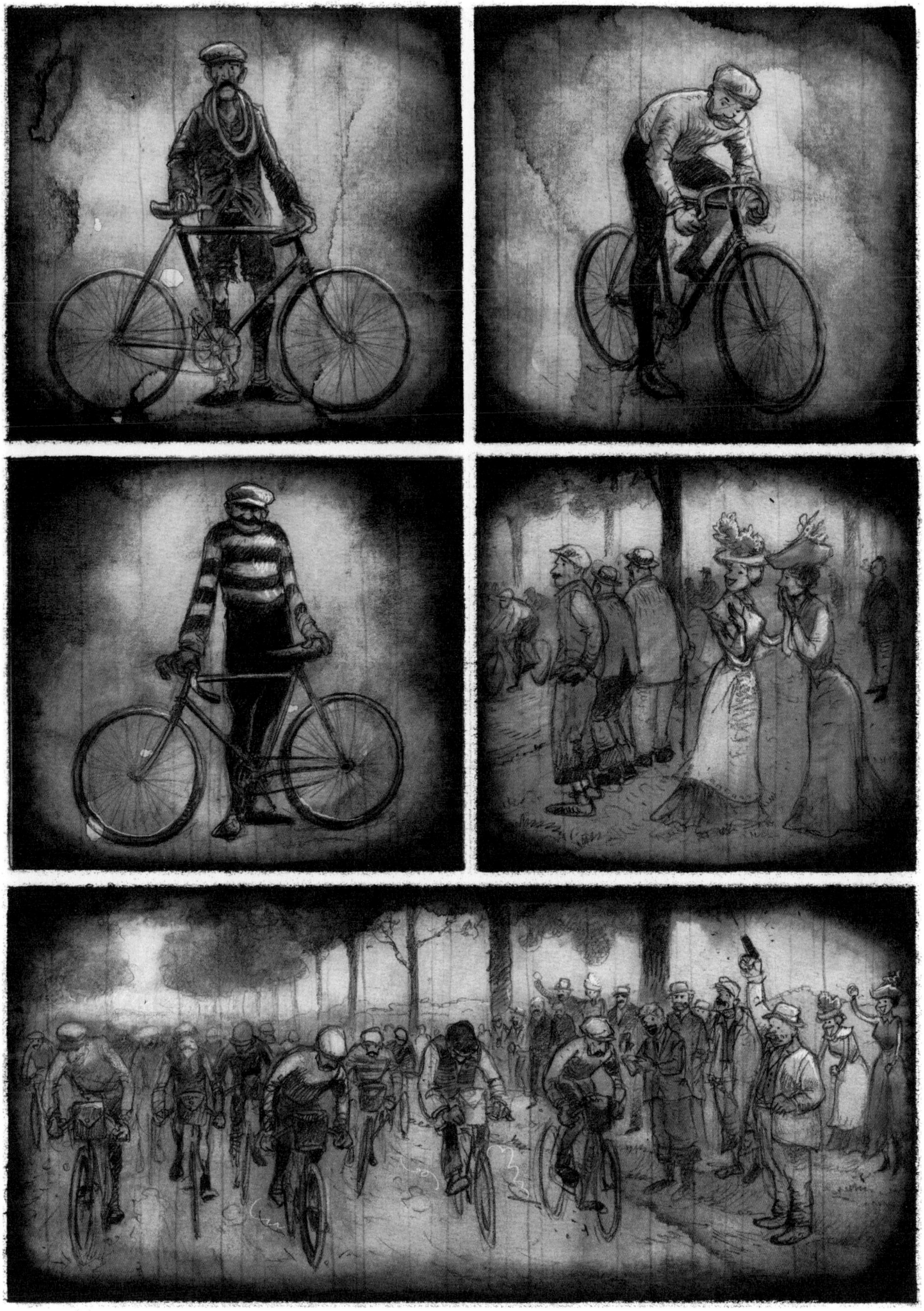

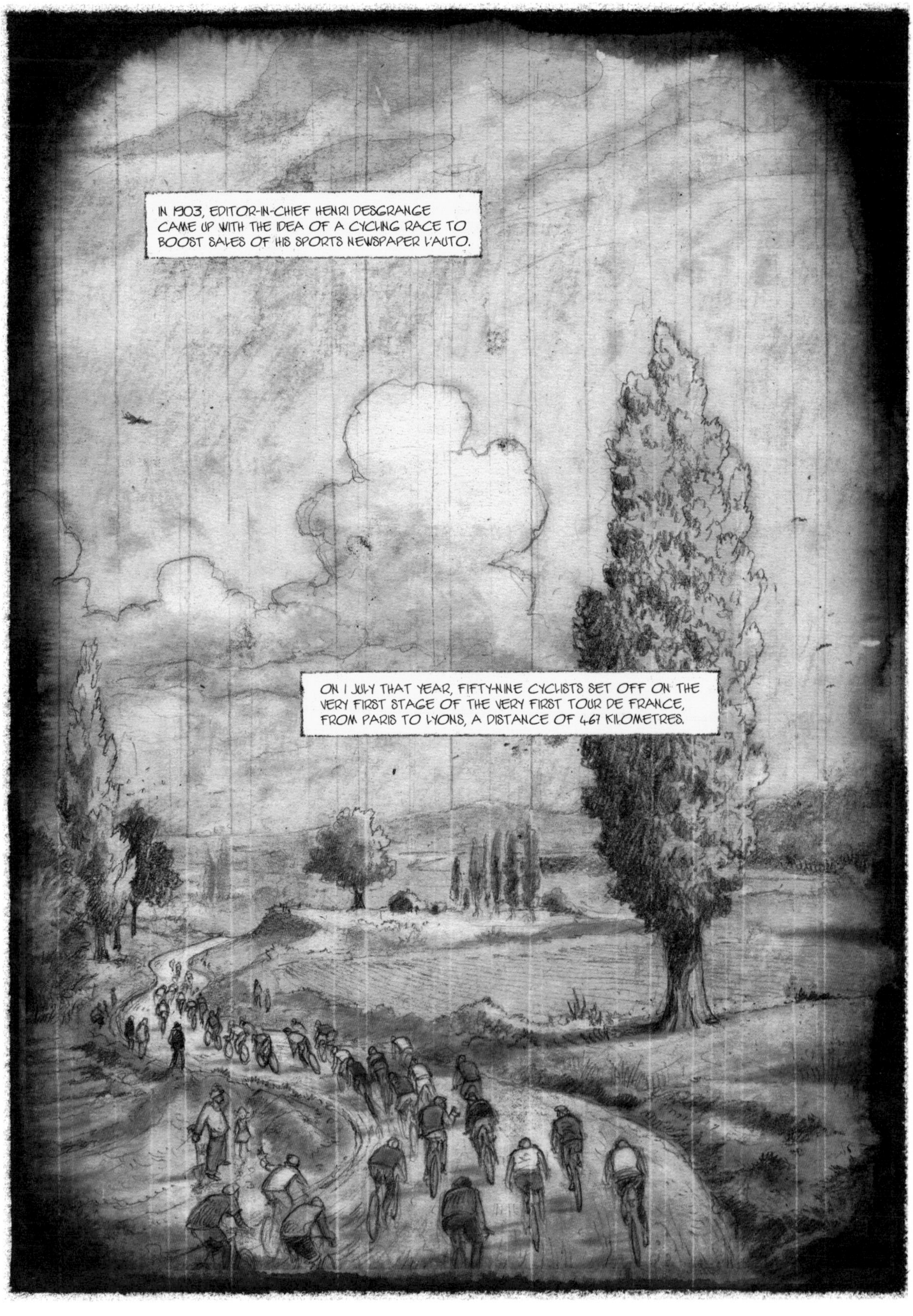
IN 1903, EDITOR-IN-CHIEF HENRI DESGRANGE CAME UP WITH THE IDEA OF A CYCLING RACE TO BOOST SALES OF HIS SPORTS NEWSPAPER L'AUTO.
ON 1 JULY THAT YEAR, FIFTY-NINE CYCLISTS SET OFF ON THE VERY FIRST STAGE OF THE VERY FIRST TOUR DE FRANCE, FROM PARIS TO LYONS, A DISTANCE OF 467 KILOMETRES.

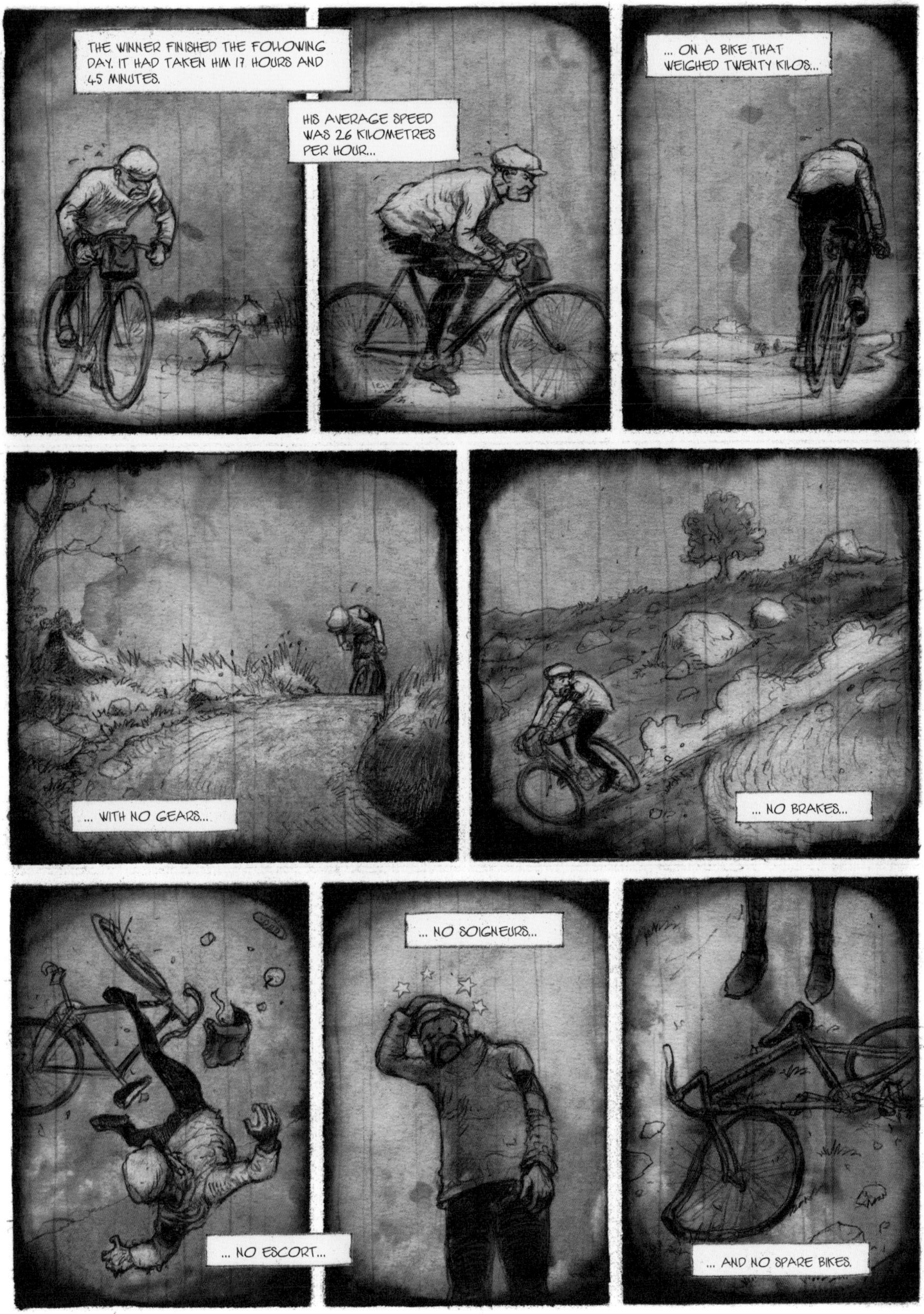
THE WINNER FINISHED THE FOLLOWING DAY. IT HAD TAKEN HIM 17 HOURS AND 45 MINUTES.
HIS AVERAGE SPEED WAS 26 KILOMETRES PER HOUR...
... ON A BIKE THAT WEIGHED TWENTY KILOS...
... WITH NO GEARS...
... NO BRAKES...
... NO ESCORT...
... NO SOIGNEURS...
... AND NO SPARE BIKES.

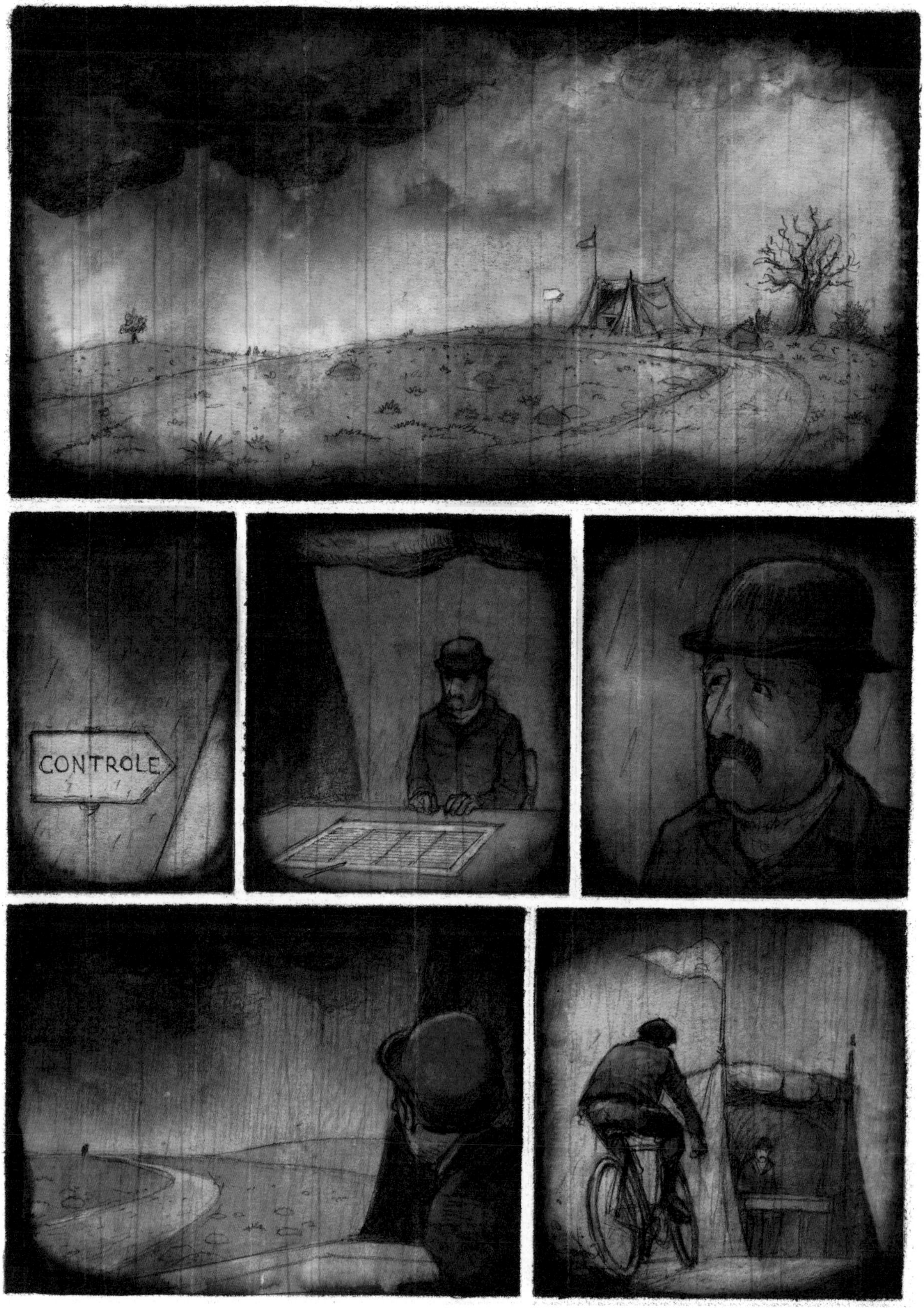
CONTROLE

'How far ahead is he?'

'I'd stay and shelter if I were you!'

MAURICE GARIN WON THE FIRST TOUR, FINISHING 2 HOURS AND 59 MINUTES AHEAD OF THE NEXT COMPETITOR, LUCIEN POTHIER. THIS IS STILL THE LARGEST GAP BETWEEN FIRST AND SECOND PLACES IN THE HISTORY OF THE TOUR DE FRANCE.

FEWER THAN ONE HUNDRED SPECTATORS WATCHED THE FIRST STAGE, BUT DESGRANGE WHIPPED UP INTEREST WITH DAILY REPORTS OF MAN VERSUS FRANCE IN L'AUTO. THREE WEEKS LATER, TEN THOUSAND PEOPLE CHEERED GARIN AS HE TOOK HIS VICTORY LAP. THE LEGEND WAS BORN.

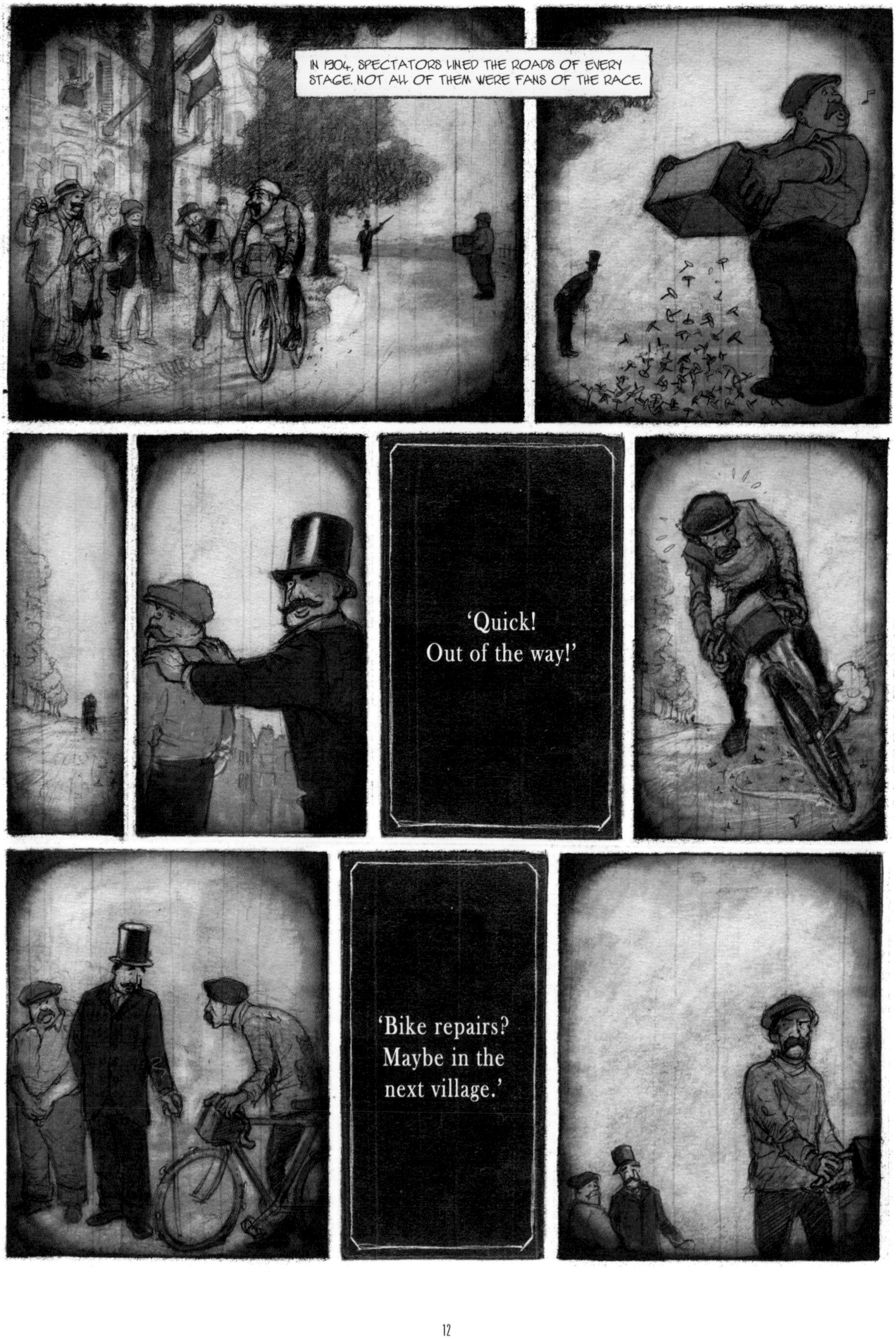
IN 1904, SPECTATORS LINED THE ROADS OF EVERY STAGE. NOT ALL OF THEM WERE FANS OF THE RACE.
'Quick! Out of the way!'
'Bike repairs? Maybe in the next village.'

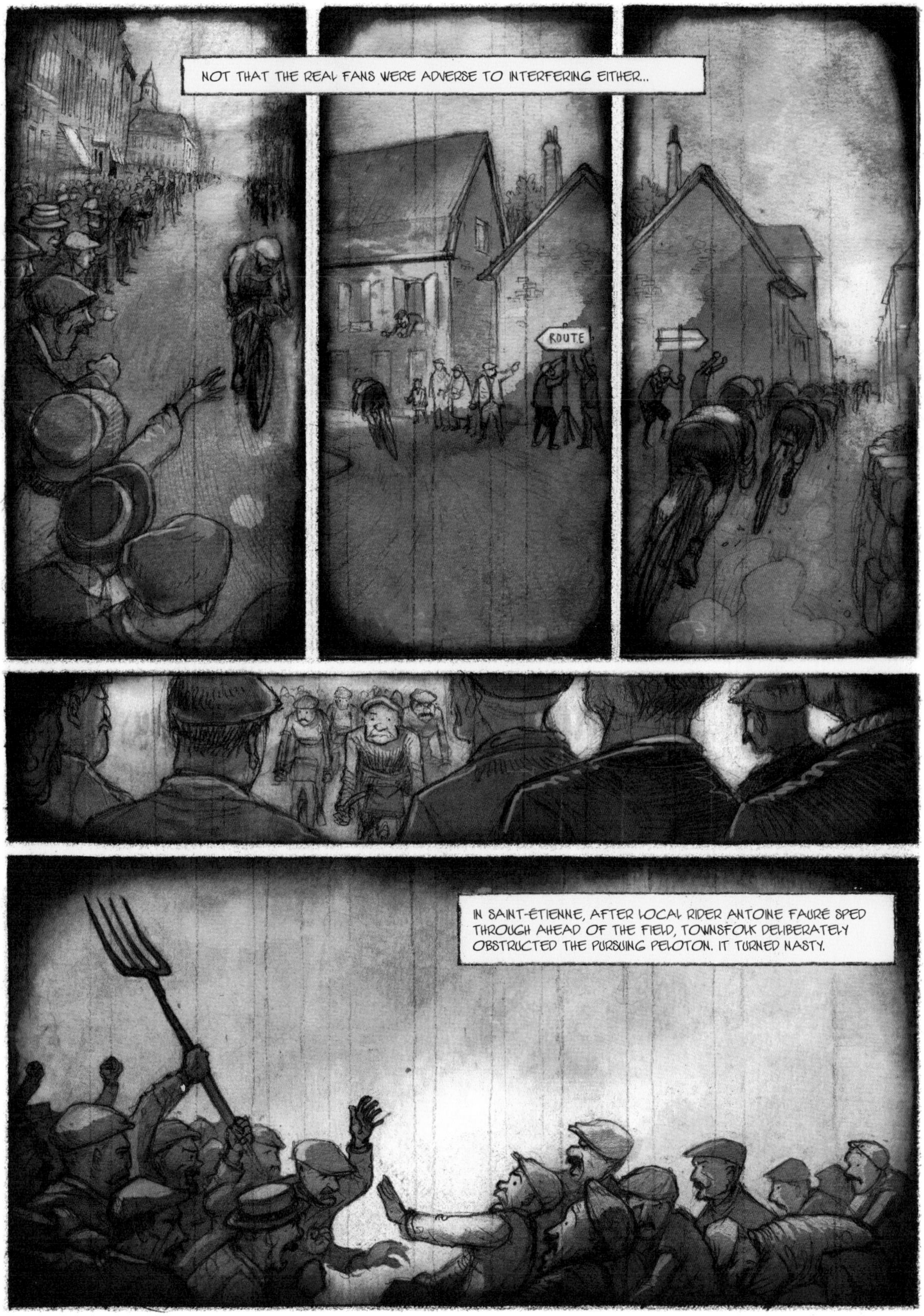
NOT THAT THE REAL FANS WERE ADVERSE TO INTERFERING EITHER...
ROUTE
IN SAINT-ÉTIENNE, AFTER LOCAL RIDER ANTOINE FAURE SPED THROUGH AHEAD OF THE FIELD, TOWNSFOLK DELIBERATELY OBSTRUCTED THE PURSUING PELOTON. IT TURNED NASTY.

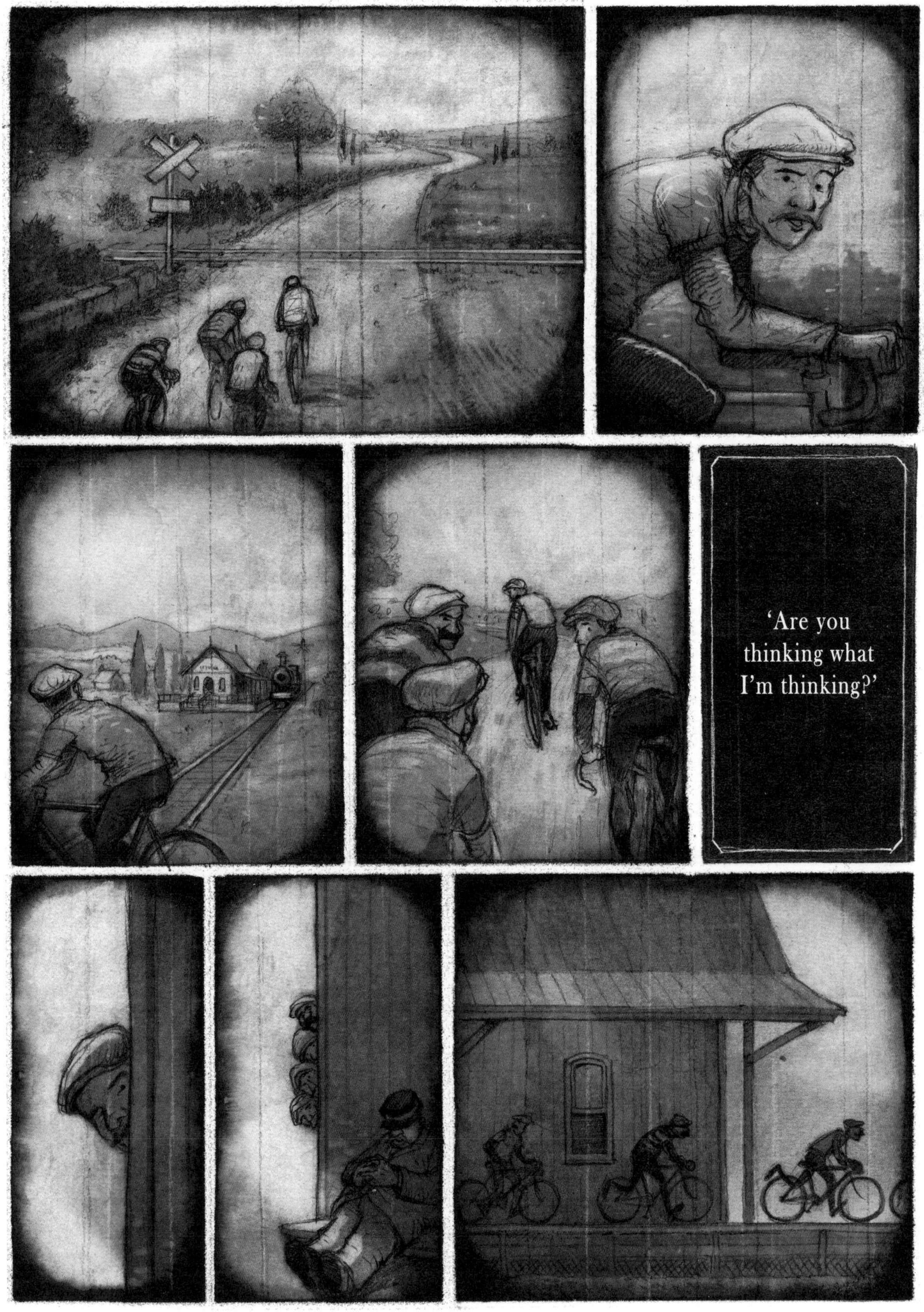
'Are you thinking what I'm thinking?'

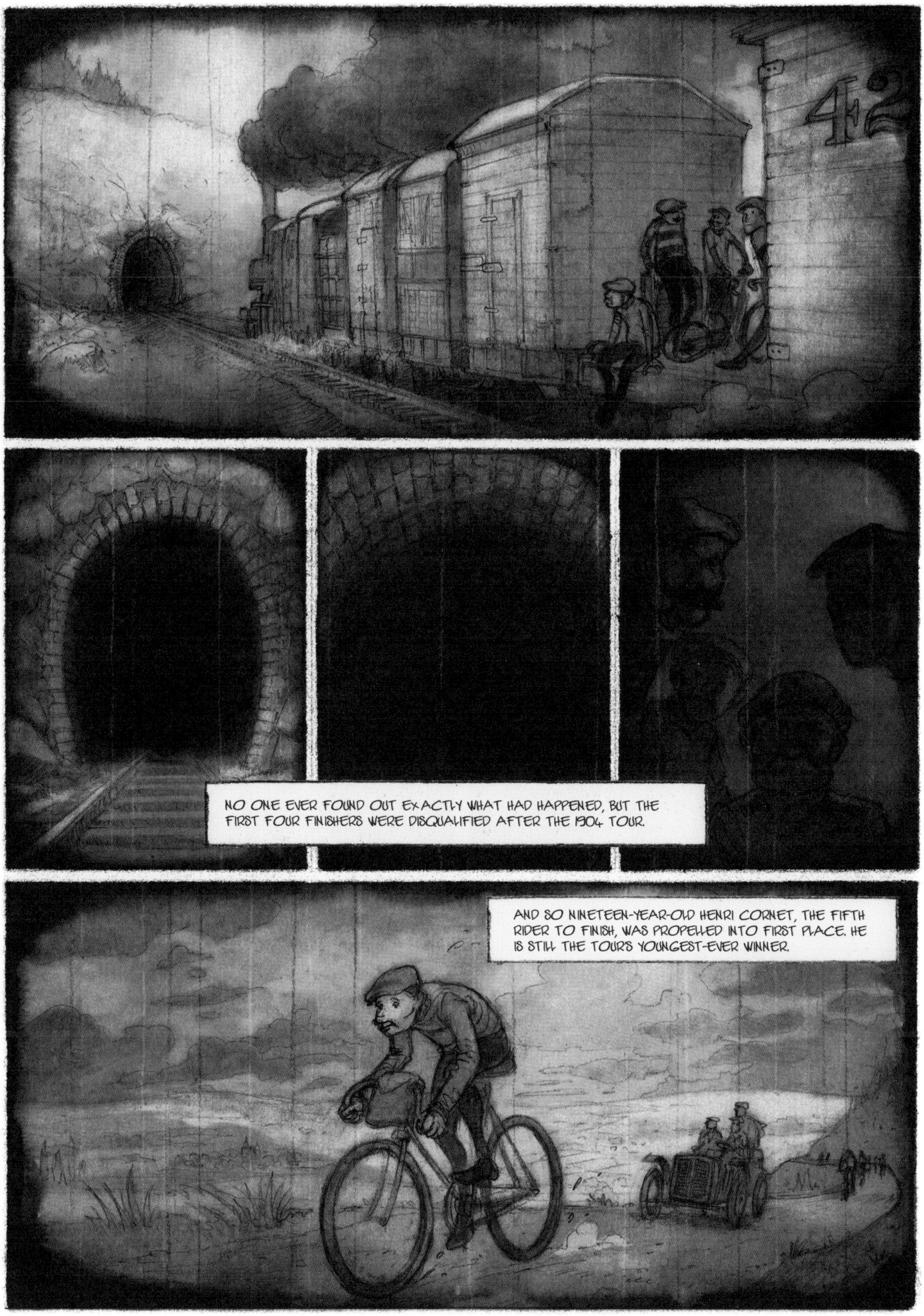
42
NO ONE EVER FOUND OUT EXACTLY WHAT HAD HAPPENED, BUT THE FIRST FOUR FINISHERS WERE DISQUALIFIED AFTER THE 1904 TOUR.
AND SO NINETEEN-YEAR-OLD HENRI CORNET, THE FIFTH RIDER TO FINISH, WAS PROPELLED INTO FIRST PLACE. HE IS STILL THE TOUR'S YOUNGEST-EVER WINNER.

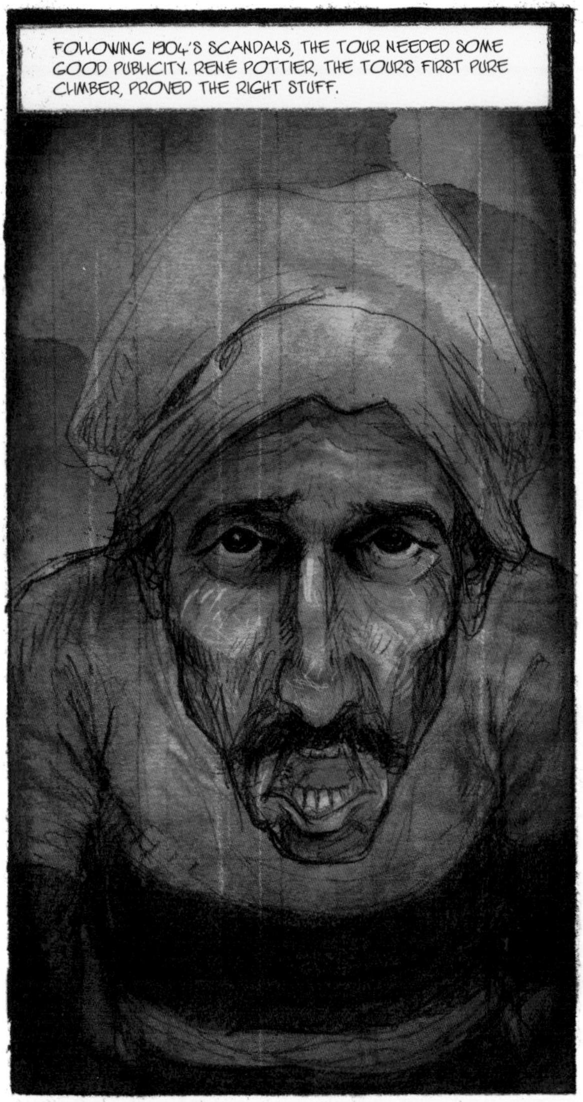
FOLLOWING 1904'S SCANDALS, THE TOUR NEEDED SOME GOOD PUBLICITY. RENÉ POTTIER, THE TOUR'S FIRST PURE CLIMBER, PROVED THE RIGHT STUFF.

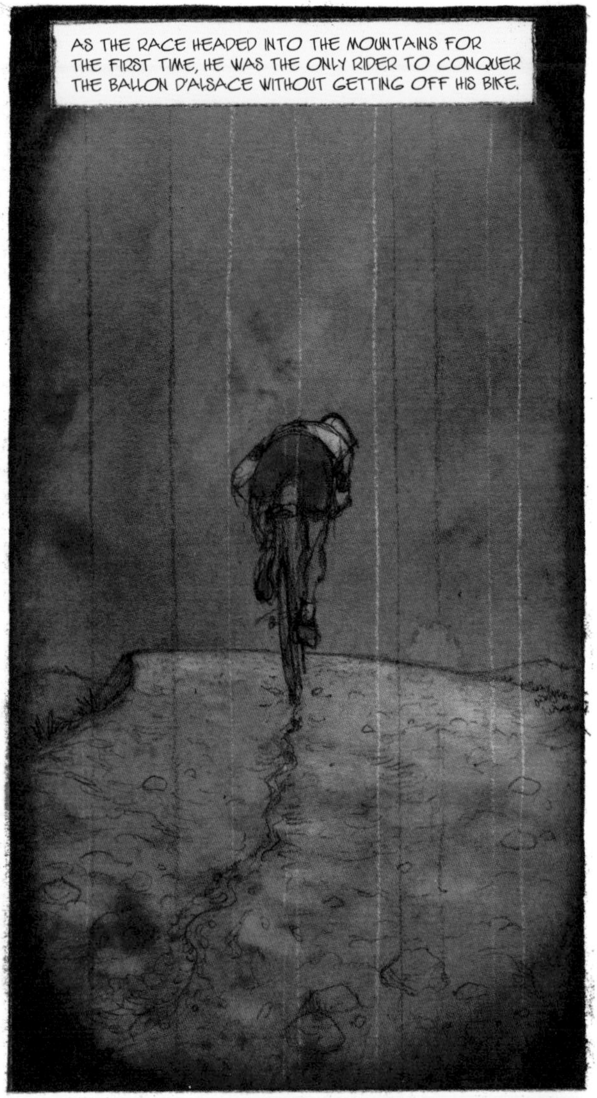
AS THE RACE HEADED INTO THE MOUNTAINS FOR THE FIRST TIME, HE WAS THE ONLY RIDER TO CONQUER THE BALLON D'ALSACE WITHOUT GETTING OFF HIS BIKE.

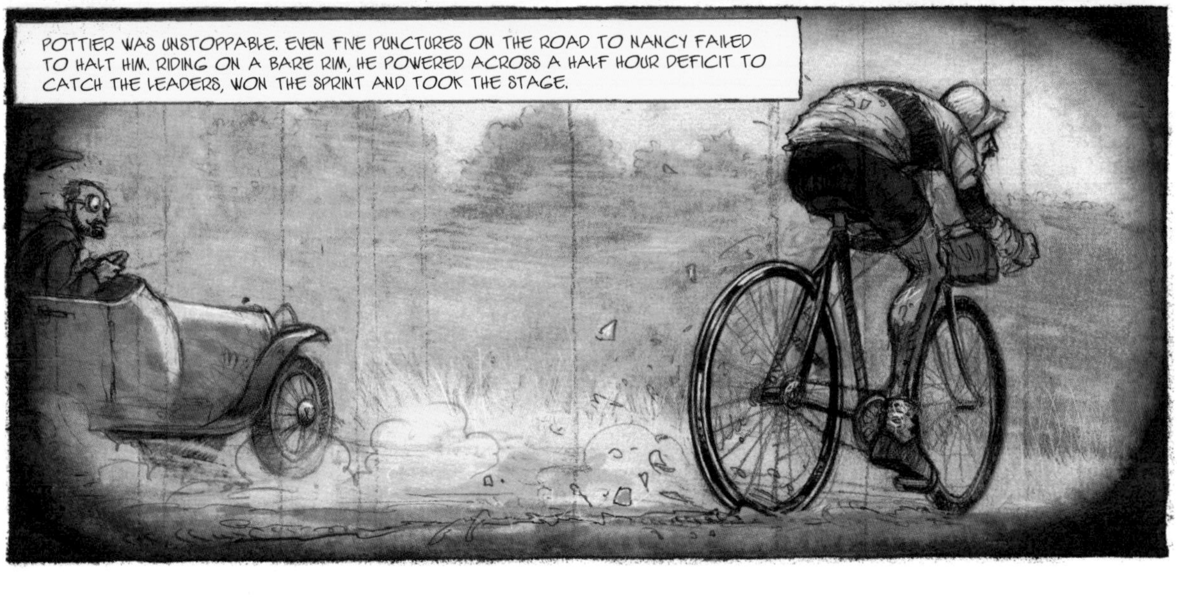
POTTIER WAS UNSTOPPABLE. EVEN FIVE PUNCTURES ON THE ROAD TO NANCY FAILED TO HALT HIM. RIDING ON A BARE RIM, HE POWERED ACROSS A HALF HOUR DEFICIT TO CATCH THE LEADERS, WON THE SPRINT AND TOOK THE STAGE.

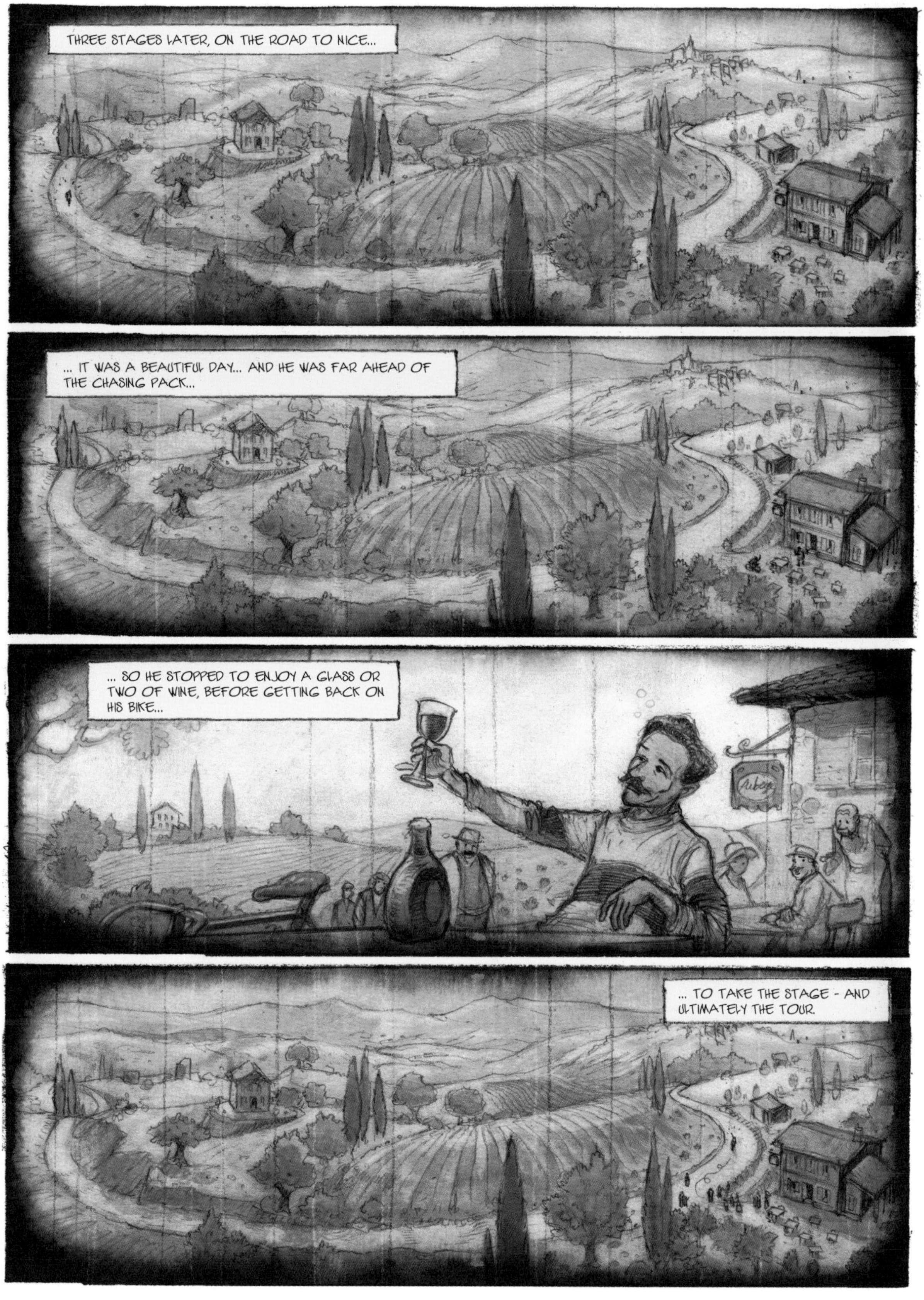
THREE STAGES LATER, ON THE ROAD TO NICE...
... IT WAS A BEAUTIFUL DAY... AND HE WAS FAR AHEAD OF THE CHASING PACK...
... SO HE STOPPED TO ENJOY A GLASS OR TWO OF WINE, BEFORE GETTING BACK ON HIS BIKE...
... TO TAKE THE STAGE - AND ULTIMATELY THE TOUR.

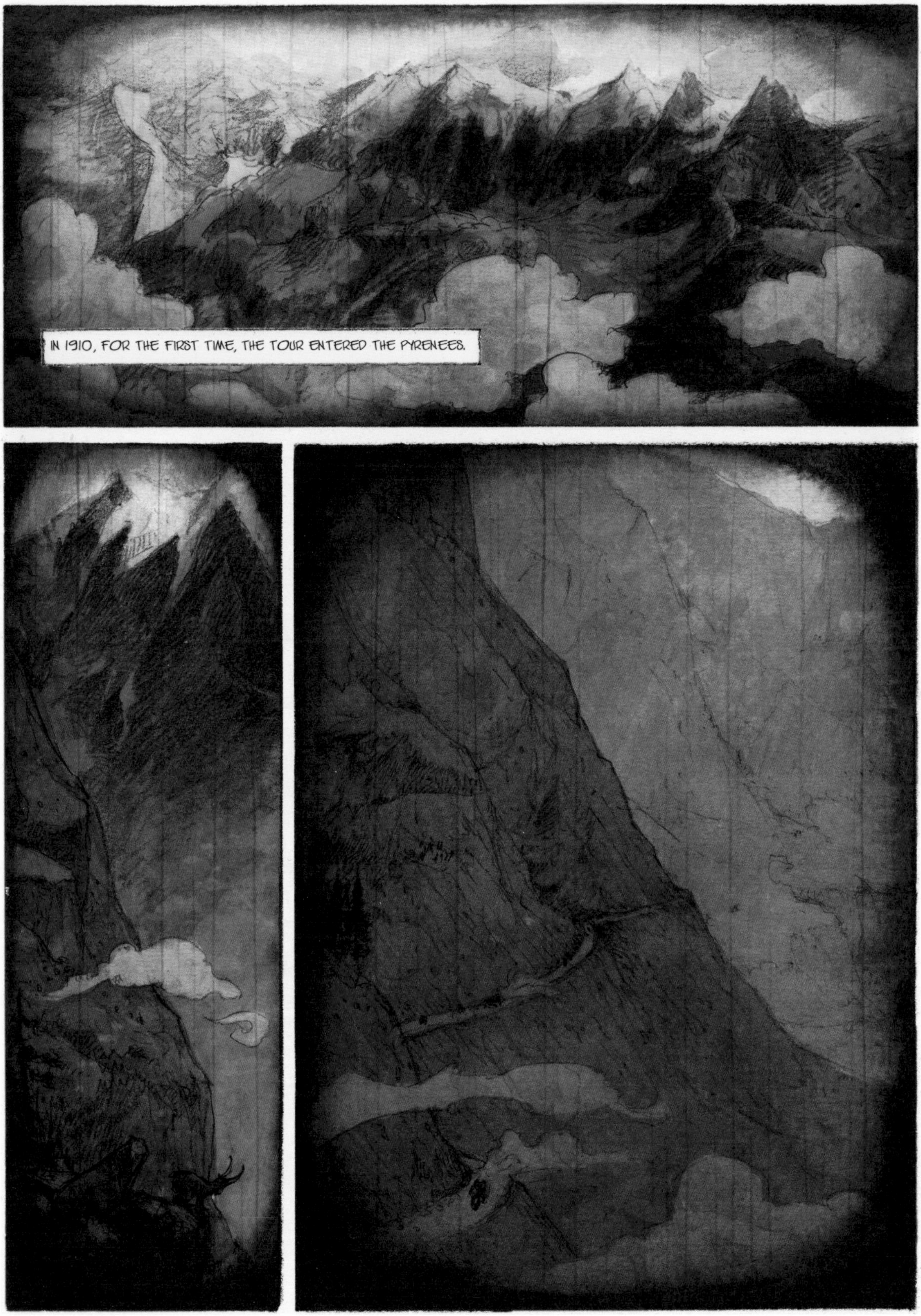
IN 1910, FOR THE FIRST TIME, THE TOUR ENTERED THE PYRENEES.

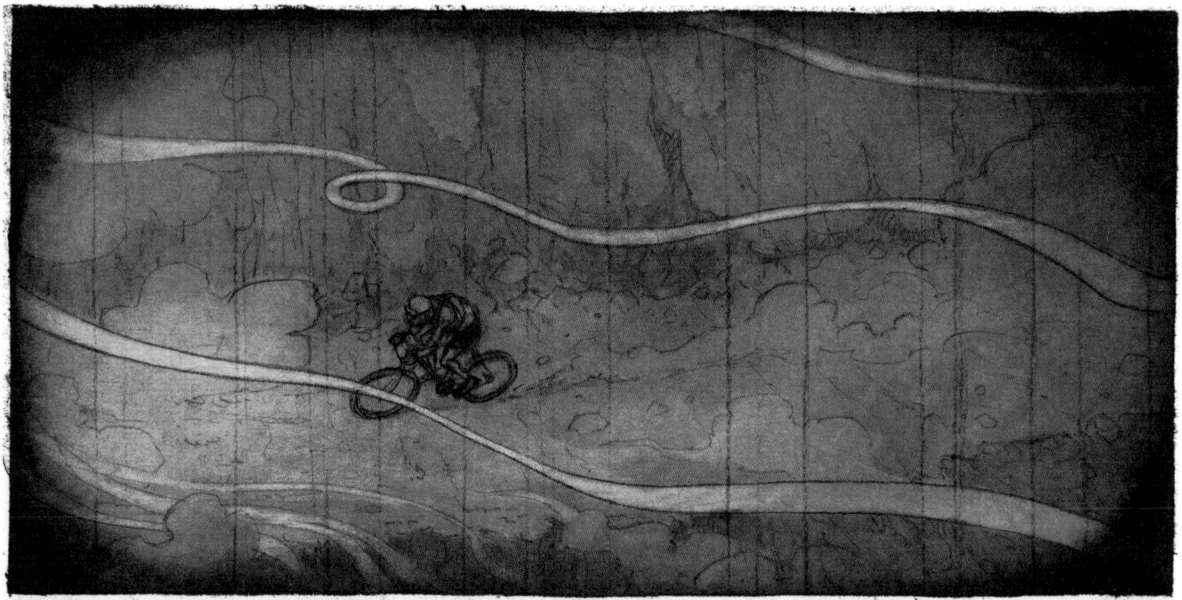

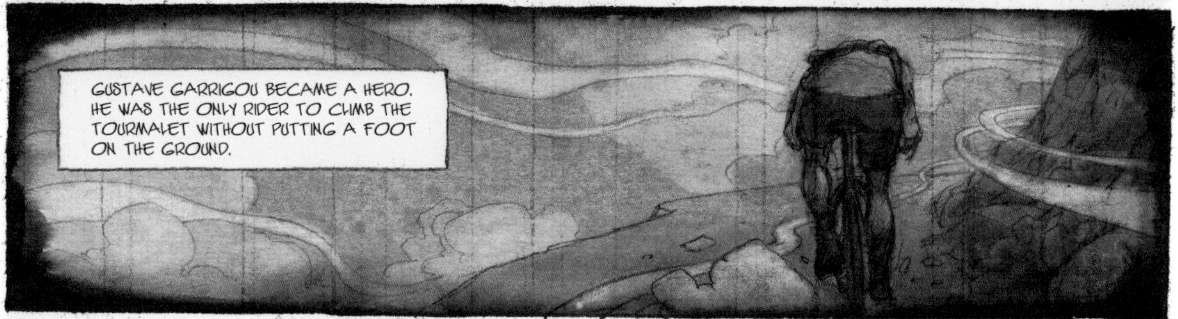
GUSTAVE GARRIGOU BECAME A HERO. HE WAS THE ONLY RIDER TO CLIMB THE TOURMALET WITHOUT PUTTING A FOOT ON THE GROUND.

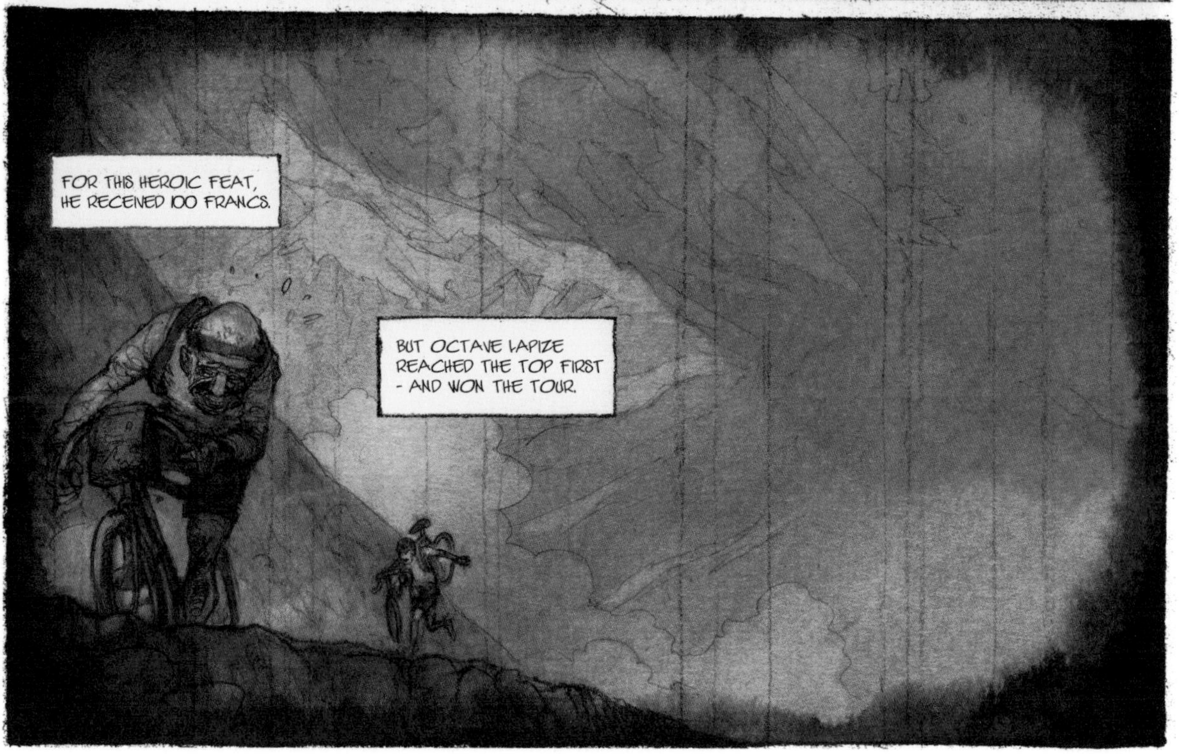
FOR THIS HEROIC FEAT, HE RECEIVED 100 FRANCS.
BUT OCTAVE LAPIZE REACHED THE TOP FIRST - AND WON THE TOUR.

THERE WERE OTHER WAYS OF BECOMING A LEGEND.

AS EUGENE CHRISTOPHE PROVED IN 1913.

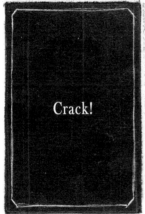

Crack!

DURING THE FIRST MOUNTAIN STAGE, WHILE HE WAS IN THE LEAD, HIS FORKS BROKE. NO HELP WAS ALLOWED. HE HAD TO WALK TO THE NEAREST VILLAGE, FIFTEEN KILOMETRES AWAY IN THE VALLEY BELOW.

CHRISTOPHE REPAIRED HIS BIKE HIMSELF AT THE FORGE IN SAINTE-MARIE-DE-CAMPAN, WITHOUT HELP OR INSTRUCTION.

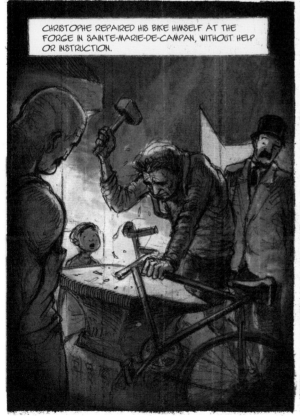

HE LOST THREE HOURS - AND THE TOUR.

TO ADD INSULT TO INJURY, A TOUR OFFICIAL SPOTTED A YOUNG BOY HELPING WITH THE FORGE BELLOWS. ANY ASSISTANCE WHATSOEVER WAS AGAINST THE RULES, SO CHRISTOPHE RECEIVED AN EXTRA TIME PENALTY OF THREE MINUTES.

TRUE HEROES

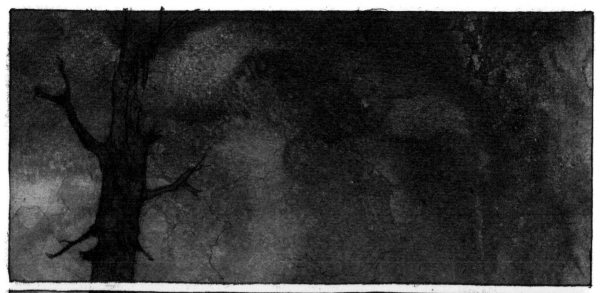

THERE WAS NO TOUR
BETWEEN 1914 AND 1918.

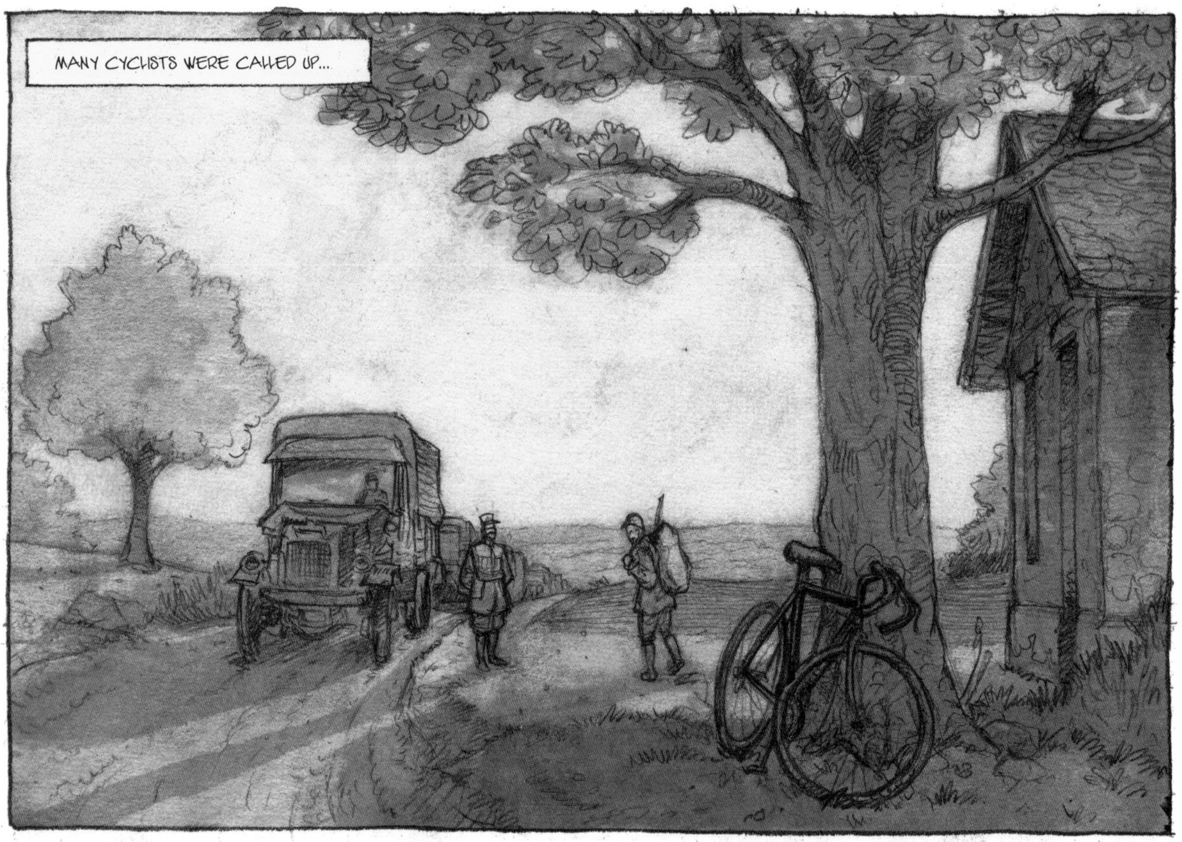
MANY CYCLISTS WERE CALLED UP...

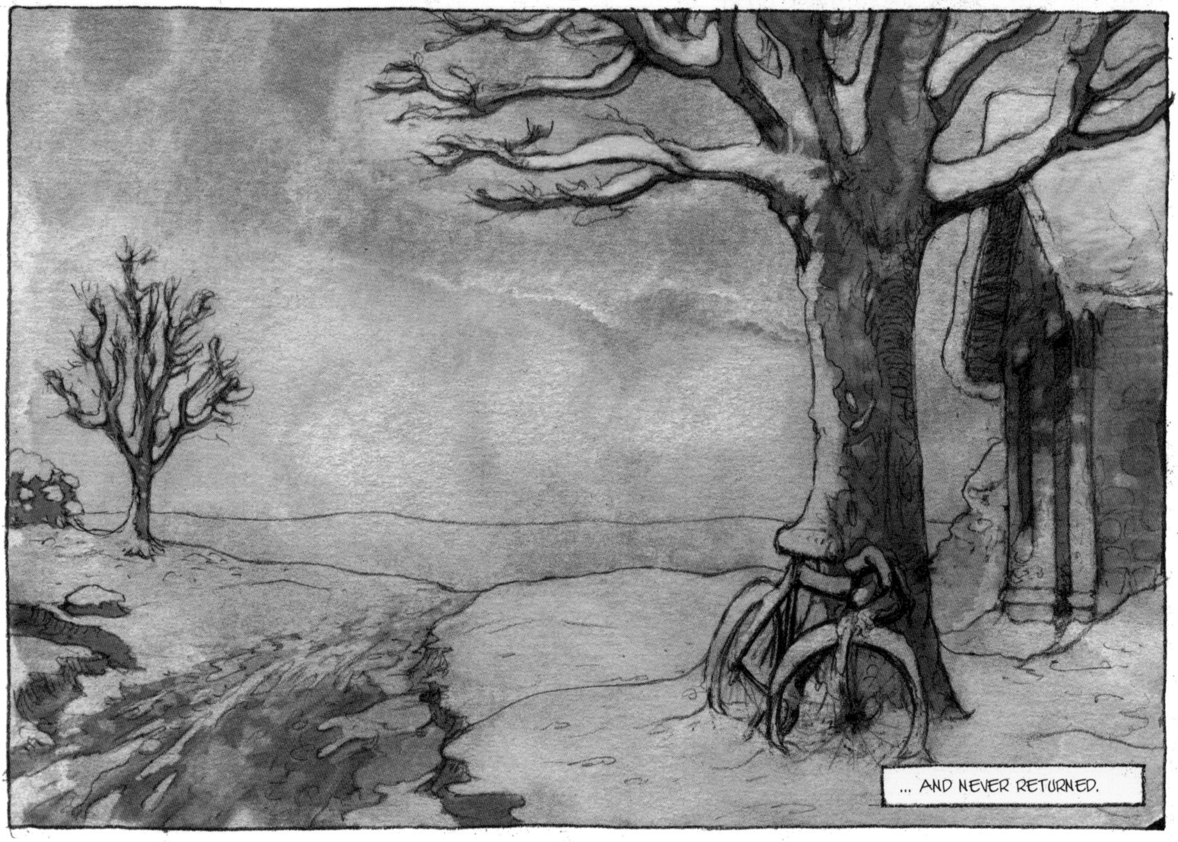
... AND NEVER RETURNED.

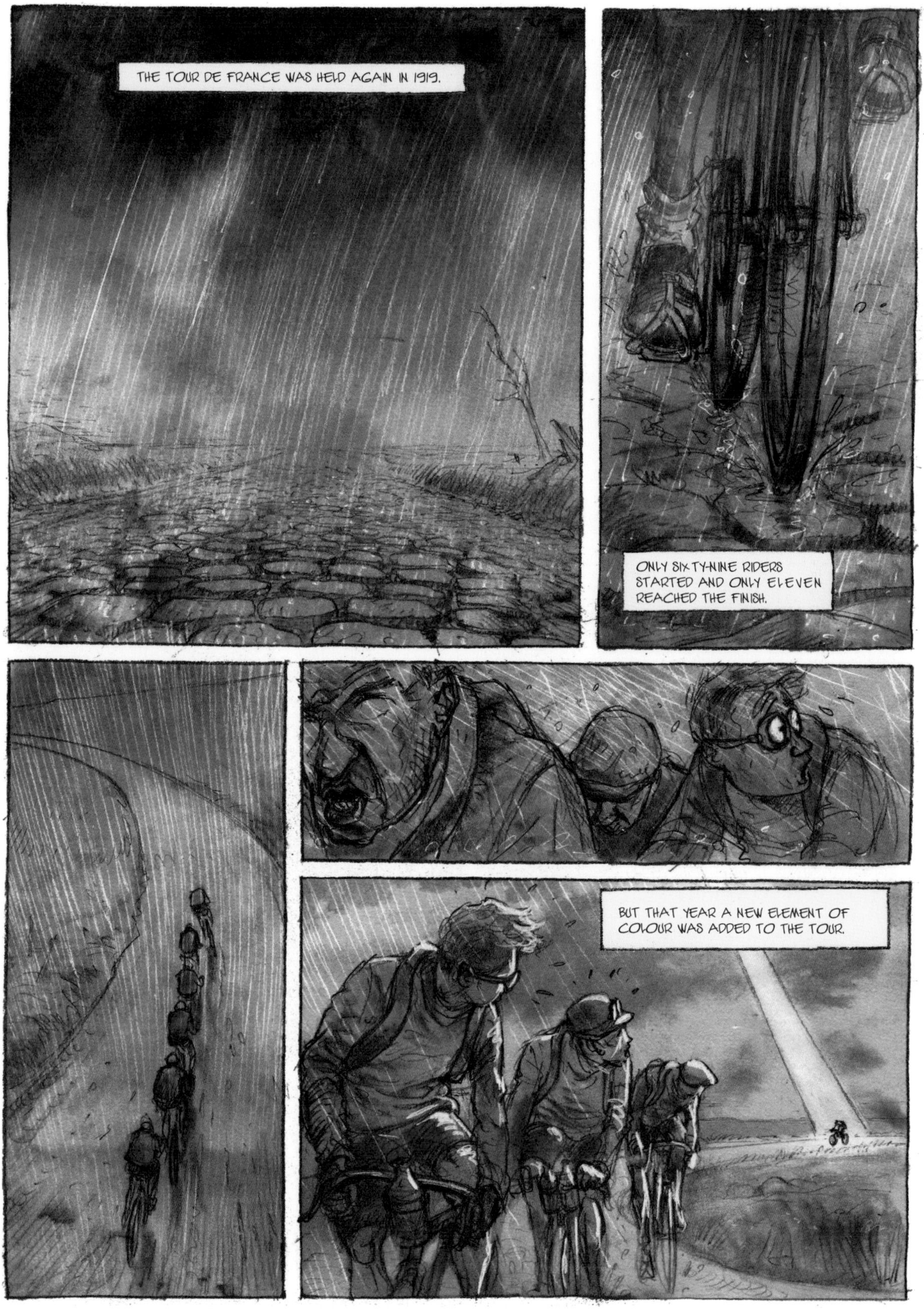
THE TOUR DE FRANCE WAS HELD AGAIN IN 1919.
ONLY SIXTY-NINE RIDERS STARTED AND ONLY ELEVEN REACHED THE FINISH.
BUT THAT YEAR A NEW ELEMENT OF COLOUR WAS ADDED TO THE TOUR.

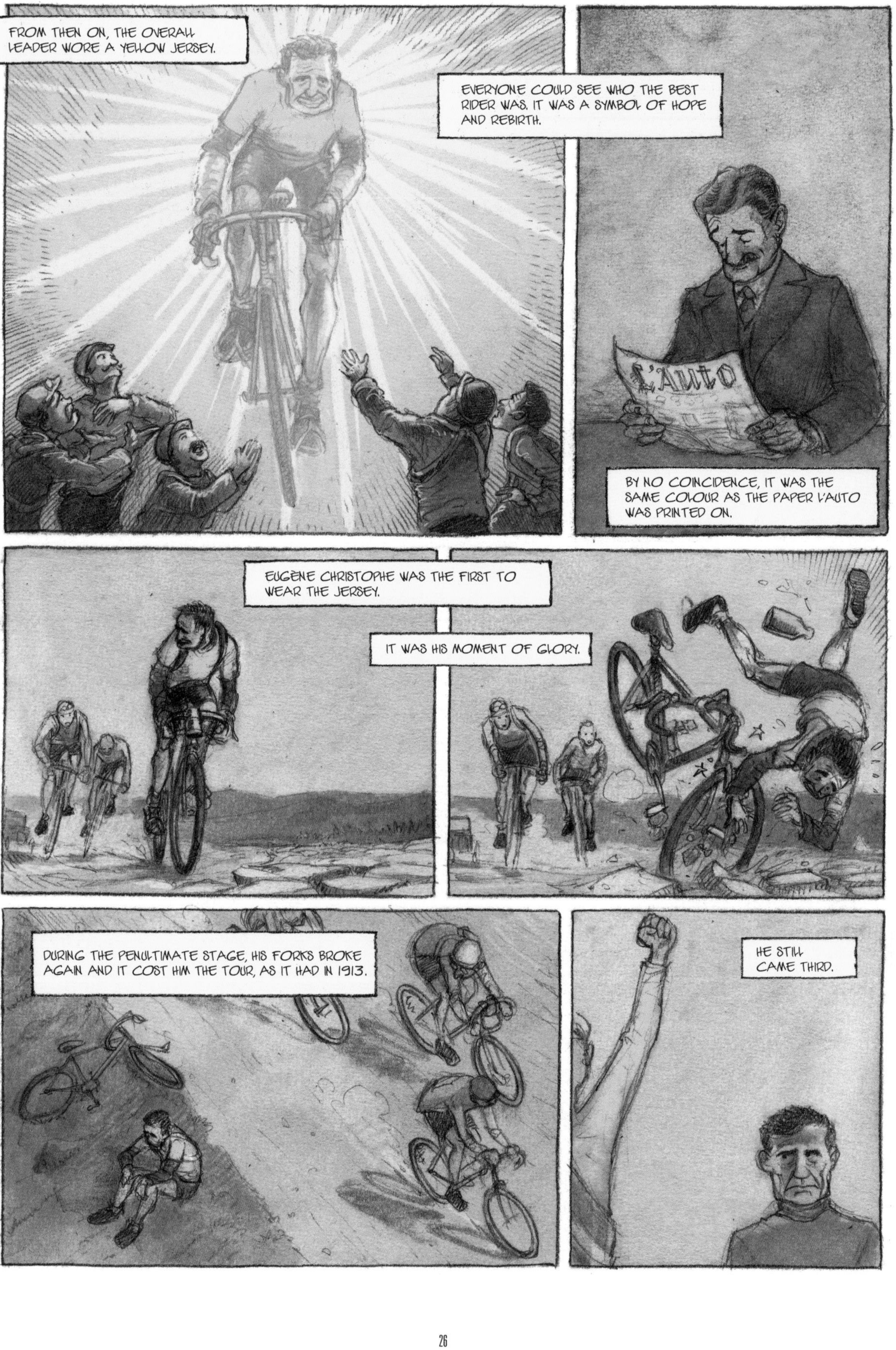
FROM THEN ON, THE OVERALL LEADER WORE A YELLOW JERSEY.
EVERYONE COULD SEE WHO THE BEST RIDER WAS. IT WAS A SYMBOL OF HOPE AND REBIRTH.
L'Auto
BY NO COINCIDENCE, IT WAS THE SAME COLOUR AS THE PAPER L'AUTO WAS PRINTED ON.
EUGÈNE CHRISTOPHE WAS THE FIRST TO WEAR THE JERSEY.
IT WAS HIS MOMENT OF GLORY.
DURING THE PENULTIMATE STAGE, HIS FORKS BROKE AGAIN AND IT COST HIM THE TOUR, AS IT HAD IN 1913.
HE STILL CAME THIRD.

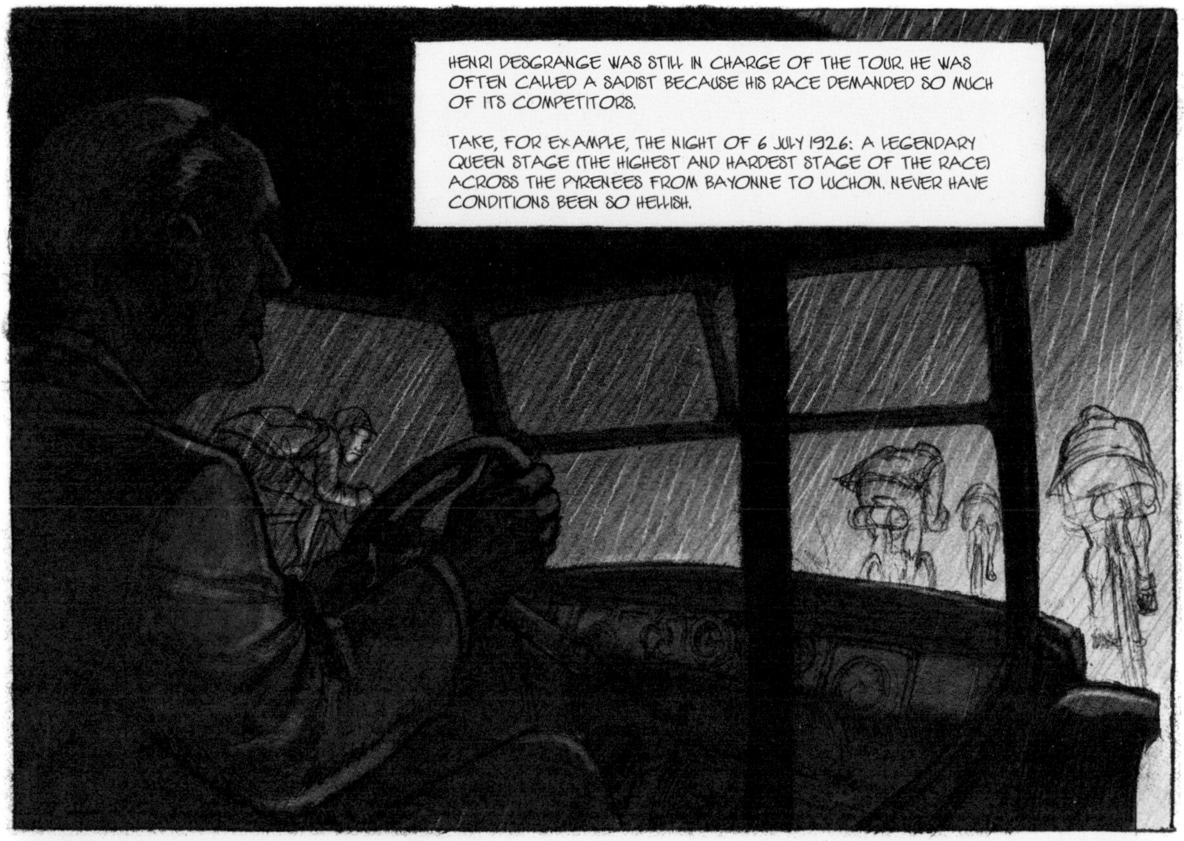
HENRI DESGRANGE WAS STILL IN CHARGE OF THE TOUR. HE WAS OFTEN CALLED A SADIST BECAUSE HIS RACE DEMANDED SO MUCH OF ITS COMPETITORS.
TAKE, FOR EXAMPLE, THE NIGHT OF 6 JULY 1926: A LEGENDARY QUEEN STAGE (THE HIGHEST AND HARDEST STAGE OF THE RACE) ACROSS THE PYRENEES FROM BAYONNE TO LUCHON. NEVER HAVE CONDITIONS BEEN SO HELLISH.

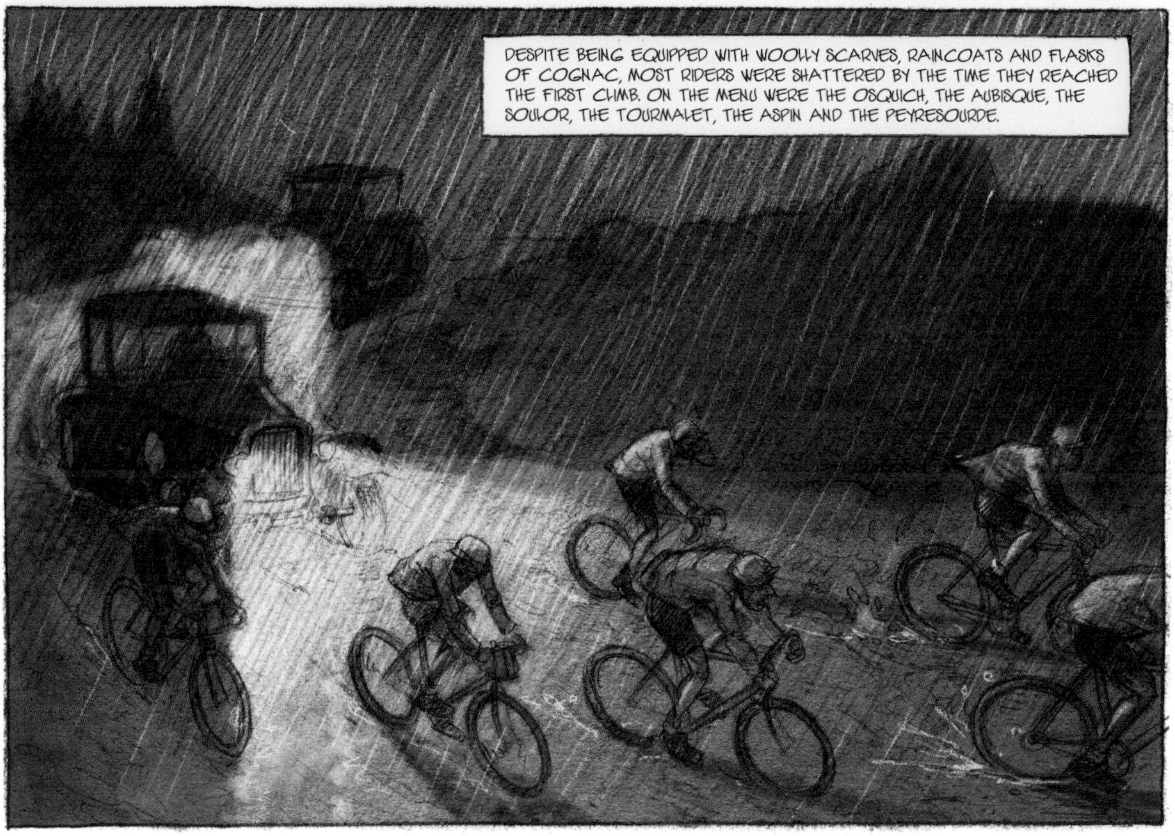
DESPITE BEING EQUIPPED WITH WOOLLY SCARVES, RAINCOATS AND FLASKS OF COGNAC, MOST RIDERS WERE SHATTERED BY THE TIME THEY REACHED THE FIRST CLIMB. ON THE MENU WERE THE OSQUICH, THE AUBISQUE, THE SOULOR, THE TOURMALET, THE ASPIN AND THE PEYRESOURDE.

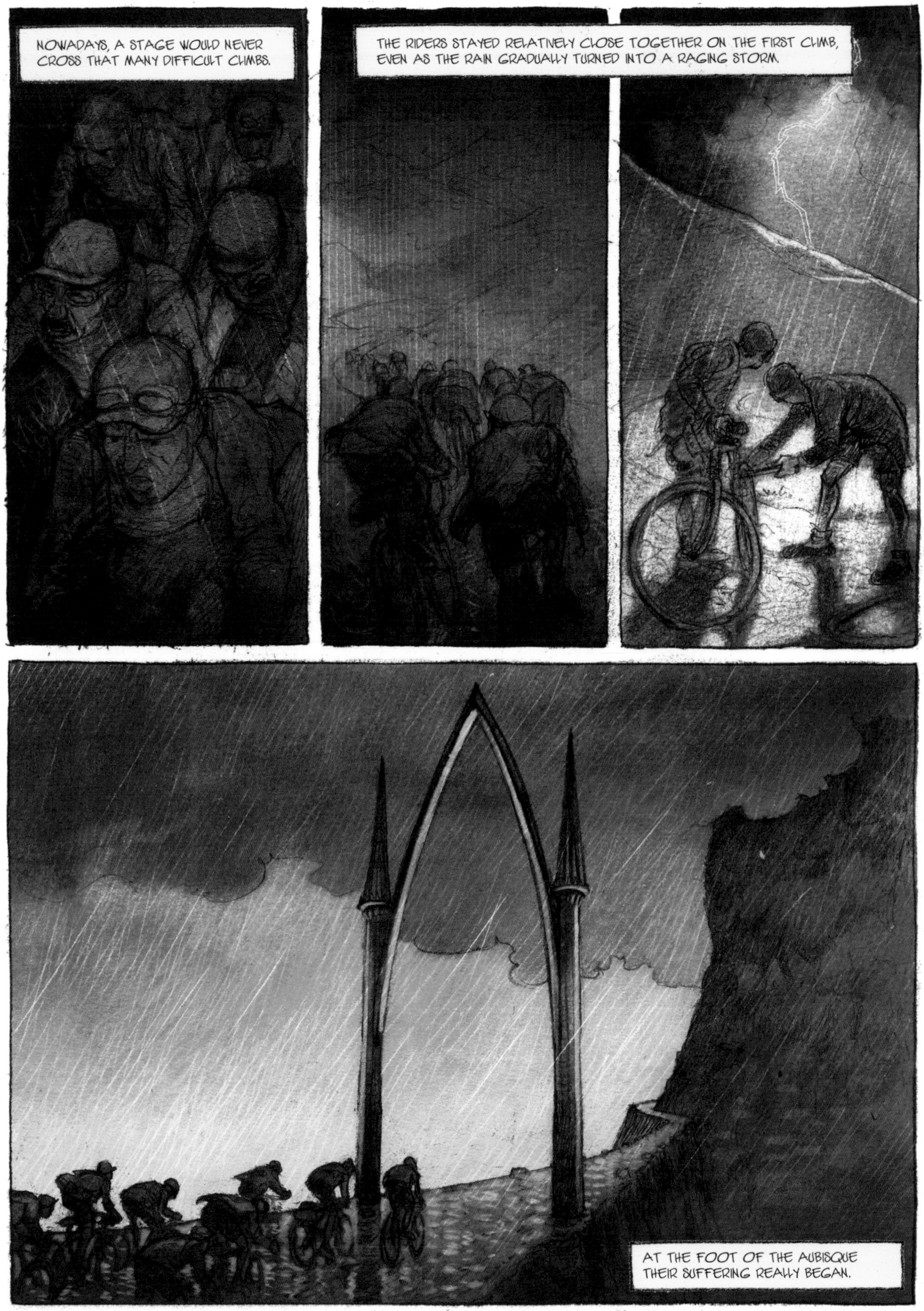
NOWADAYS, A STAGE WOULD NEVER CROSS THAT MANY DIFFICULT CLIMBS.
THE RIDERS STAYED RELATIVELY CLOSE TOGETHER ON THE FIRST CLIMB, EVEN AS THE RAIN GRADUALLY TURNED INTO A RAGING STORM.
AT THE FOOT OF THE AUBISQUE THEIR SUFFERING REALLY BEGAN.

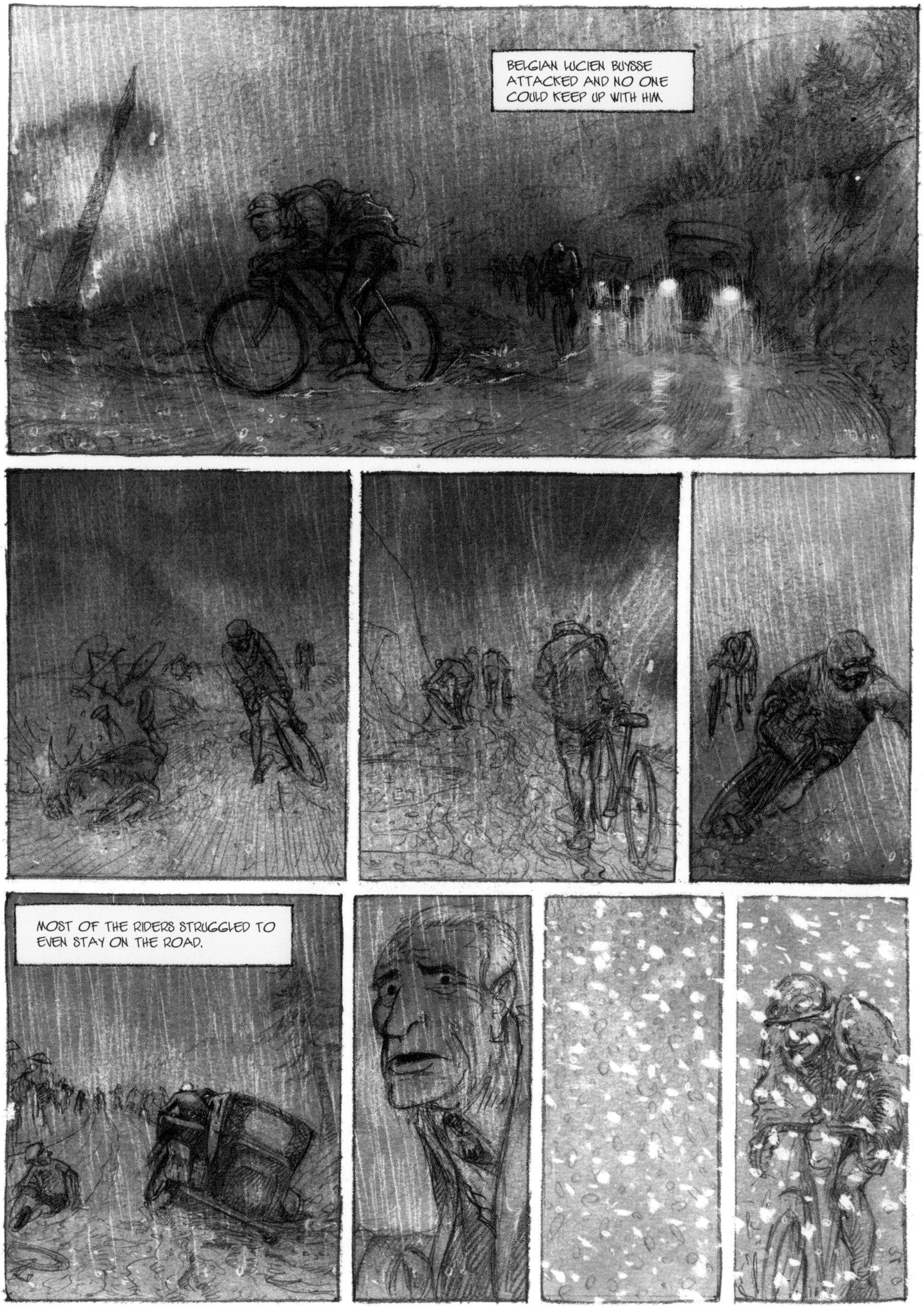
BELGIAN LUCIEN BUYSSE ATTACKED AND NO ONE COULD KEEP UP WITH HIM.
MOST OF THE RIDERS STRUGGLED TO EVEN STAY ON THE ROAD.

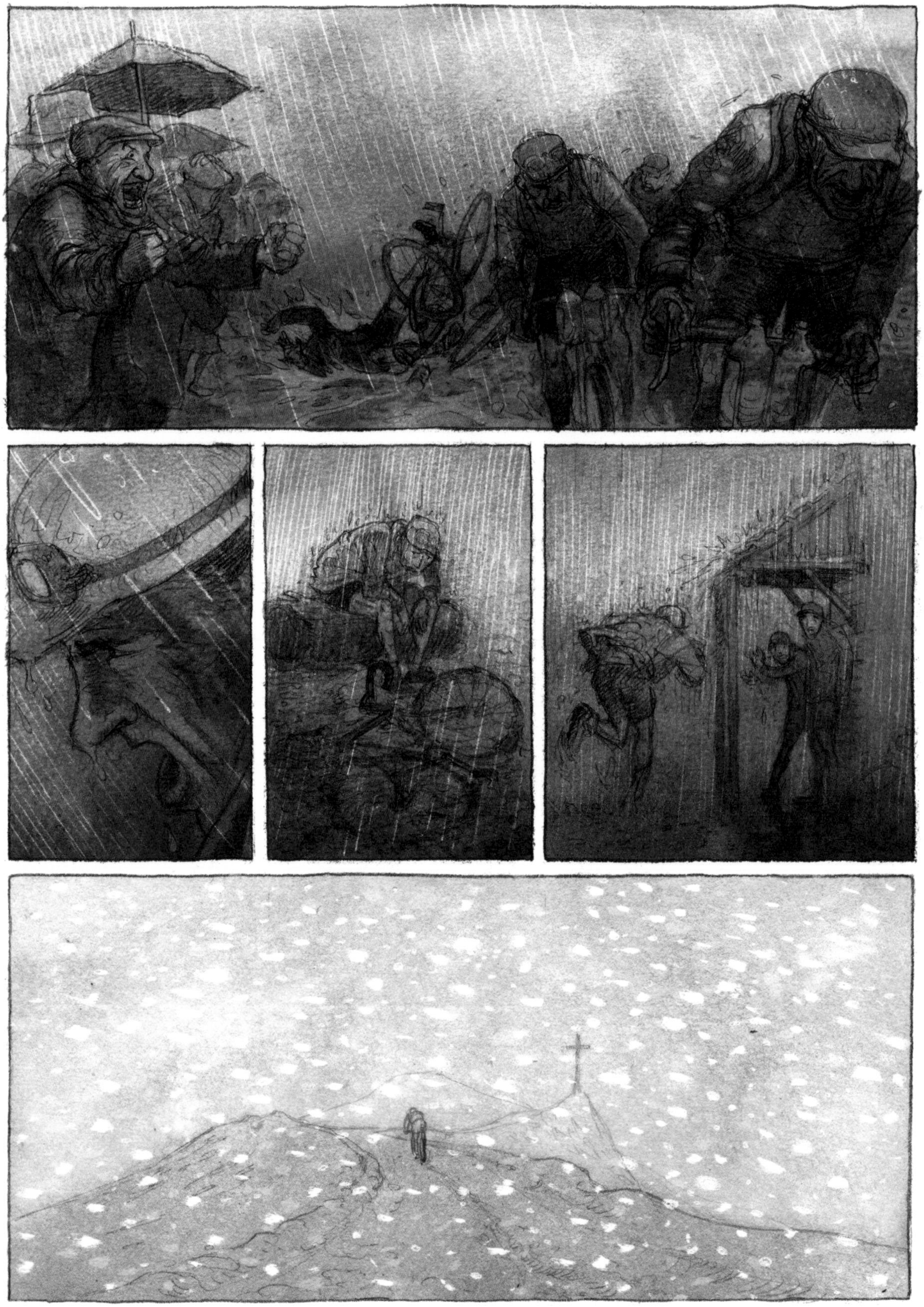

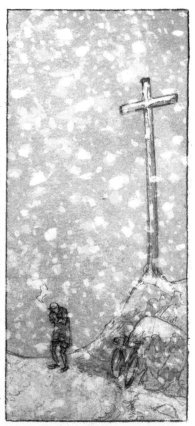

AFTER AN UNCHALLENGED SOLO RIDE, BUYSSE WAS THE FIRST TO CROSS THE FINISH LINE. HE'D BEEN ON HIS BIKE FOR SEVENTEEN HOURS.

THE OTHERS, EVEN LONGER...

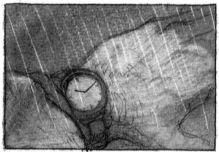

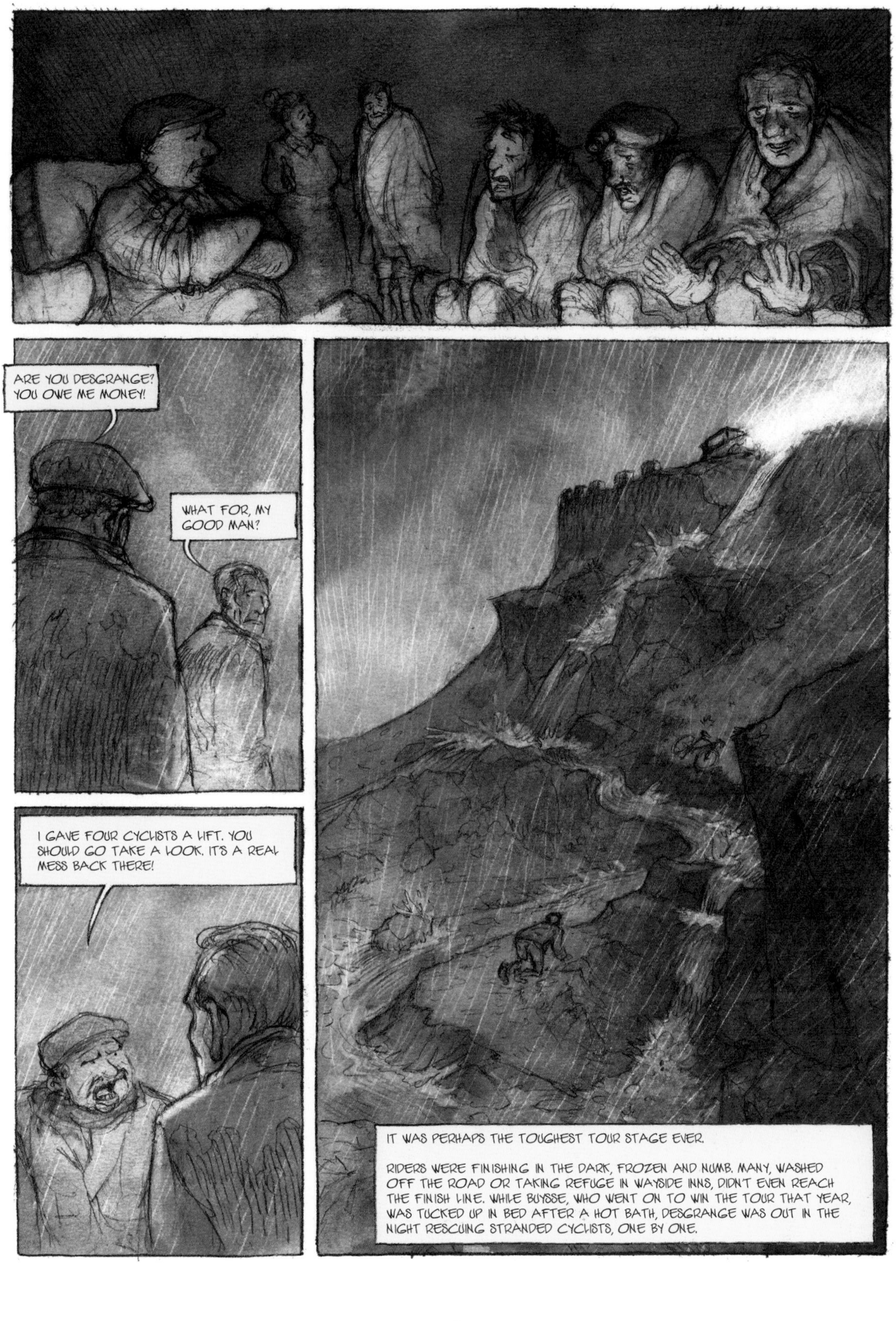
ARE YOU DESGRANGE? YOU OWE ME MONEY!
WHAT FOR, MY GOOD MAN?
I GAVE FOUR CYCLISTS A LIFT. YOU SHOULD GO TAKE A LOOK. IT'S A REAL MESS BACK THERE!
IT WAS PERHAPS THE TOUGHEST TOUR STAGE EVER.
RIDERS WERE FINISHING IN THE DARK, FROZEN AND NUMB. MANY, WASHED OFF THE ROAD OR TAKING REFUGE IN WAYSIDE INNS, DIDN'T EVEN REACH THE FINISH LINE. WHILE BUYSSE, WHO WENT ON TO WIN THE TOUR THAT YEAR, WAS TUCKED UP IN BED AFTER A HOT BATH, DESGRANGE WAS OUT IN THE NIGHT RESCUING STRANDED CYCLISTS, ONE BY ONE.

IN 1930, CHANGES WERE MADE, PAVING THE WAY FOR THE MODERN TOUR.

SPECTATORS WERE INTRODUCED TO A LIVELY MOTORIZED CAVALCADE OF ADVERTISERS THAT PRECEDED THE RACE. AND THE TOUR WAS RESTRICTED TO OFFICE HOURS.

PREVIOUSLY, THE TEAMS HAD BEEN SPONSORED BY MAJOR BICYCLE MANUFACTURERS, WHOSE HOLD ON THE TOUR WAS GROWING.

DESGRANGE DIDN'T APPROVE. HIS IDEAL TOUR WAS A HEROIC STRUGGLE BETWEEN INDIVIDUAL RIDERS, FREE OF COMMERCIAL INTERFERENCE.

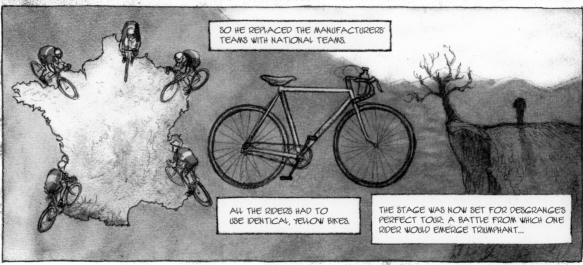

SO HE REPLACED THE MANUFACTURERS' TEAMS WITH NATIONAL TEAMS.

ALL THE RIDERS HAD TO USE IDENTICAL, YELLOW BIKES.

THE STAGE WAS NOW SET FOR DESGRANGE'S PERFECT TOUR: A BATTLE FROM WHICH ONE RIDER WOULD EMERGE TRIUMPHANT...

... A BATTLE FROM WHICH, PERHAPS, A FRENCH RIDER WOULD EMERGE TRIUMPHANT...

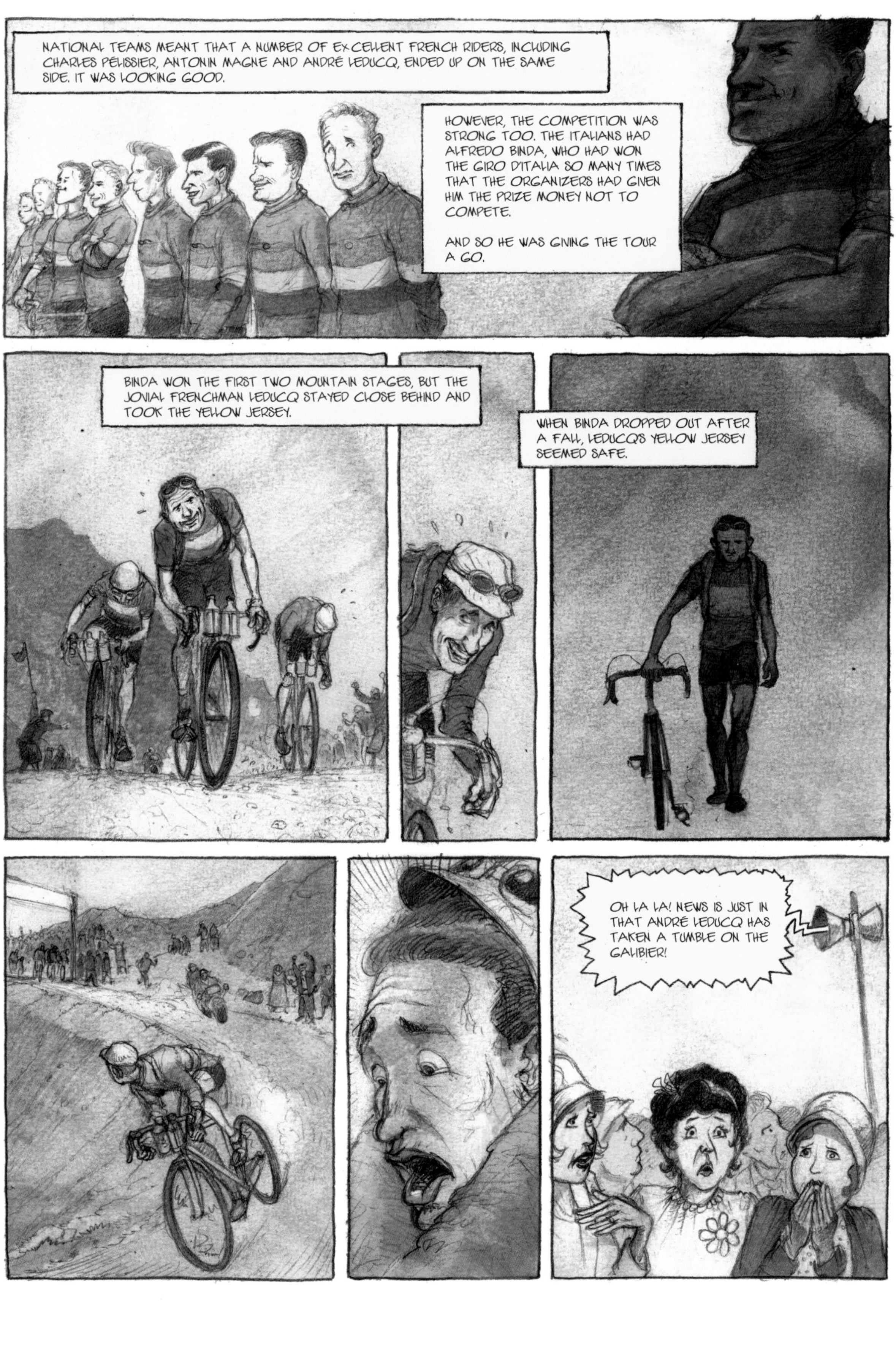
NATIONAL TEAMS MEANT THAT A NUMBER OF EXCELLENT FRENCH RIDERS, INCLUDING CHARLES PÉLISSIER, ANTONIN MAGNE AND ANDRÉ LEDUCQ, ENDED UP ON THE SAME SIDE. IT WAS LOOKING GOOD.
HOWEVER, THE COMPETITION WAS STRONG TOO. THE ITALIANS HAD ALFREDO BINDA, WHO HAD WON THE GIRO D'ITALIA SO MANY TIMES THAT THE ORGANIZERS HAD GIVEN HIM THE PRIZE MONEY NOT TO COMPETE.
AND SO HE WAS GIVING THE TOUR A GO.
BINDA WON THE FIRST TWO MOUNTAIN STAGES, BUT THE JOVIAL FRENCHMAN LEDUCQ STAYED CLOSE BEHIND AND TOOK THE YELLOW JERSEY.
WHEN BINDA DROPPED OUT AFTER A FALL, LEDUCQ'S YELLOW JERSEY SEEMED SAFE.
OH LA LA! NEWS IS JUST IN THAT ANDRÉ LEDUCQ HAS TAKEN A TUMBLE ON THE GALIBIER!

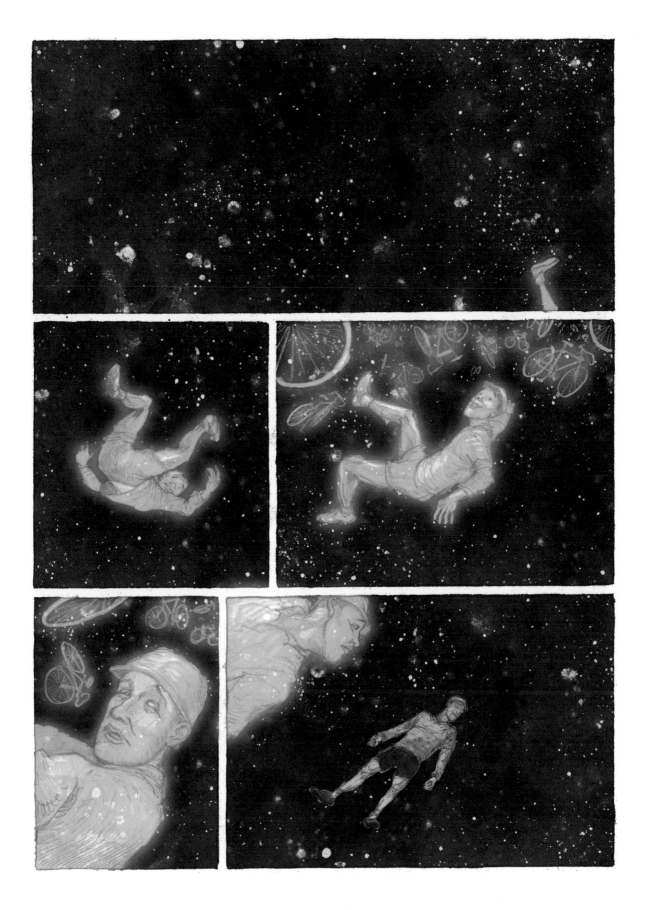

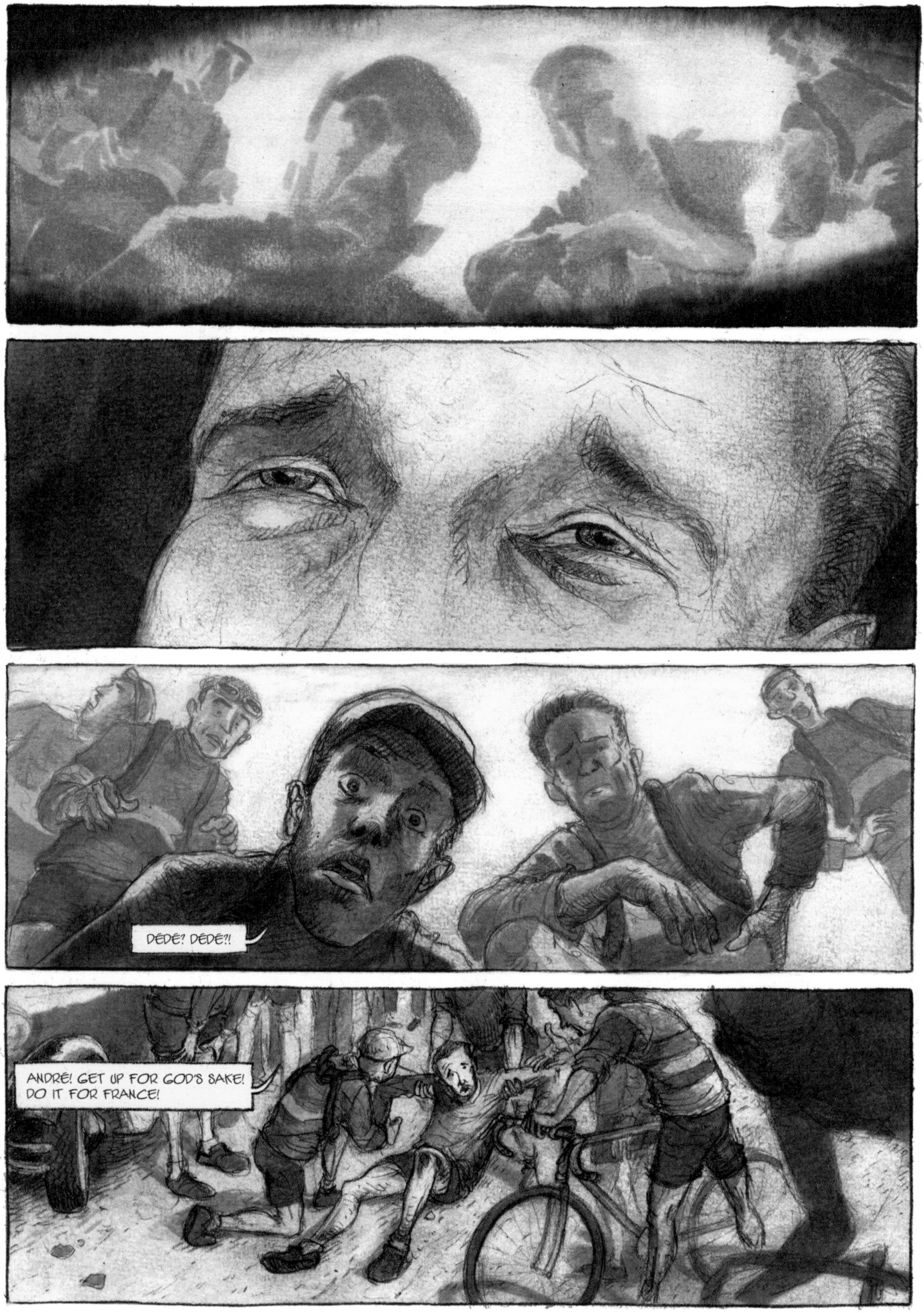
DÉDÉ? DÉDÉ?!
ANDRÉ! GET UP FOR GOD'S SAKE! DO IT FOR FRANCE!

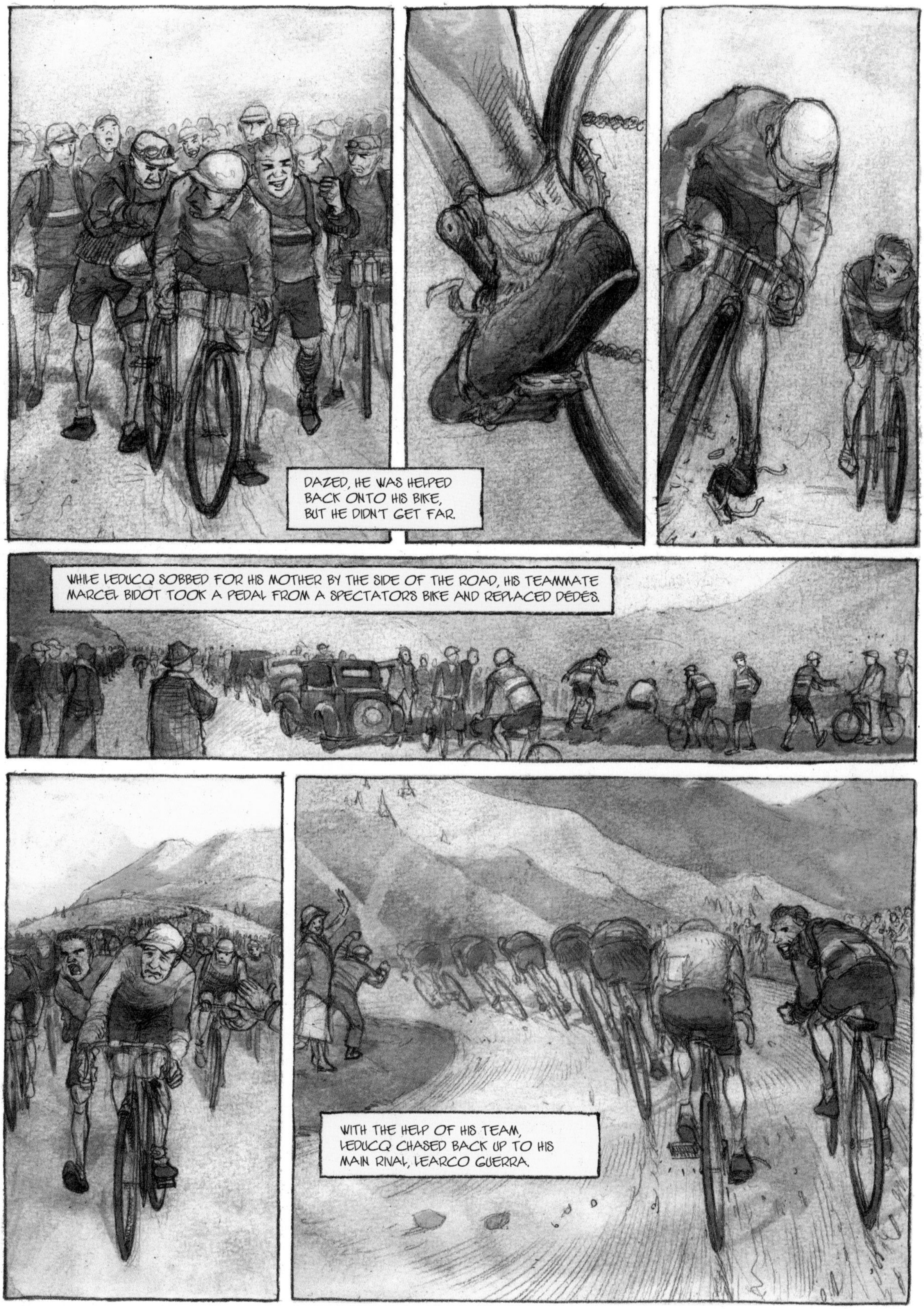
DAZED, HE WAS HELPED BACK ONTO HIS BIKE, BUT HE DIDN'T GET FAR.
WHILE LEDUCQ SOBBED FOR HIS MOTHER BY THE SIDE OF THE ROAD, HIS TEAMMATE MARCEL BIDOT TOOK A PEDAL FROM A SPECTATOR'S BIKE AND REPLACED DEDES.
WITH THE HELP OF HIS TEAM, LEDUCQ CHASED BACK UP TO HIS MAIN RIVAL, LEARCO GUERRA.

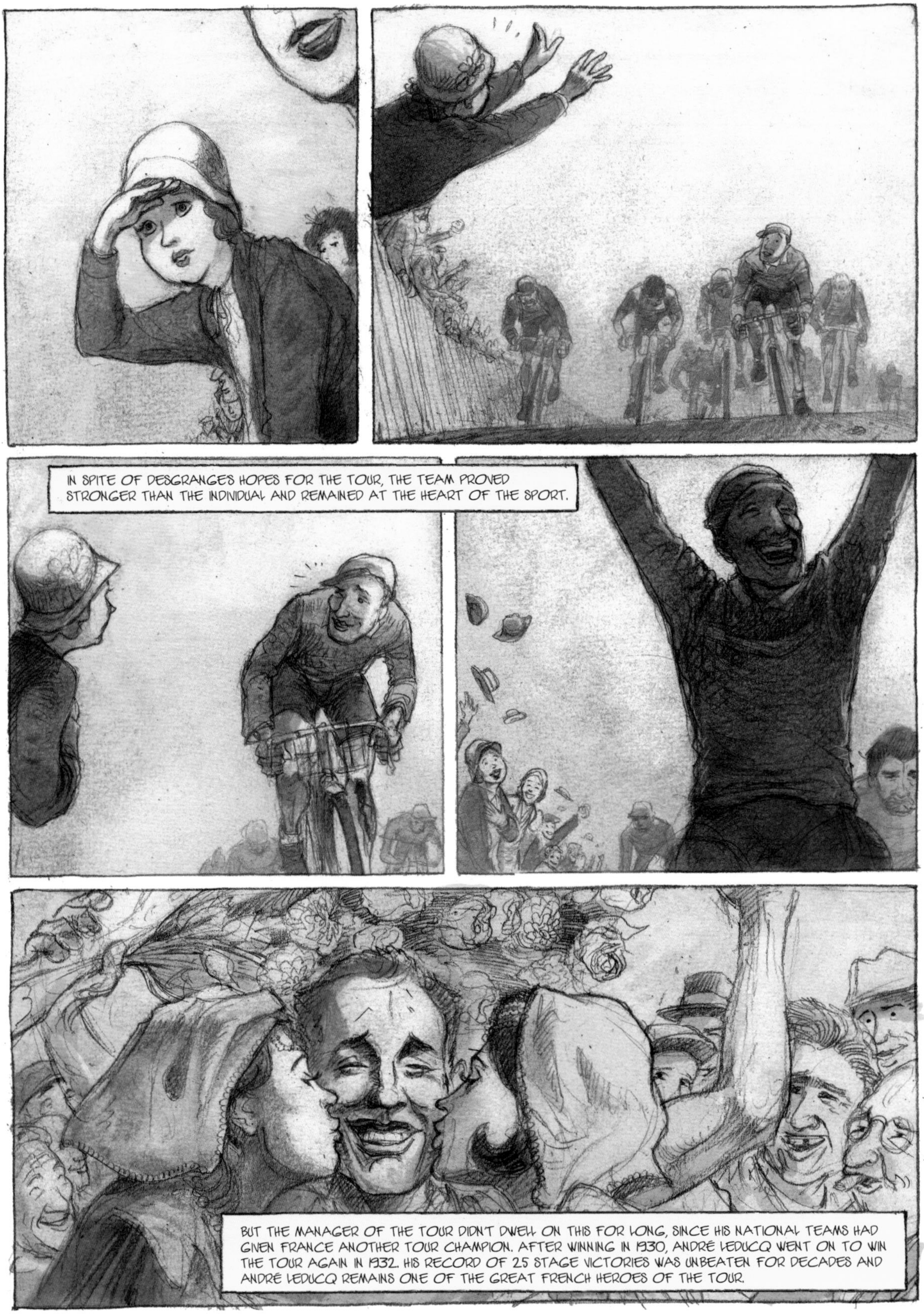
IN SPITE OF DESGRANGES HOPES FOR THE TOUR, THE TEAM PROVED STRONGER THAN THE INDIVIDUAL AND REMAINED AT THE HEART OF THE SPORT.
BUT THE MANAGER OF THE TOUR DIDN'T DWELL ON THIS FOR LONG, SINCE HIS NATIONAL TEAMS HAD GIVEN FRANCE ANOTHER TOUR CHAMPION. AFTER WINNING IN 1930, ANDRÉ LEDUCQ WENT ON TO WIN THE TOUR AGAIN IN 1932. HIS RECORD OF 25 STAGE VICTORIES WAS UNBEATEN FOR DECADES AND ANDRÉ LEDUCQ REMAINS ONE OF THE GREAT FRENCH HEROES OF THE TOUR.

THE ITALIAN DUEL

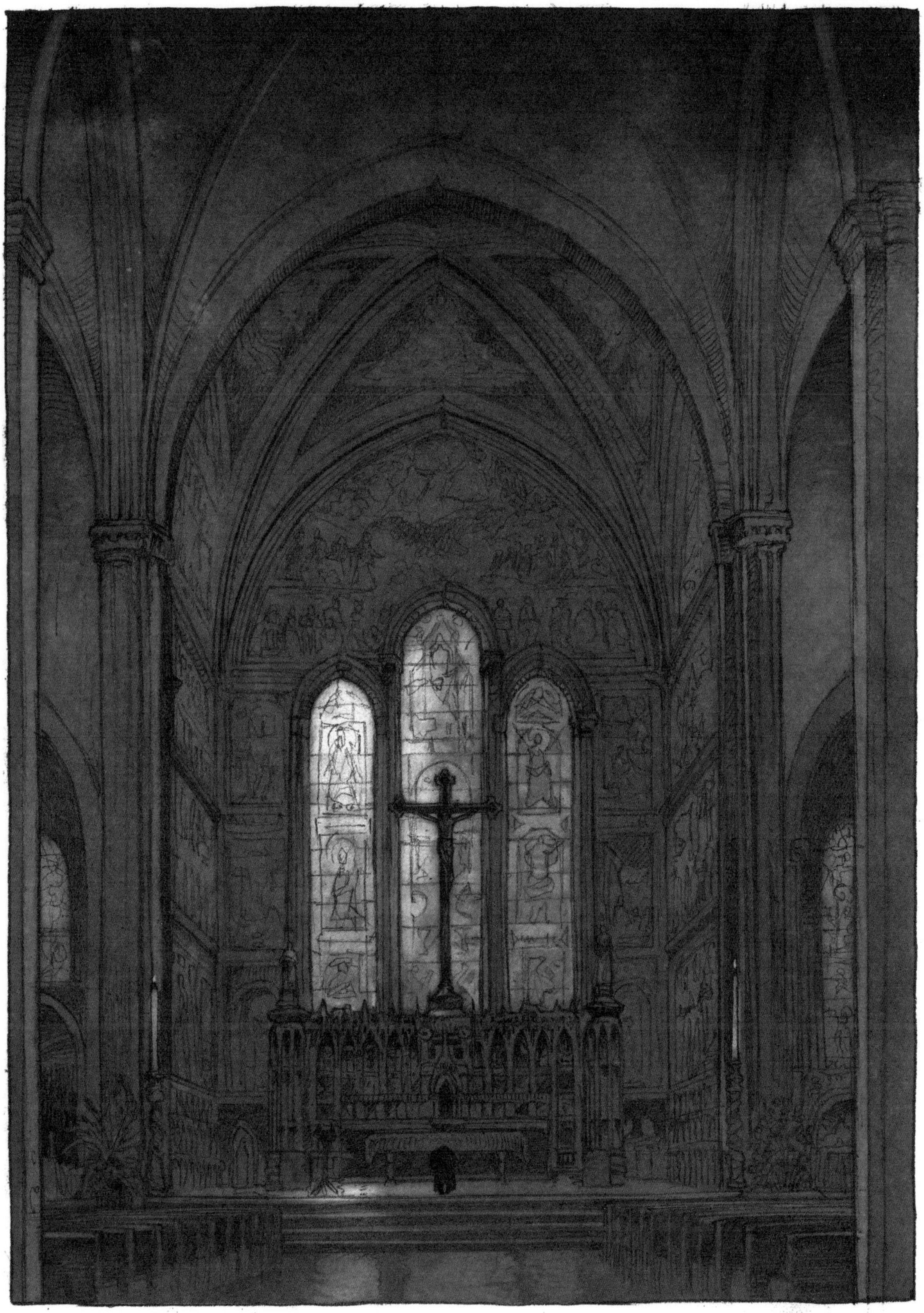

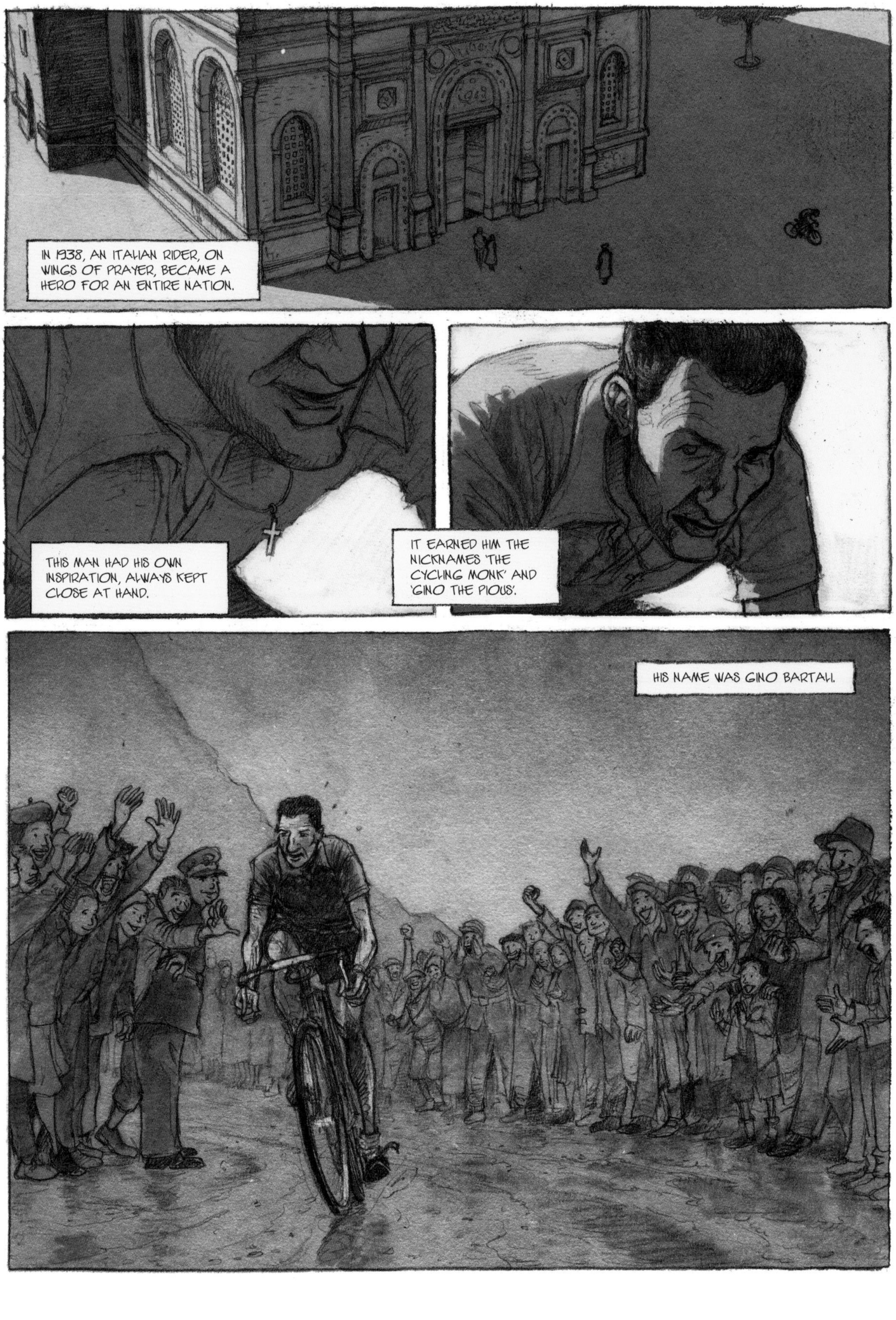
IN 1938, AN ITALIAN RIDER, ON WINGS OF PRAYER, BECAME A HERO FOR AN ENTIRE NATION.
THIS MAN HAD HIS OWN INSPIRATION, ALWAYS KEPT CLOSE AT HAND.
IT EARNED HIM THE NICKNAMES 'THE CYCLING MONK' AND 'GINO THE PIOUS'.
HIS NAME WAS GINO BARTALI.

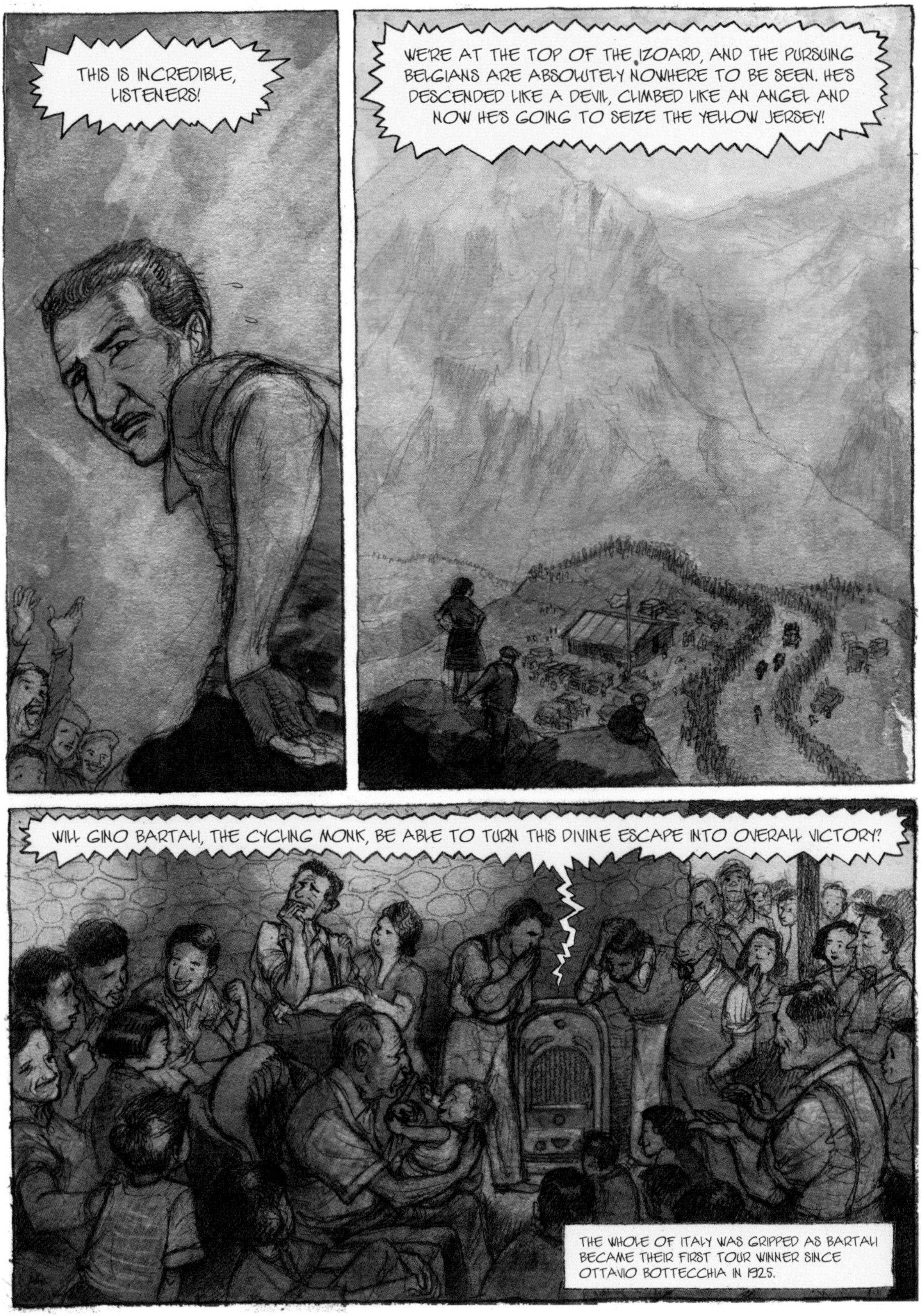
THIS IS INCREDIBLE, LISTENERS!
WE'RE AT THE TOP OF THE IZOARD, AND THE PURSUING BELGIANS ARE ABSOLUTELY NOWHERE TO BE SEEN. HE'S DESCENDED LIKE A DEVIL, CLIMBED LIKE AN ANGEL AND NOW HE'S GOING TO SEIZE THE YELLOW JERSEY!
WILL GINO BARTALI, THE CYCLING MONK, BE ABLE TO TURN THIS DIVINE ESCAPE INTO OVERALL VICTORY?
THE WHOLE OF ITALY WAS GRIPPED AS BARTALI BECAME THEIR FIRST TOUR WINNER SINCE OTTAVIO BOTTECCHIA IN 1925.

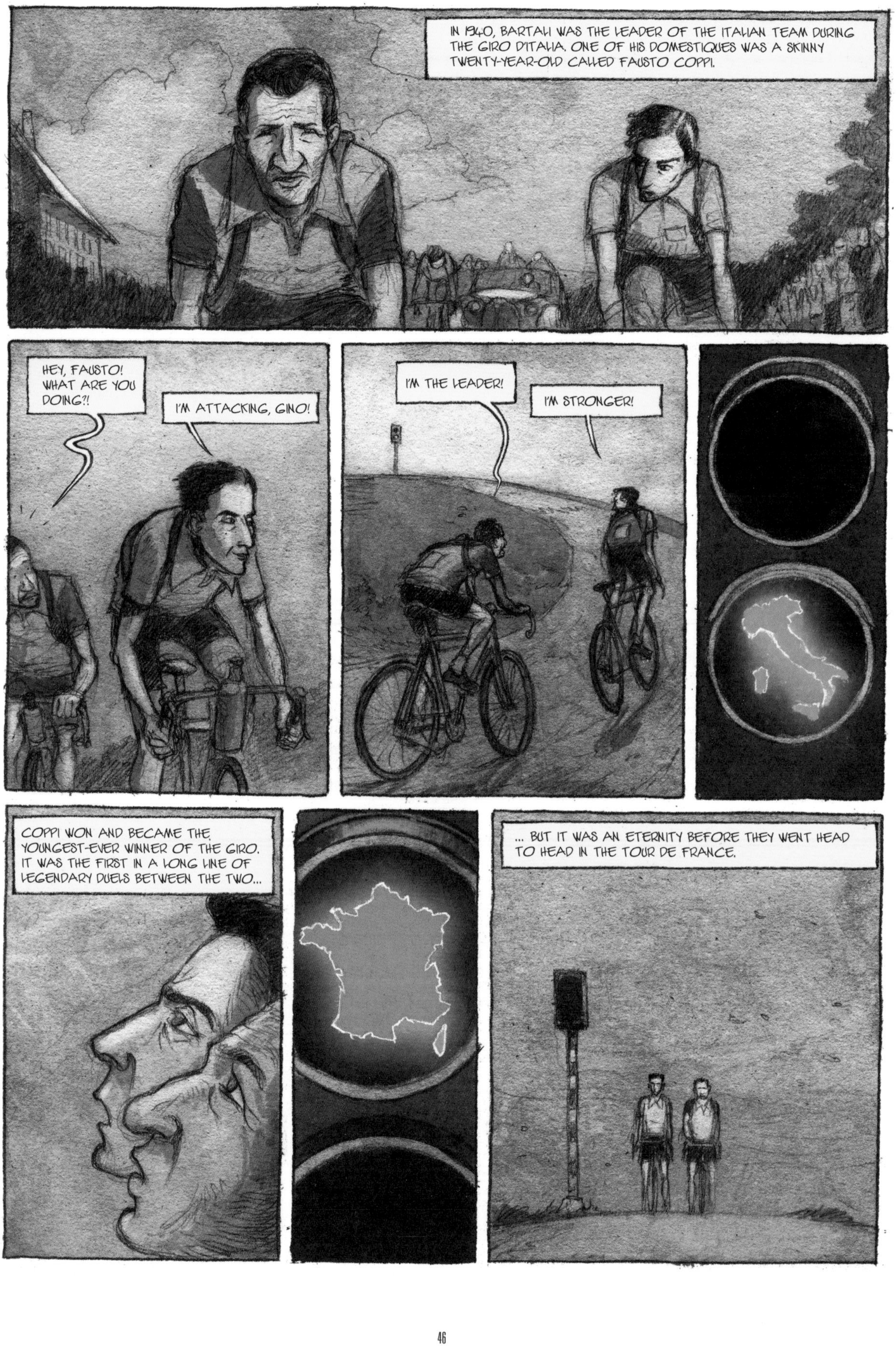
IN 1940, BARTALI WAS THE LEADER OF THE ITALIAN TEAM DURING THE GIRO D'ITALIA. ONE OF HIS DOMESTIQUES WAS A SKINNY TWENTY-YEAR-OLD CALLED FAUSTO COPPI.
HEY, FAUSTO! WHAT ARE YOU DOING?!
I'M ATTACKING, GINO!
I'M THE LEADER!
I'M STRONGER!
COPPI WON AND BECAME THE YOUNGEST-EVER WINNER OF THE GIRO. IT WAS THE FIRST IN A LONG LINE OF LEGENDARY DUELS BETWEEN THE TWO...
... BUT IT WAS AN ETERNITY BEFORE THEY WENT HEAD TO HEAD IN THE TOUR DE FRANCE.

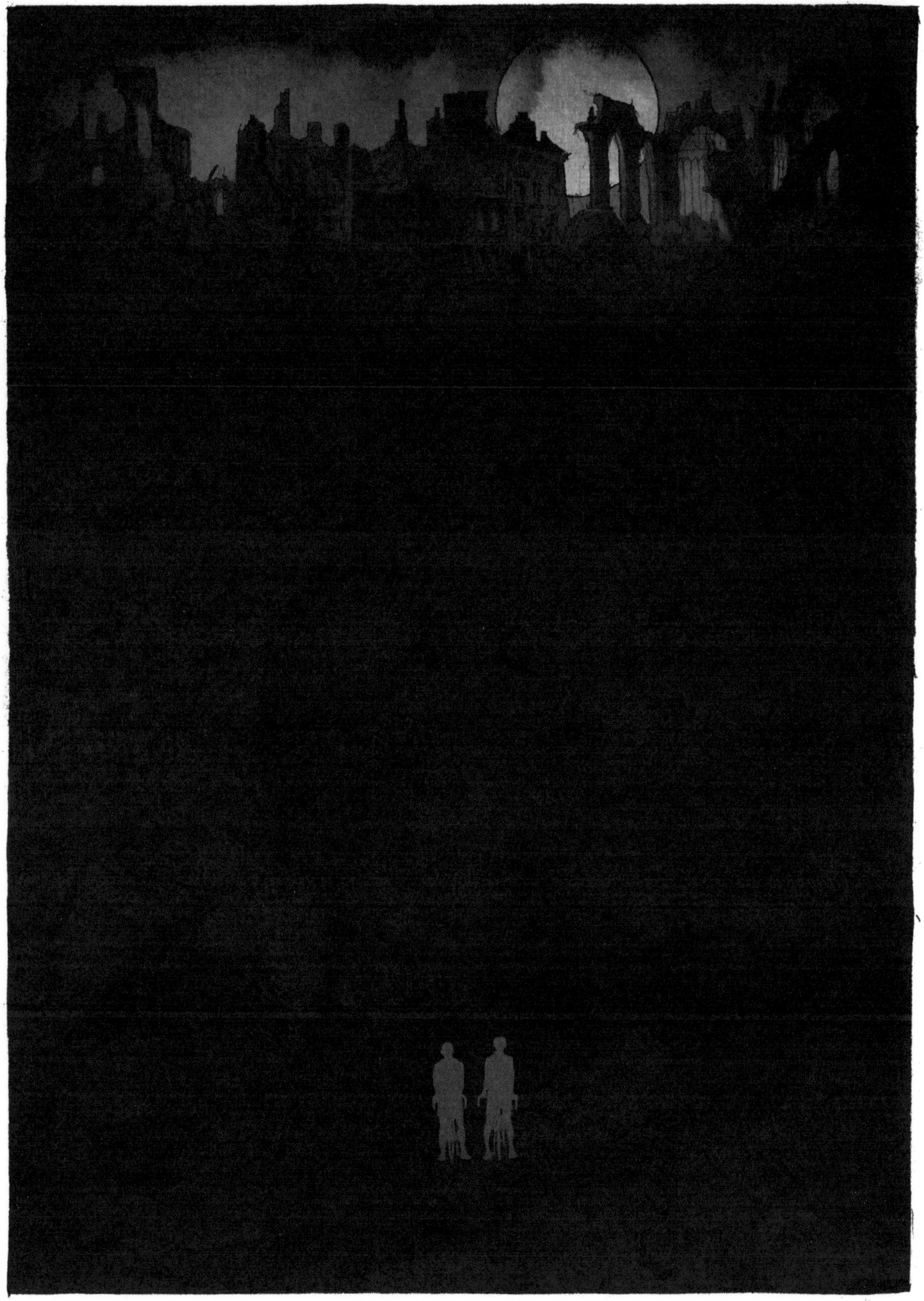

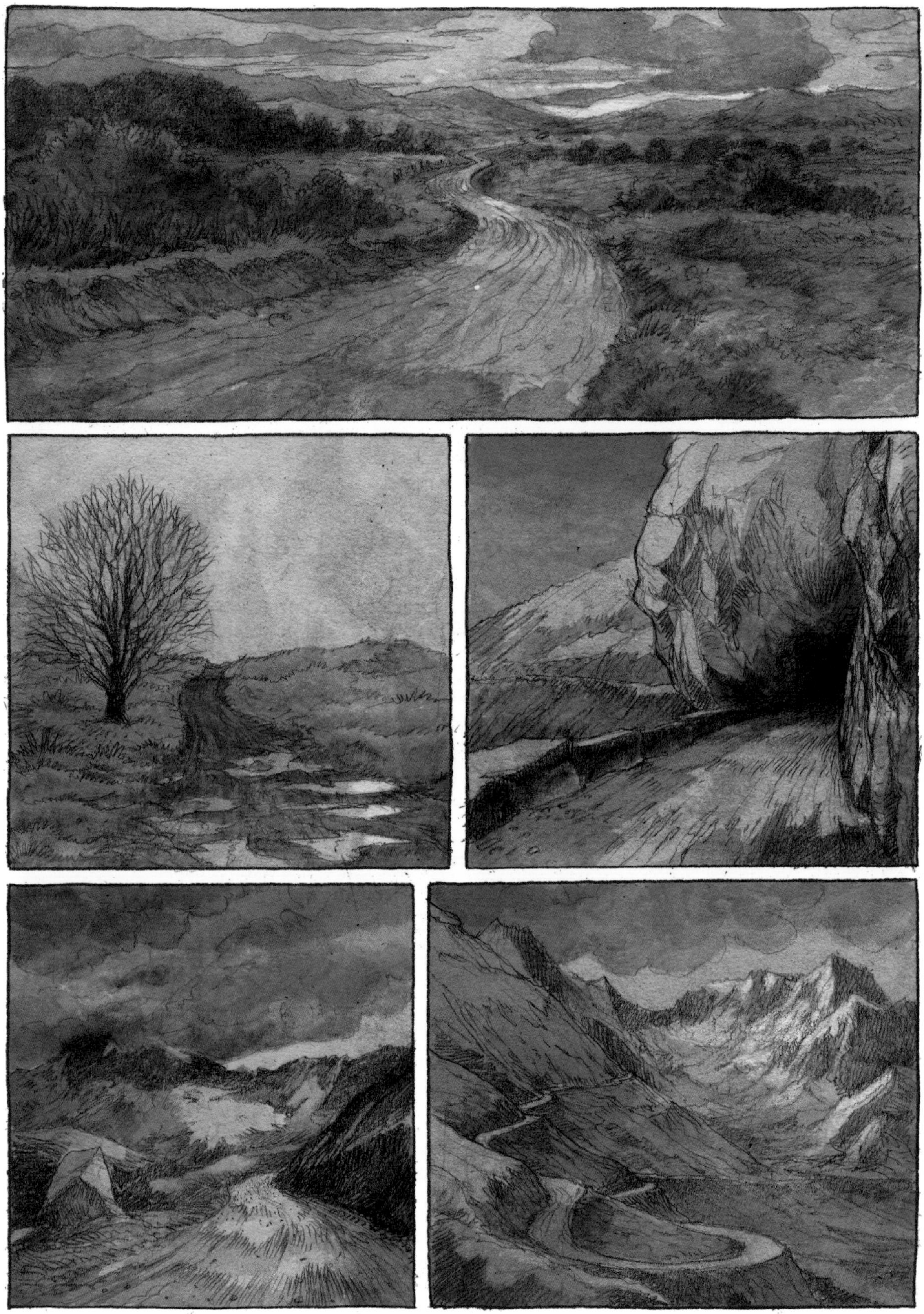

CANNES, 1948. THE EVENING BEFORE THE FIRST MOUNTAIN STAGE. BARTALI WAS LAGGING FAR BEHIND THE YELLOW-JERSEY.

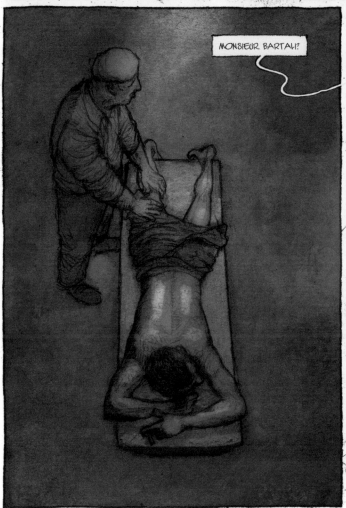

MONSIEUR. BARTALI?

TELEPHONE CALL FOR YOU.

THE SECOND WORLD WAR WAS OVER AND
MUSSOLINI'S FASCISM HAD BEEN DEFEATED.
BUT ITALY WAS FAR FROM PEACEFUL.

THERE HAD BEEN AN ASSASSINATION ATTEMPT ON
THE LEADER OF THE COMMUNIST PARTY. THE COUNTRY
WAS IN CHAOS.

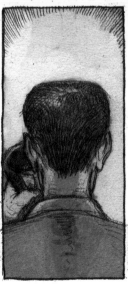

THE PRIME MINISTER CALLED BARTALI. HE TOLD HIM
HE HAD TO WIN THE STAGE IN ORDER TO AVERT THE
THREAT OF CIVIL WAR.

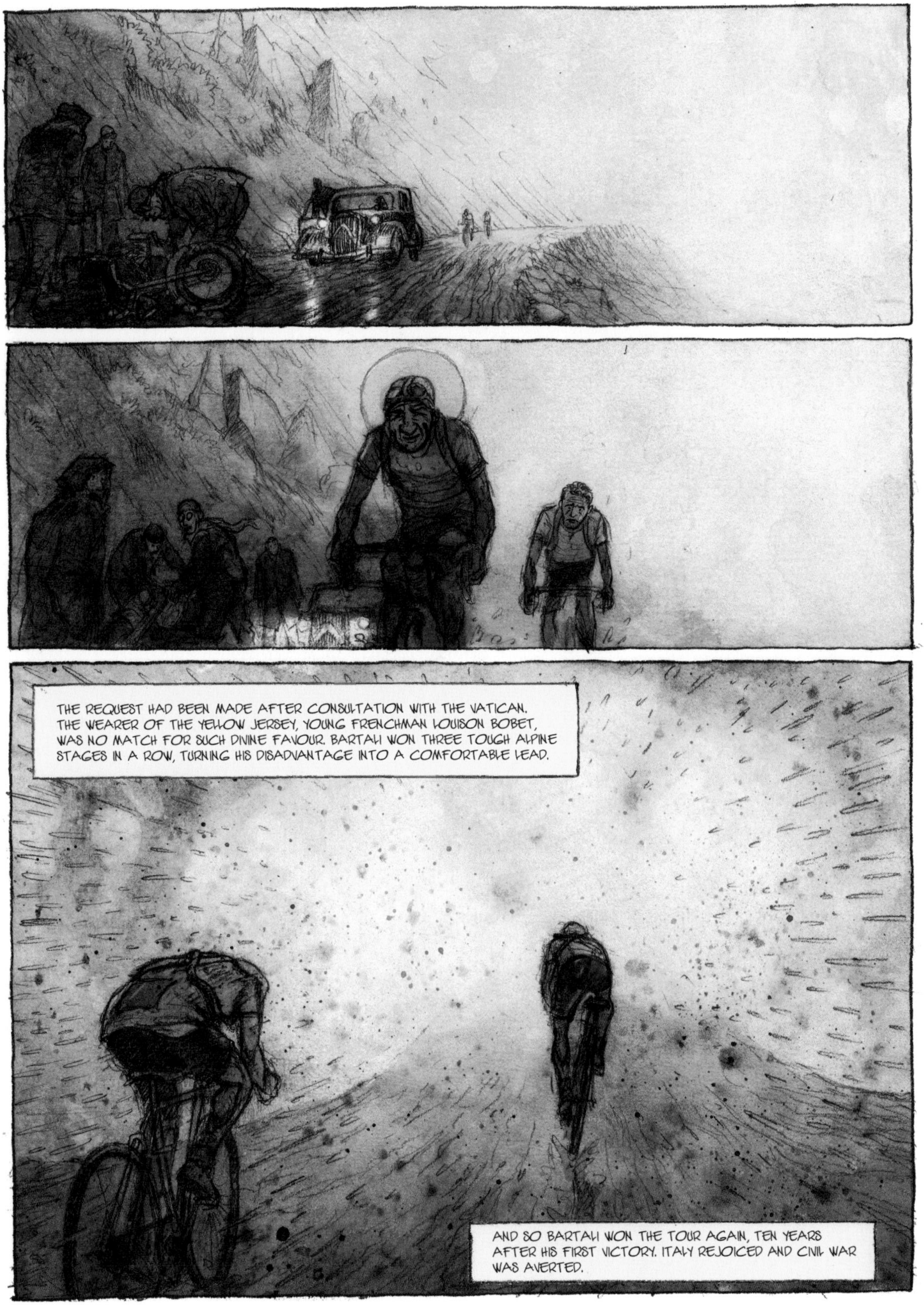

THE REQUEST HAD BEEN MADE AFTER CONSULTATION WITH THE VATICAN. THE WEARER OF THE YELLOW JERSEY, YOUNG FRENCHMAN LOUISON BOBET, WAS NO MATCH FOR SUCH DIVINE FAVOUR. BARTALI WON THREE TOUGH ALPINE STAGES IN A ROW, TURNING HIS DISADVANTAGE INTO A COMFORTABLE LEAD.
AND SO BARTALI WON THE TOUR AGAIN, TEN YEARS AFTER HIS FIRST VICTORY. ITALY REJOICED AND CIVIL WAR WAS AVERTED.

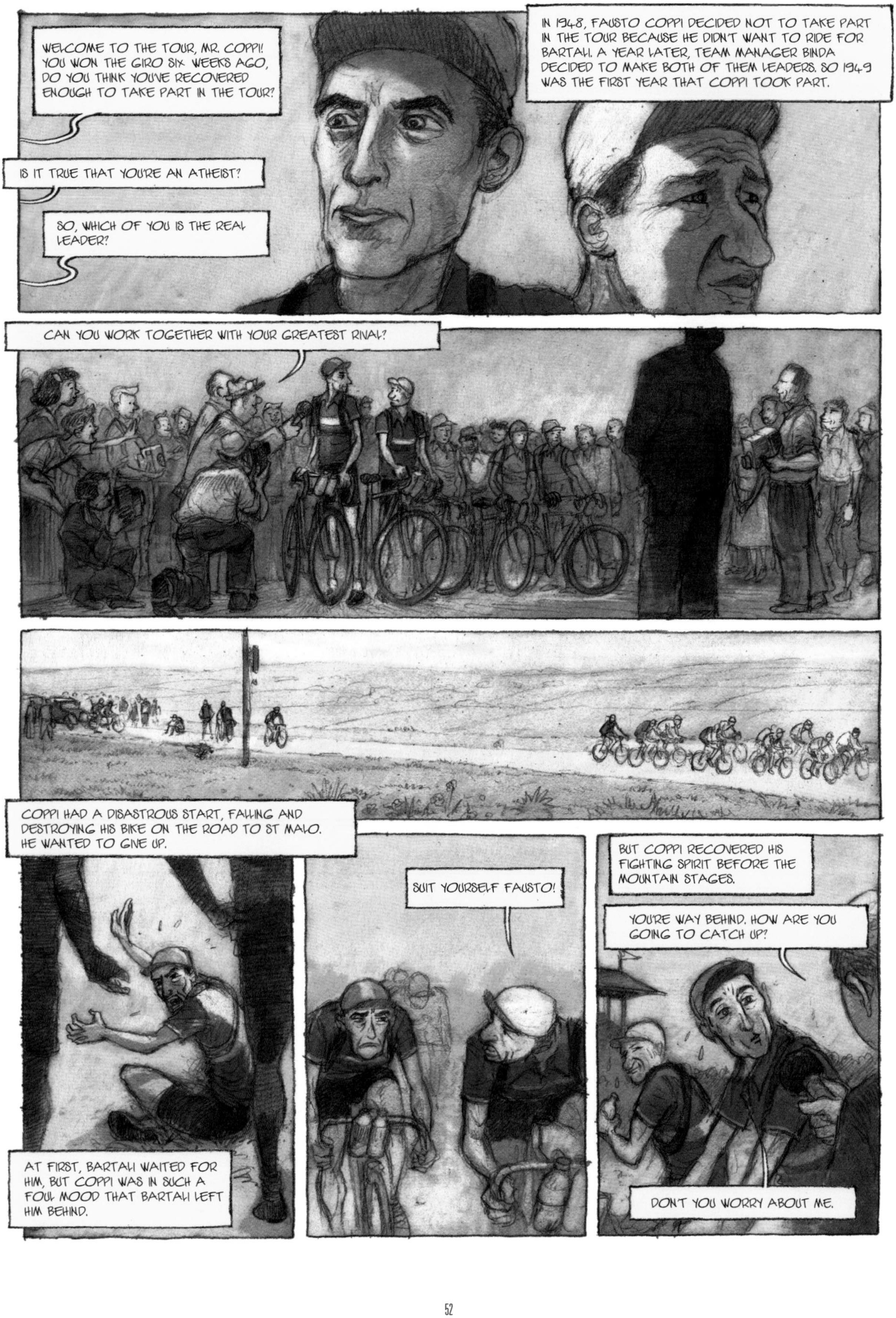
WELCOME TO THE TOUR, MR. COPPI! YOU WON THE GIRO SIX WEEKS AGO, DO YOU THINK YOU'VE RECOVERED ENOUGH TO TAKE PART IN THE TOUR?
IN 1948, FAUSTO COPPI DECIDED NOT TO TAKE PART IN THE TOUR BECAUSE HE DIDN'T WANT TO RIDE FOR BARTALI. A YEAR LATER, TEAM MANAGER BINDA DECIDED TO MAKE BOTH OF THEM LEADERS. SO 1949 WAS THE FIRST YEAR THAT COPPI TOOK PART.
IS IT TRUE THAT YOU'RE AN ATHEIST?
SO, WHICH OF YOU IS THE REAL LEADER?
CAN YOU WORK TOGETHER WITH YOUR GREATEST RIVAL?
COPPI HAD A DISASTROUS START, FALLING AND DESTROYING HIS BIKE ON THE ROAD TO ST MALO. HE WANTED TO GIVE UP.
AT FIRST, BARTALI WAITED FOR HIM, BUT COPPI WAS IN SUCH A FOUL MOOD THAT BARTALI LEFT HIM BEHIND.
SUIT YOURSELF FAUSTO!
BUT COPPI RECOVERED HIS FIGHTING SPIRIT BEFORE THE MOUNTAIN STAGES.
YOU'RE WAY BEHIND. HOW ARE YOU GOING TO CATCH UP?
DON'T YOU WORRY ABOUT ME.

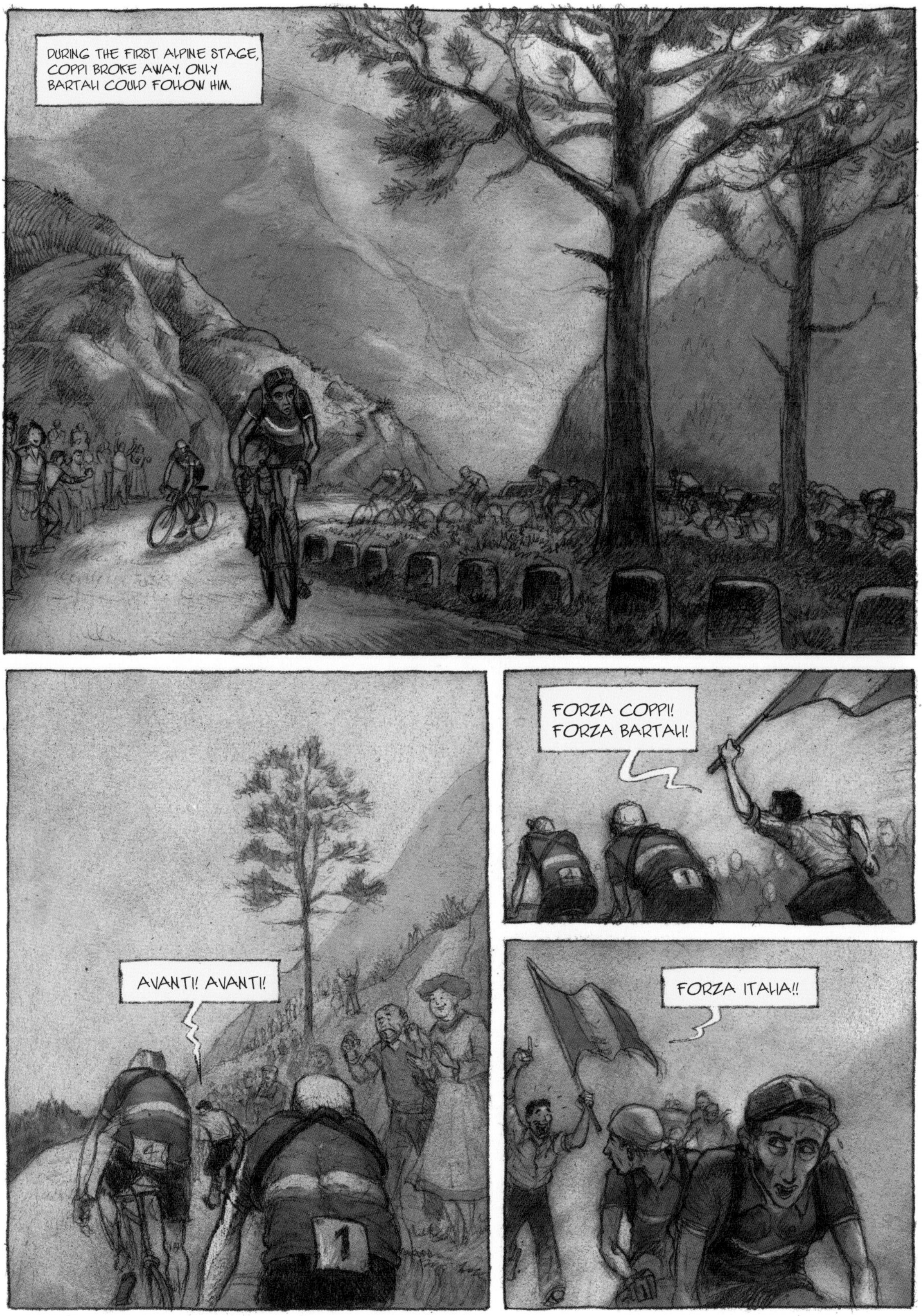
DURING THE FIRST ALPINE STAGE, COPPI BROKE AWAY. ONLY BARTALI COULD FOLLOW HIM.
AVANTI! AVANTI!
FORZA COPPI! FORZA BARTALI!
FORZA ITALIA!!

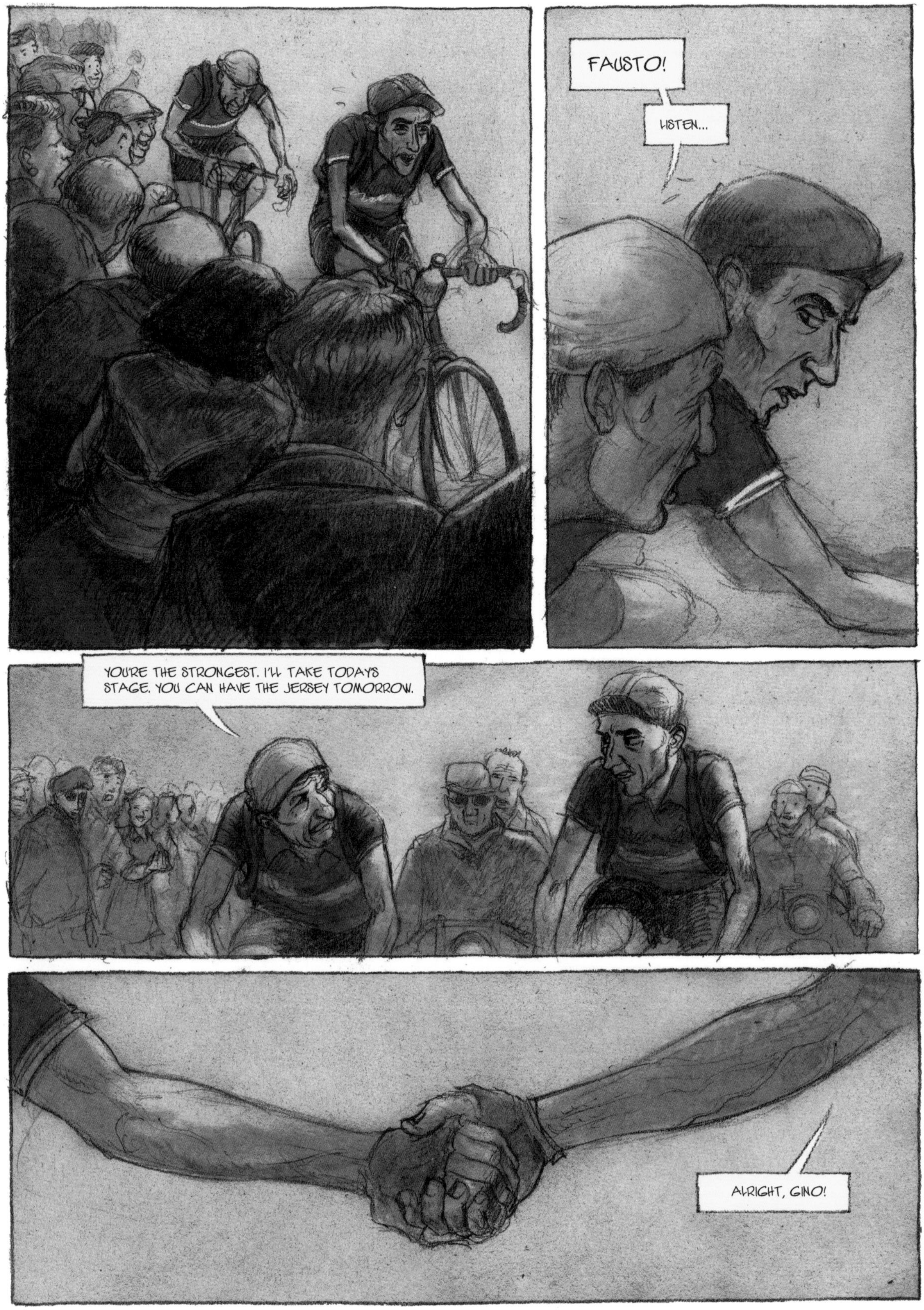
FAUSTO!
LISTEN...
YOU'RE THE STRONGEST. I'LL TAKE TODAYS STAGE. YOU CAN HAVE THE JERSEY TOMORROW.
ALRIGHT, GINO!

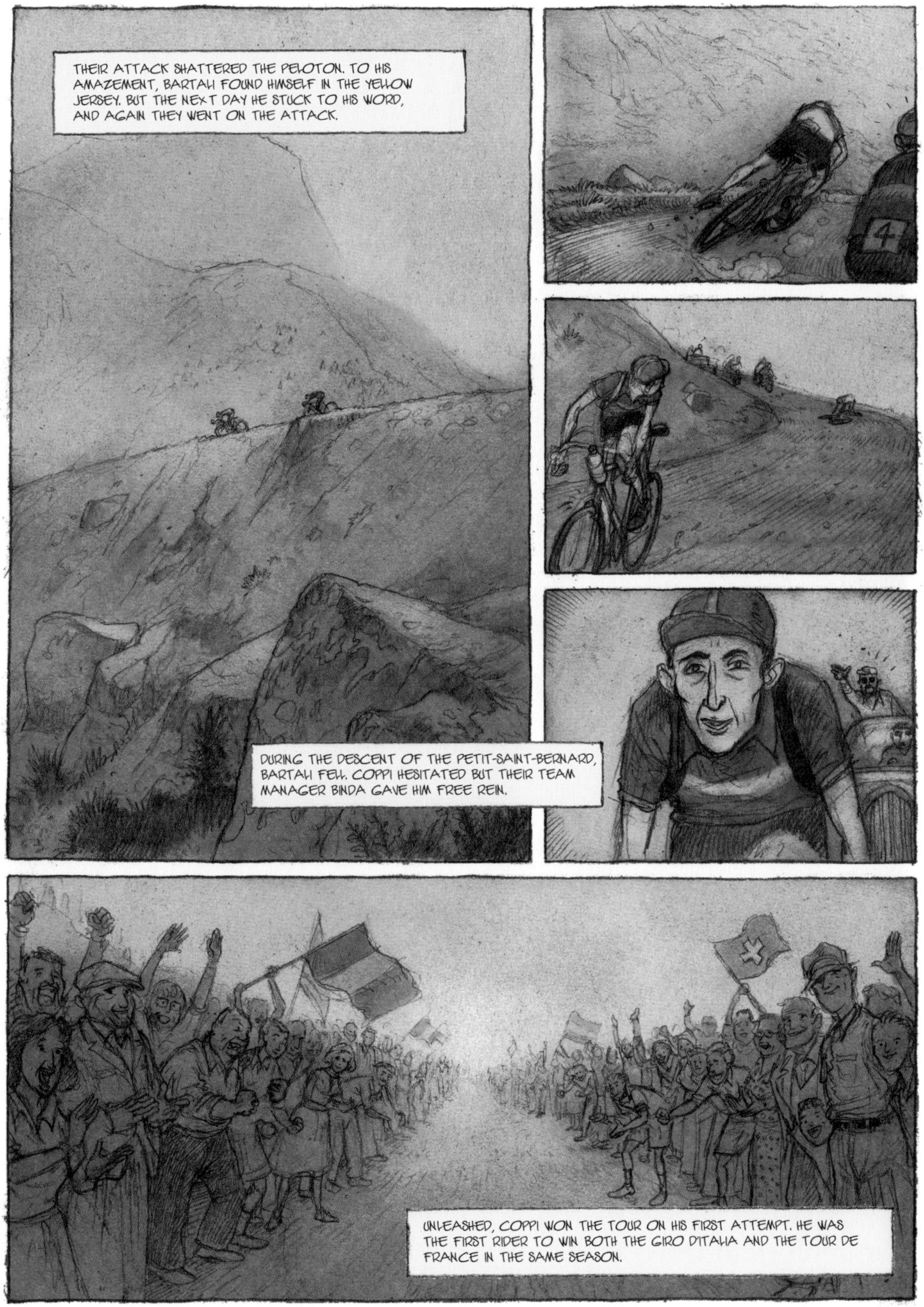
THEIR ATTACK SHATTERED THE PELOTON. TO HIS AMAZEMENT, BARTALI FOUND HIMSELF IN THE YELLOW JERSEY. BUT THE NEXT DAY HE STUCK TO HIS WORD, AND AGAIN THEY WENT ON THE ATTACK.
DURING THE DESCENT OF THE PETIT-SAINT-BERNARD, BARTALI FELL. COPPI HESITATED BUT THEIR TEAM MANAGER BINDA GAVE HIM FREE REIN.
UNLEASHED, COPPI WON THE TOUR ON HIS FIRST ATTEMPT. HE WAS THE FIRST RIDER TO WIN BOTH THE GIRO D'ITALIA AND THE TOUR DE FRANCE IN THE SAME SEASON.

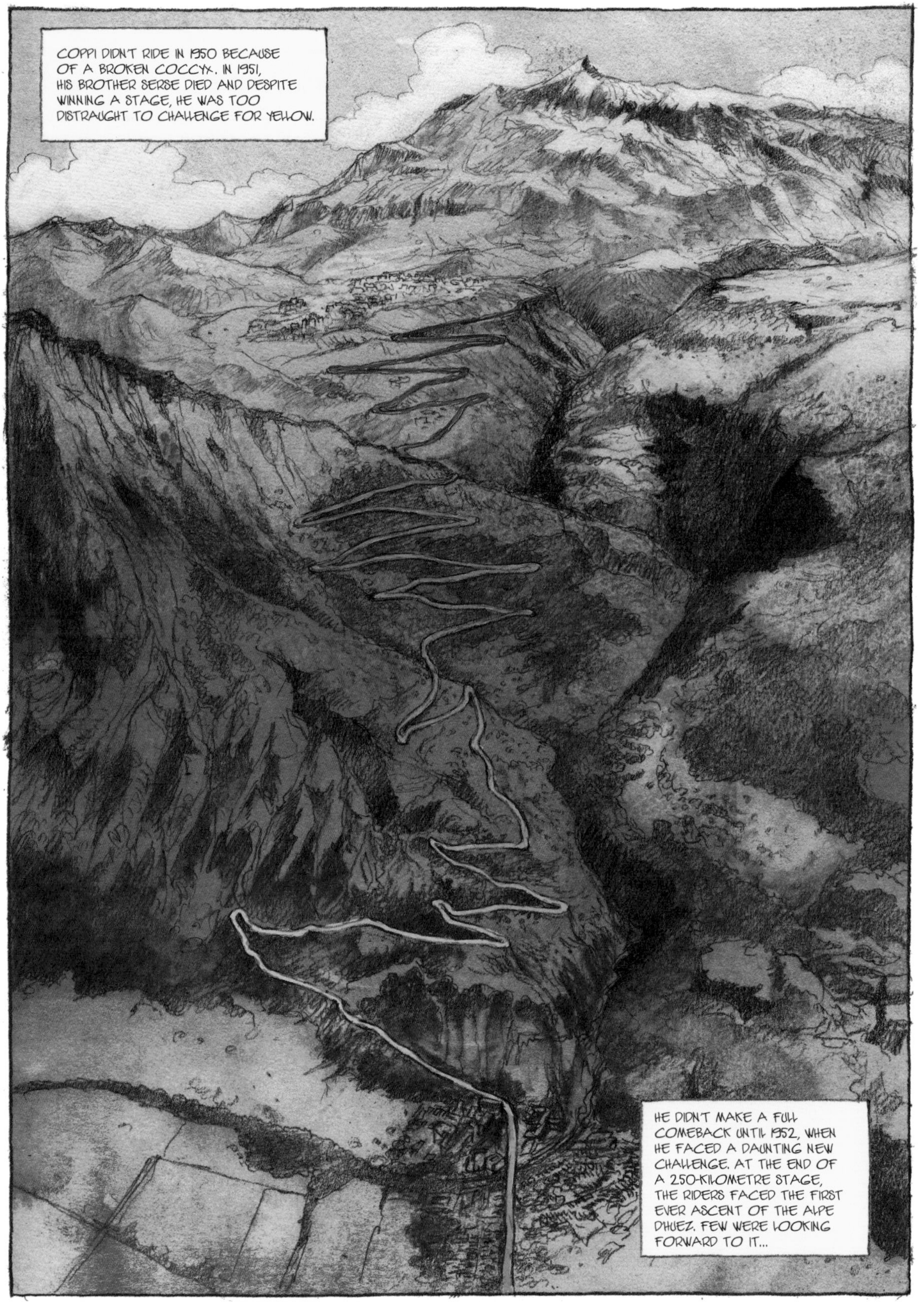
COPPI DIDN'T RIDE IN 1950 BECAUSE OF A BROKEN COCCYX. IN 1951, HIS BROTHER SERSE DIED AND DESPITE WINNING A STAGE, HE WAS TOO DISTRAUGHT TO CHALLENGE FOR YELLOW.
HE DIDN'T MAKE A FULL COMEBACK UNTIL 1952, WHEN HE FACED A DAUNTING NEW CHALLENGE. AT THE END OF A 250-KILOMETRE STAGE, THE RIDERS FACED THE FIRST EVER ASCENT OF THE ALPE D'HUEZ. FEW WERE LOOKING FORWARD TO IT...

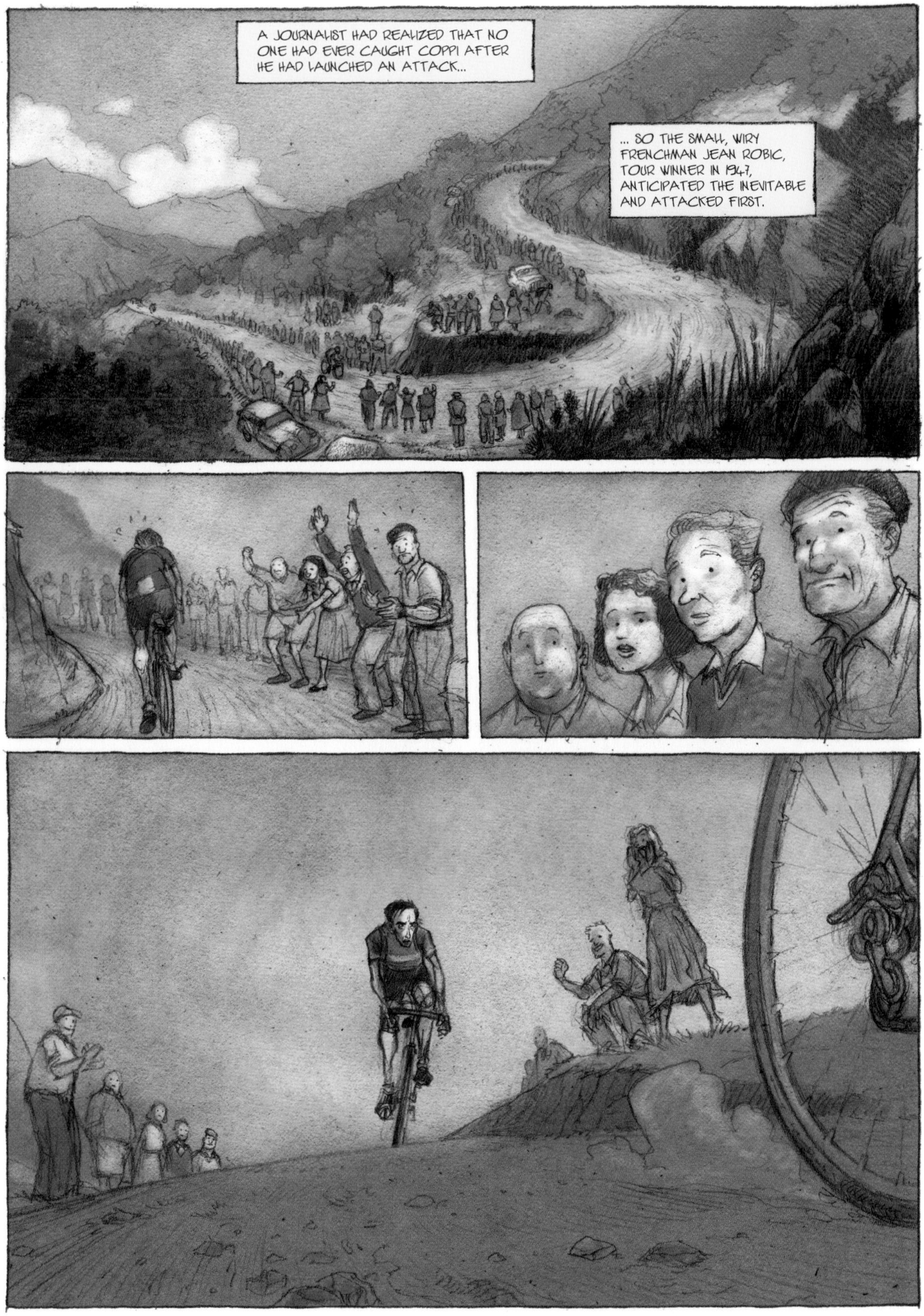
A JOURNALIST HAD REALIZED THAT NO ONE HAD EVER CAUGHT COPPI AFTER HE HAD LAUNCHED AN ATTACK...
... SO THE SMALL, WIRY FRENCHMAN JEAN ROBIC, TOUR WINNER IN 1947, ANTICIPATED THE INEVITABLE AND ATTACKED FIRST.

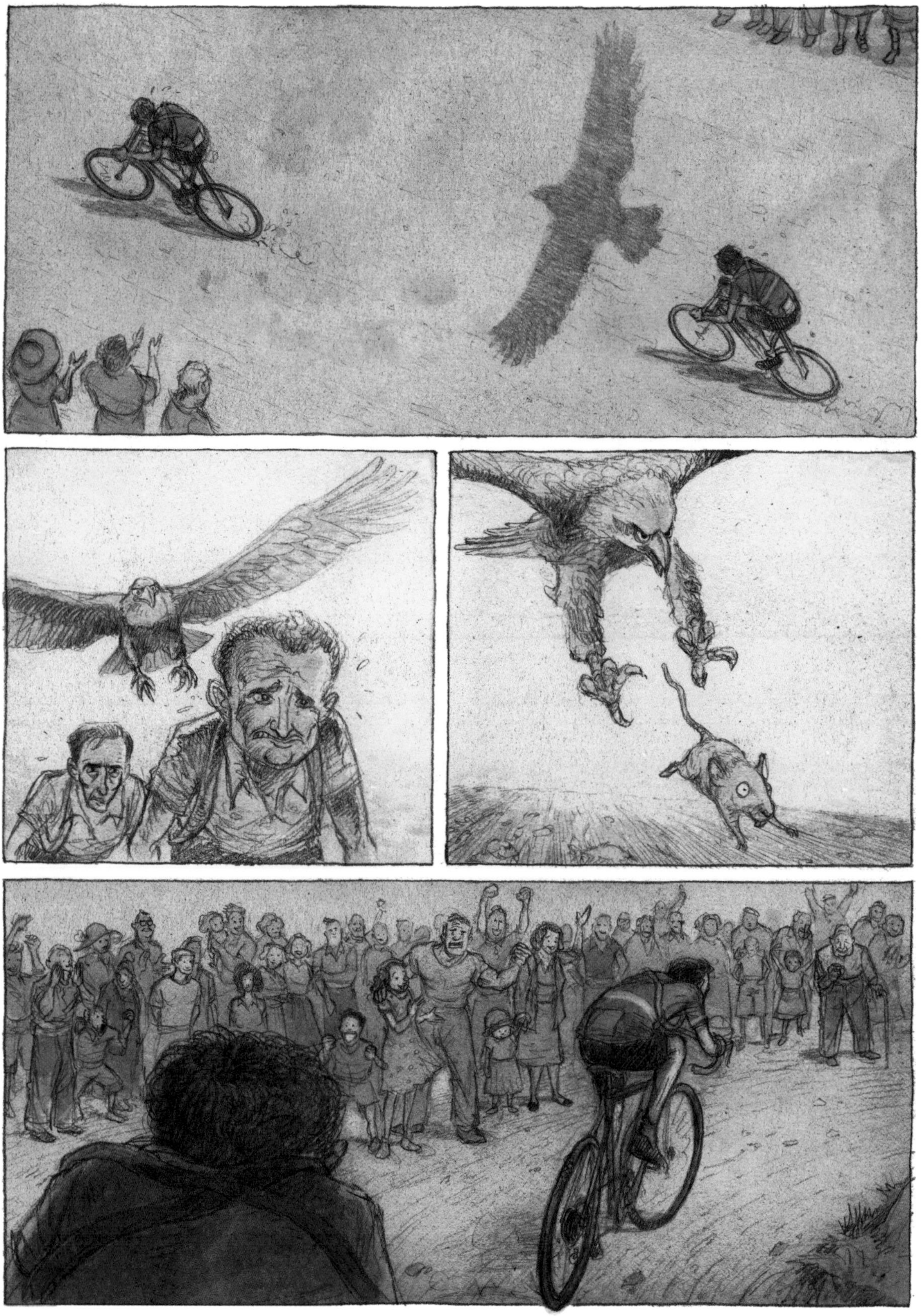

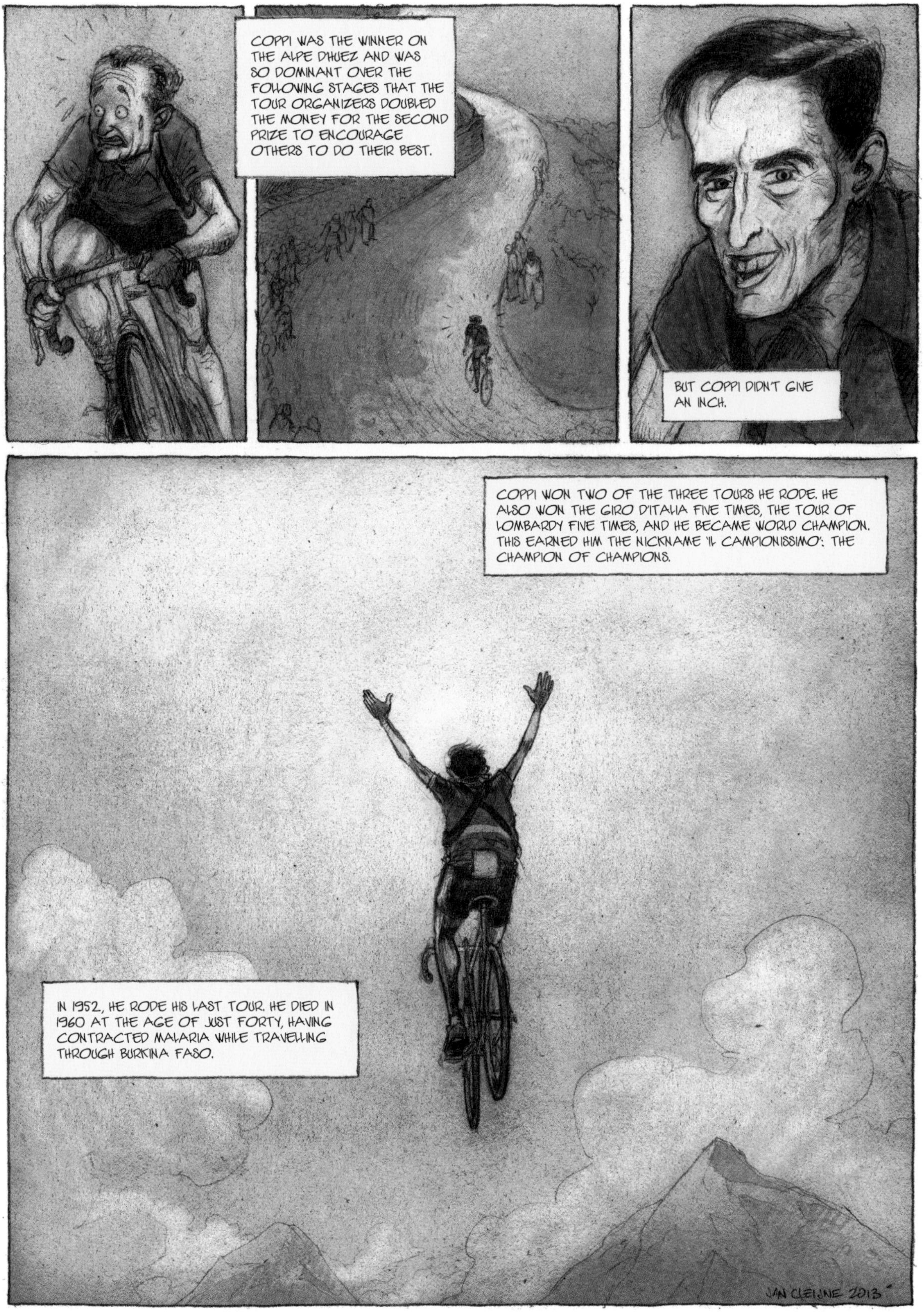
COPPI WAS THE WINNER ON THE ALPE DHUEZ AND WAS SO DOMINANT OVER THE FOLLOWING STAGES THAT THE TOUR ORGANIZERS DOUBLED THE MONEY FOR THE SECOND PRIZE TO ENCOURAGE OTHERS TO DO THEIR BEST.
BUT COPPI DIDN'T GIVE AN INCH.
COPPI WON TWO OF THE THREE TOURS HE RODE. HE ALSO WON THE GIRO D'ITALIA FIVE TIMES, THE TOUR OF LOMBARDY FIVE TIMES, AND HE BECAME WORLD CHAMPION. THIS EARNED HIM THE NICKNAME 'IL CAMPIONISSIMO': THE CHAMPION OF CHAMPIONS.
IN 1952, HE RODE HIS LAST TOUR. HE DIED IN 1960 AT THE AGE OF JUST FORTY, HAVING CONTRACTED MALARIA WHILE TRAVELLING THROUGH BURKINA FASO.
JAN CLEIJNE 2013

4

A DUTCH MOUNTAINEER

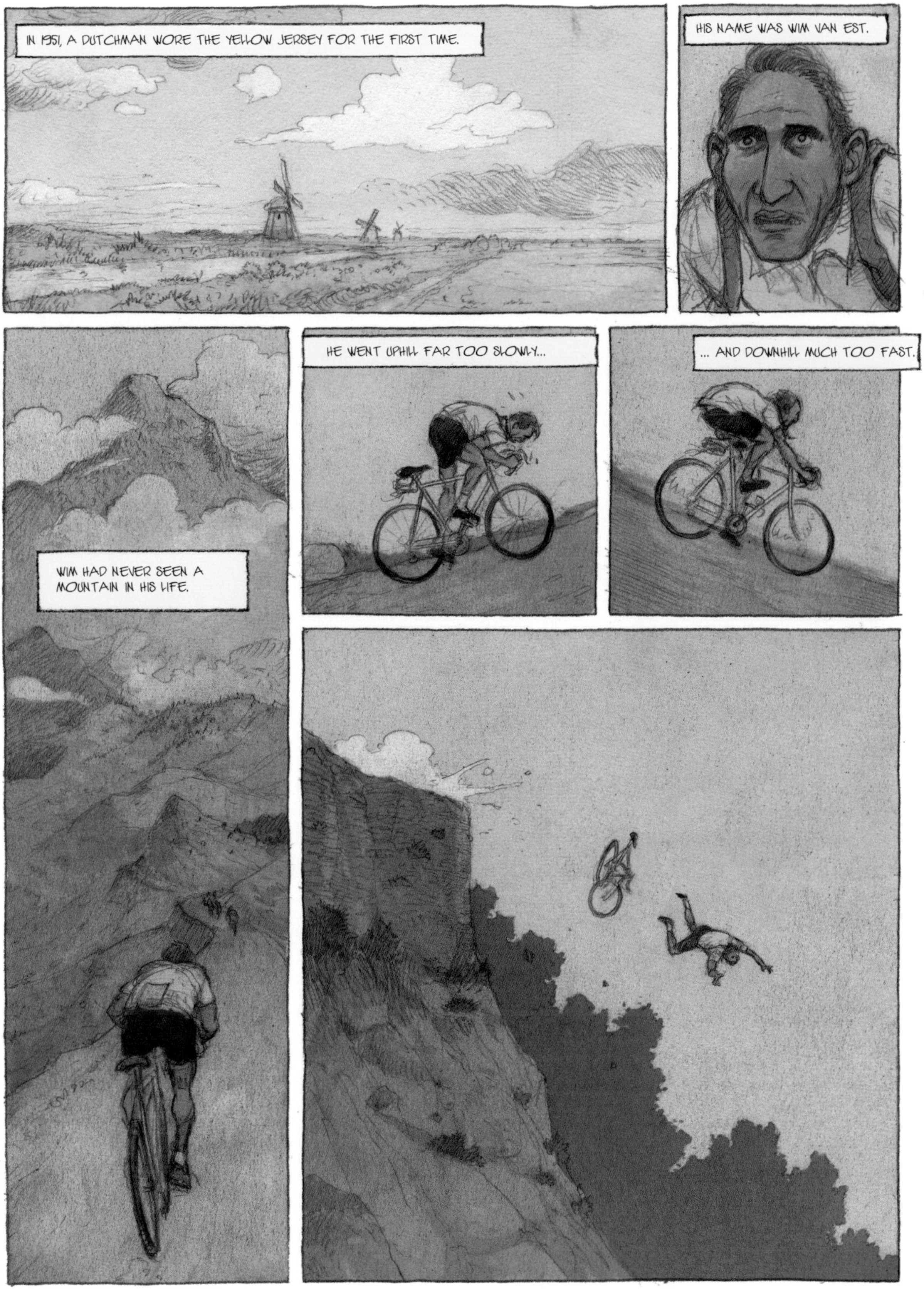
IN 1951, A DUTCHMAN WORE THE YELLOW JERSEY FOR THE FIRST TIME.
HIS NAME WAS WIM VAN EST.
WIM HAD NEVER SEEN A MOUNTAIN IN HIS LIFE.
HE WENT UPHILL FAR TOO SLOWLY...
... AND DOWNHILL MUCH TOO FAST.

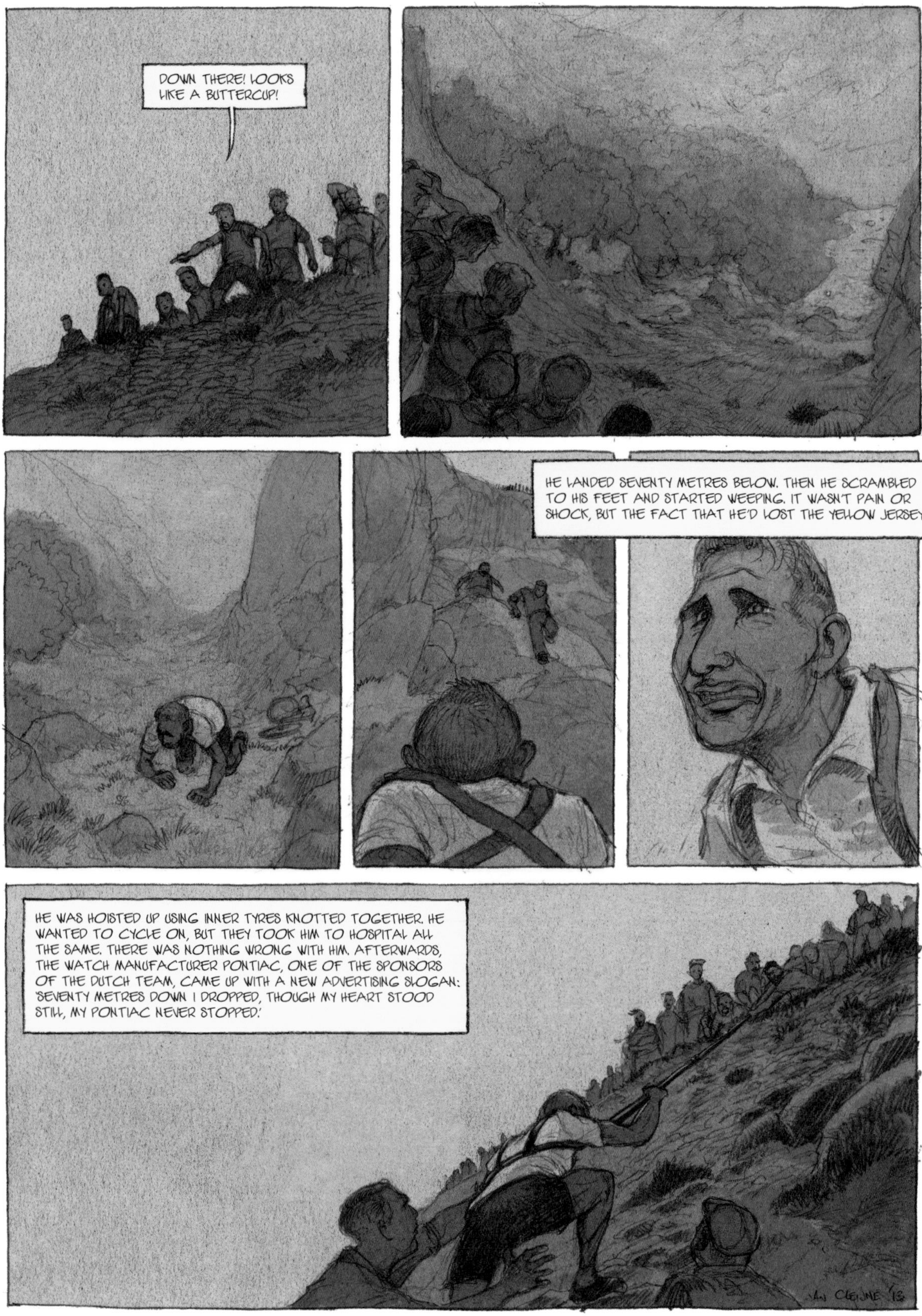
DOWN THERE! LOOKS LIKE A BUTTERCUP!
HE LANDED SEVENTY METRES BELOW. THEN HE SCRAMBLED TO HIS FEET AND STARTED WEEPING. IT WASN'T PAIN OR SHOCK, BUT THE FACT THAT HE'D LOST THE YELLOW JERSEY.
HE WAS HOISTED UP USING INNER TYRES KNOTTED TOGETHER. HE WANTED TO CYCLE ON, BUT THEY TOOK HIM TO HOSPITAL ALL THE SAME. THERE WAS NOTHING WRONG WITH HIM. AFTERWARDS, THE WATCH MANUFACTURER PONTIAC, ONE OF THE SPONSORS OF THE DUTCH TEAM, CAME UP WITH A NEW ADVERTISING SLOGAN: 'SEVENTY METRES DOWN I DROPPED, THOUGH MY HEART STOOD STILL, MY PONTIAC NEVER STOPPED.'
VAN CLEIJNE '13

5

MONSIEUR CHRONO

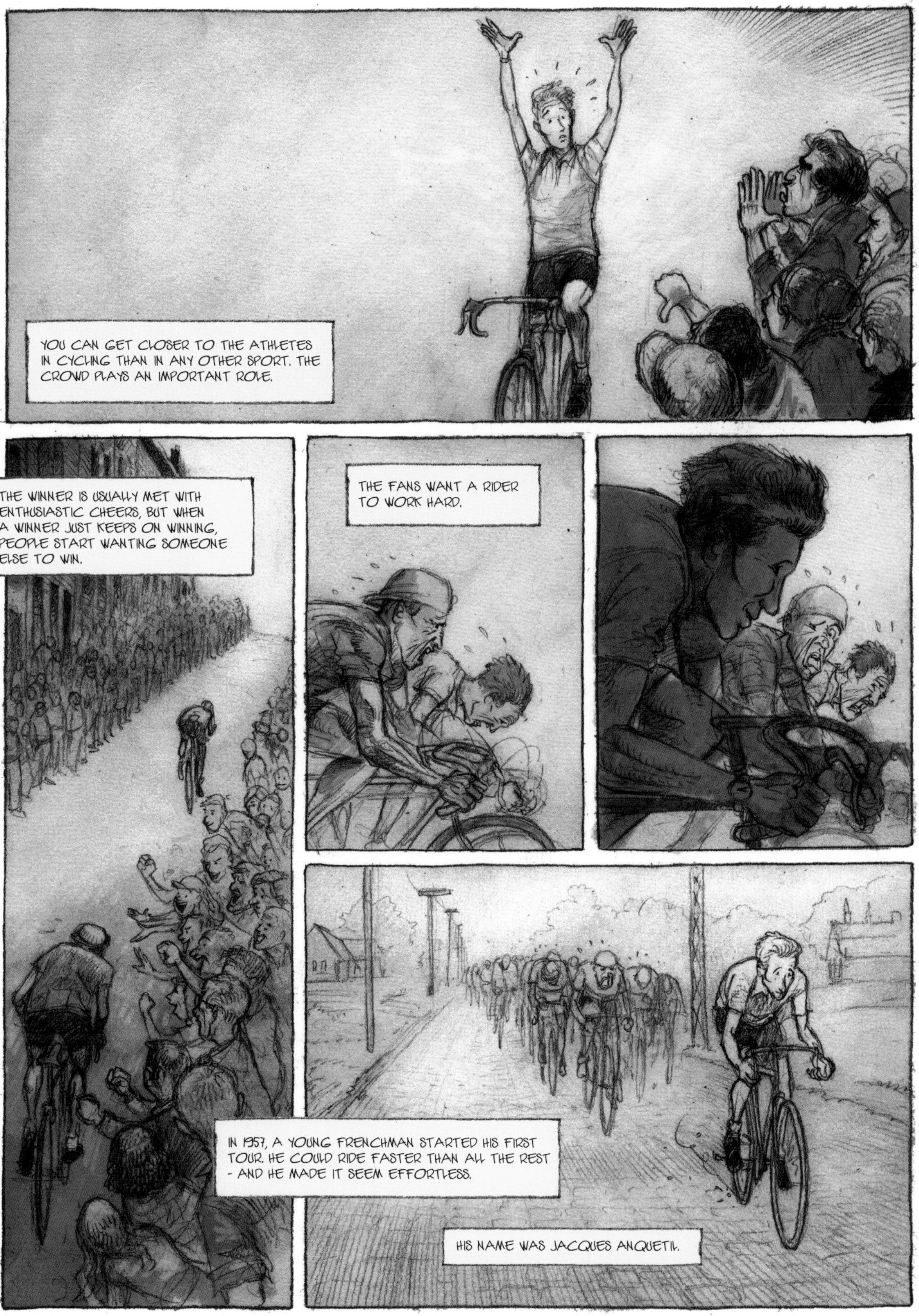
YOU CAN GET CLOSER TO THE ATHLETES IN CYCLING THAN IN ANY OTHER SPORT. THE CROWD PLAYS AN IMPORTANT ROLE.
THE WINNER IS USUALLY MET WITH ENTHUSIASTIC CHEERS, BUT WHEN A WINNER JUST KEEPS ON WINNING, PEOPLE START WANTING SOMEONE ELSE TO WIN.
THE FANS WANT A RIDER TO WORK HARD.
IN 1957, A YOUNG FRENCHMAN STARTED HIS FIRST TOUR. HE COULD RIDE FASTER THAN ALL THE REST - AND HE MADE IT SEEM EFFORTLESS.
HIS NAME WAS JACQUES ANQUETIL.

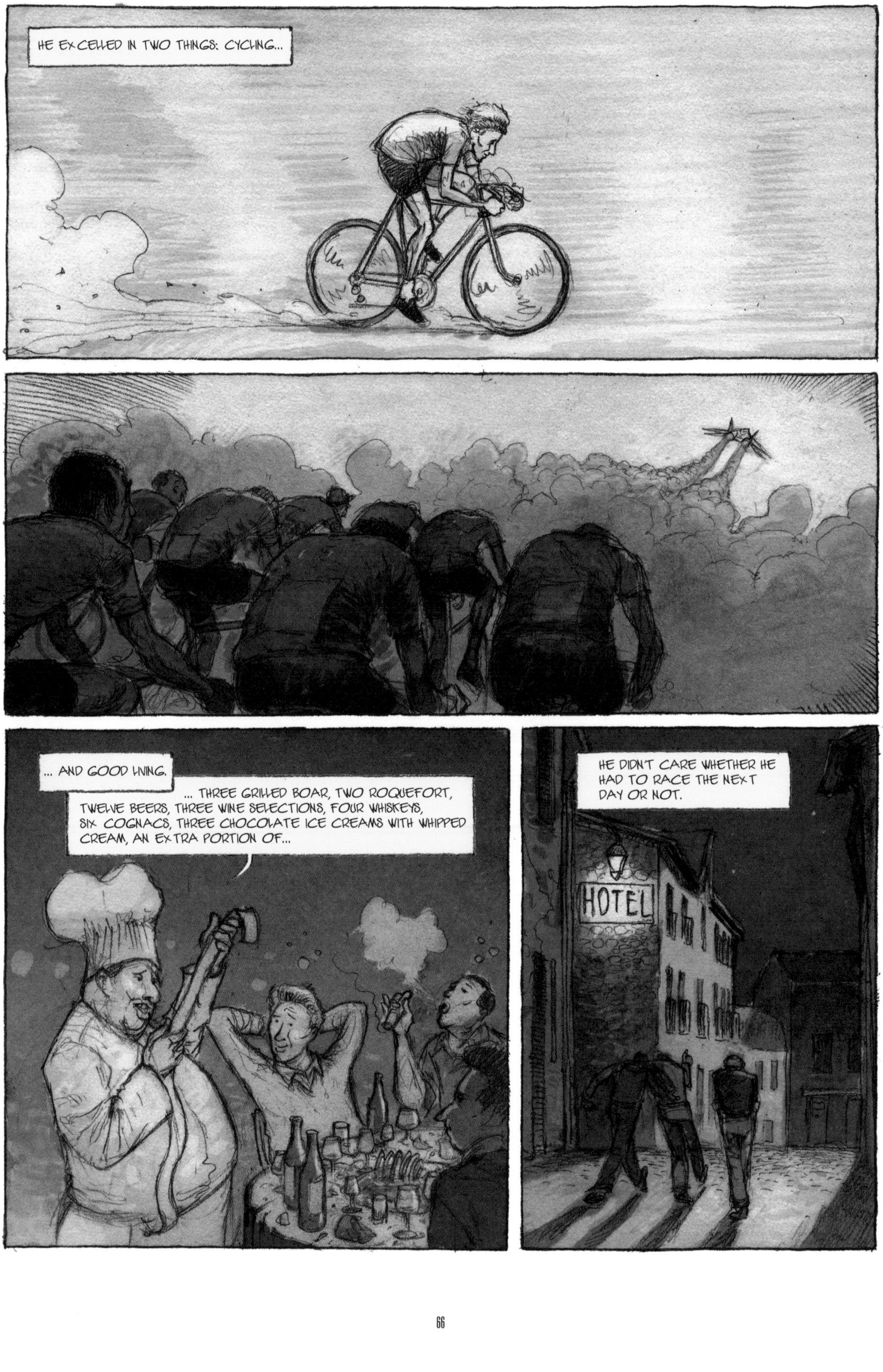
HE EXCELLED IN TWO THINGS: CYCLING...
... AND GOOD LIVING.
... THREE GRILLED BOAR, TWO ROQUEFORT, TWELVE BEERS, THREE WINE SELECTIONS, FOUR WHISKEYS, SIX COGNACS, THREE CHOCOLATE ICE CREAMS WITH WHIPPED CREAM, AN EXTRA PORTION OF...
HOTEL
HE DIDN'T CARE WHETHER HE HAD TO RACE THE NEXT DAY OR NOT.

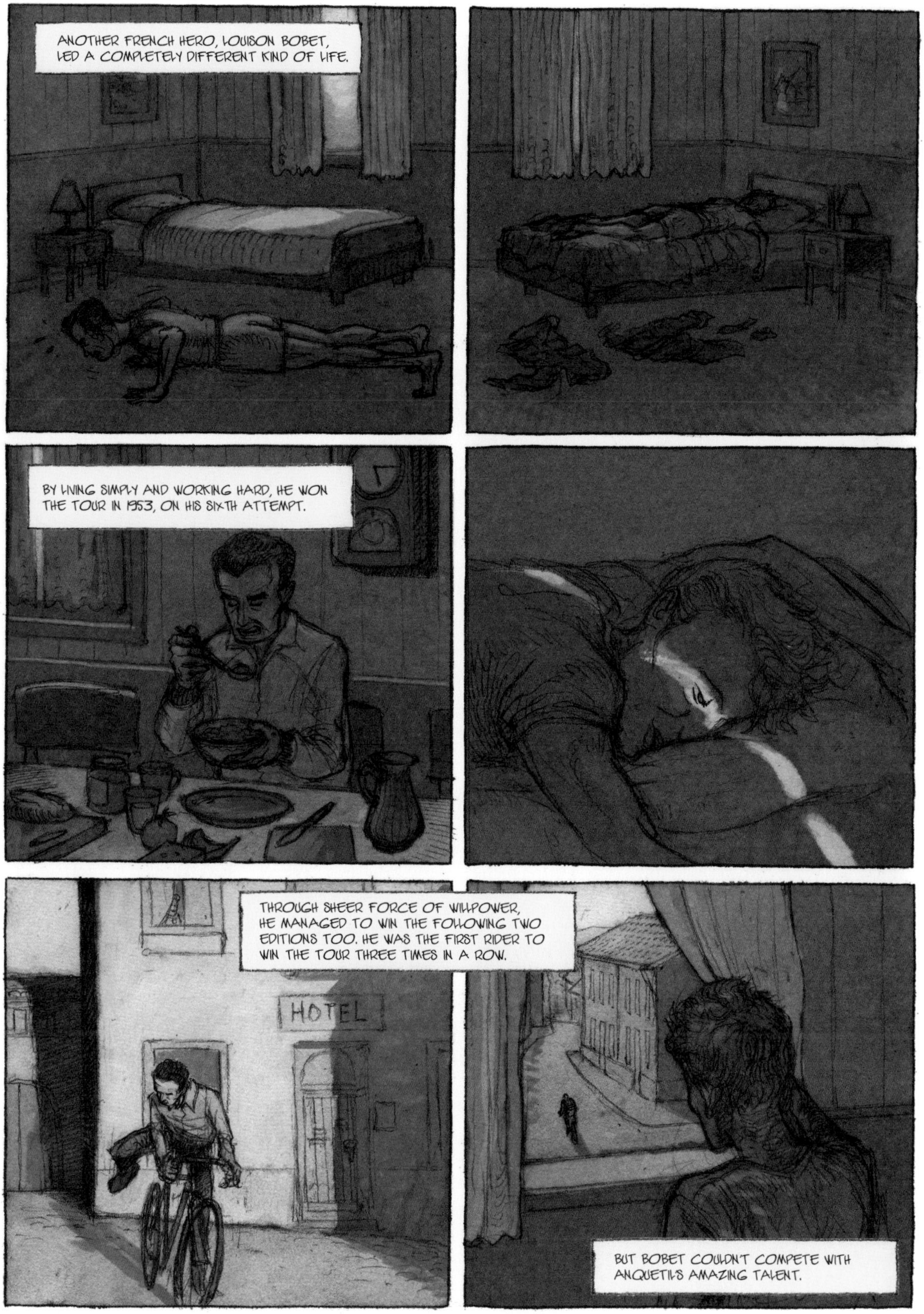
ANOTHER FRENCH HERO, LOUISON BOBET, LED A COMPLETELY DIFFERENT KIND OF LIFE.
BY LIVING SIMPLY AND WORKING HARD, HE WON THE TOUR IN 1953, ON HIS SIXTH ATTEMPT.
THROUGH SHEER FORCE OF WILLPOWER, HE MANAGED TO WIN THE FOLLOWING TWO EDITIONS TOO. HE WAS THE FIRST RIDER TO WIN THE TOUR THREE TIMES IN A ROW.
HOTEL
BUT BOBET COULDN'T COMPETE WITH ANQUETIL'S AMAZING TALENT.

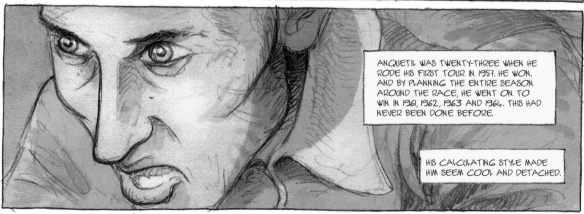

ANQUETIL WAS TWENTY-THREE WHEN HE RODE HIS FIRST TOUR IN 1957. HE WON. AND BY PLANNING THE ENTIRE SEASON AROUND THE RACE, HE WENT ON TO WIN IN 1961, 1962, 1963 AND 1964. THIS HAD NEVER BEEN DONE BEFORE.

HIS CALCULATING STYLE MADE HIM SEEM *COOL* AND DETACHED.

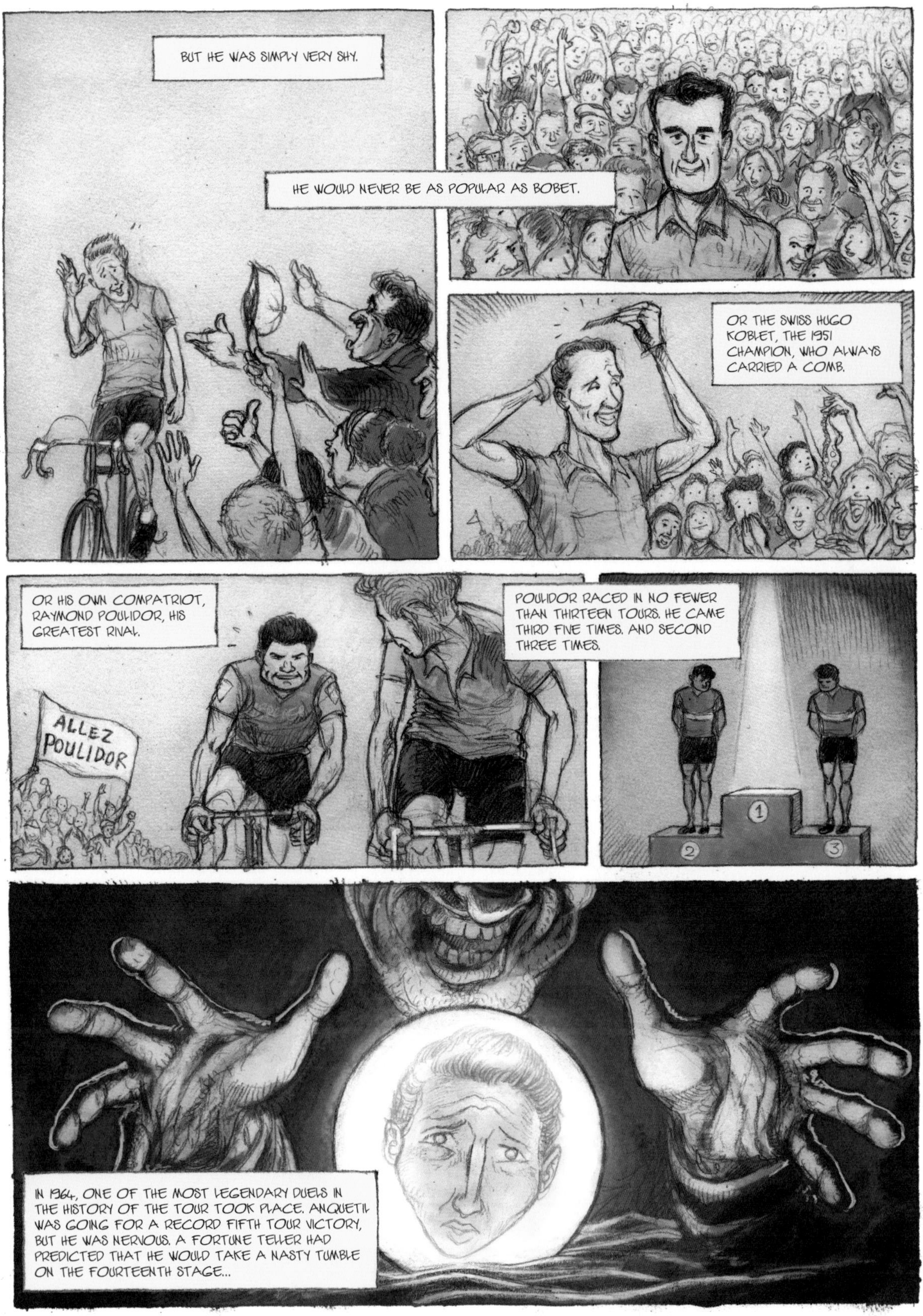
BUT HE WAS SIMPLY VERY SHY.
HE WOULD NEVER BE AS POPULAR AS BOBET.
OR THE SWISS HUGO KOBLET, THE 1951 CHAMPION, WHO ALWAYS CARRIED A COMB.
OR HIS OWN COMPATRIOT, RAYMOND POULIDOR, HIS GREATEST RIVAL.
ALLEZ POULIDOR
POULIDOR RACED IN NO FEWER THAN THIRTEEN TOURS. HE CAME THIRD FIVE TIMES. AND SECOND THREE TIMES.
1
2
3
IN 1964, ONE OF THE MOST LEGENDARY DUELS IN THE HISTORY OF THE TOUR TOOK PLACE. ANQUETIL WAS GOING FOR A RECORD FIFTH TOUR VICTORY, BUT HE WAS NERVOUS. A FORTUNE TELLER HAD PREDICTED THAT HE WOULD TAKE A NASTY TUMBLE ON THE FOURTEENTH STAGE...

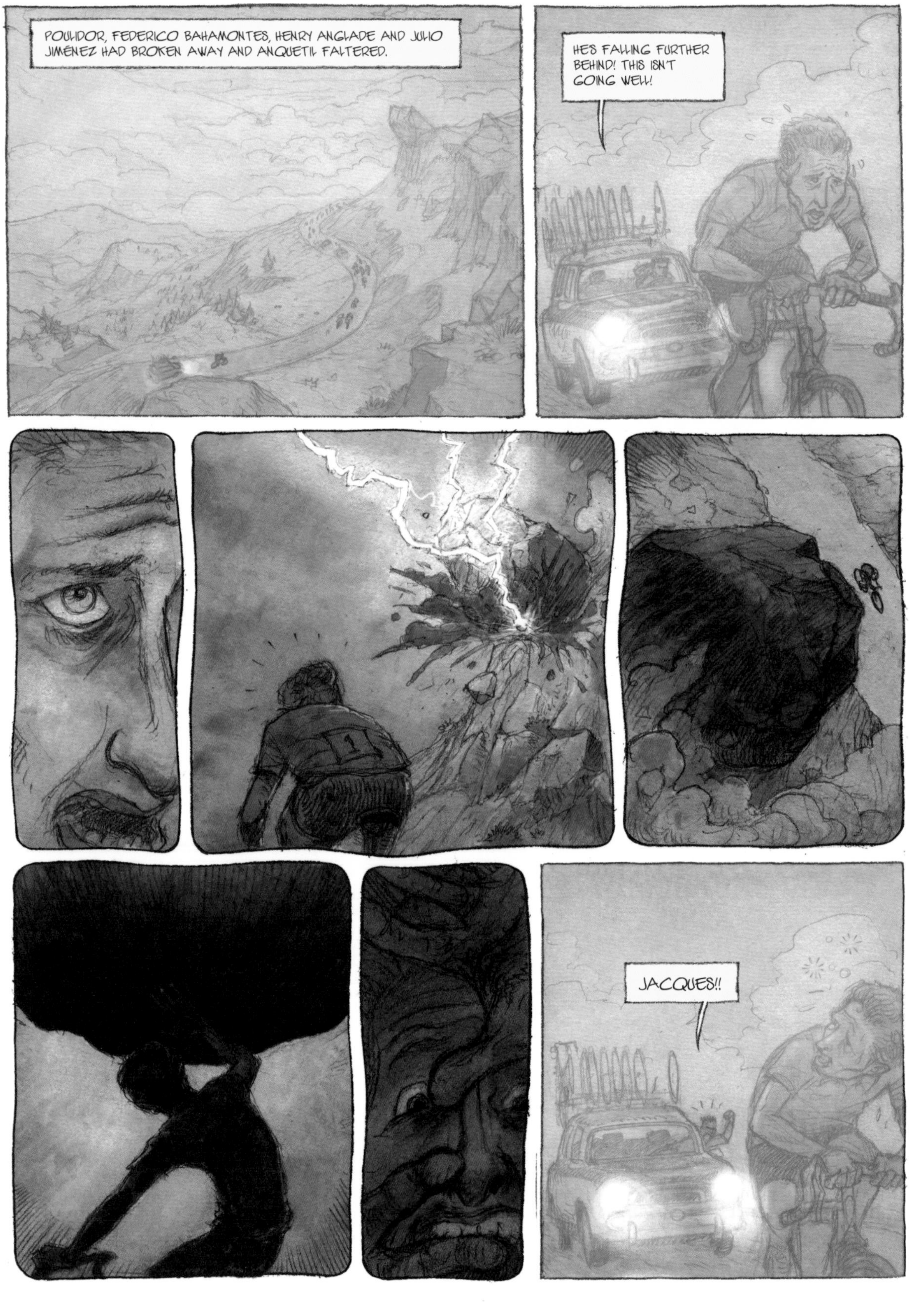
POULIDOR, FEDERICO BAHAMONTES, HENRY ANGLADE AND JULIO JIMÉNEZ HAD BROKEN AWAY AND ANQUETIL FALTERED.
HE'S FALLING FURTHER BEHIND! THIS ISN'T GOING WELL!
JACQUES!!

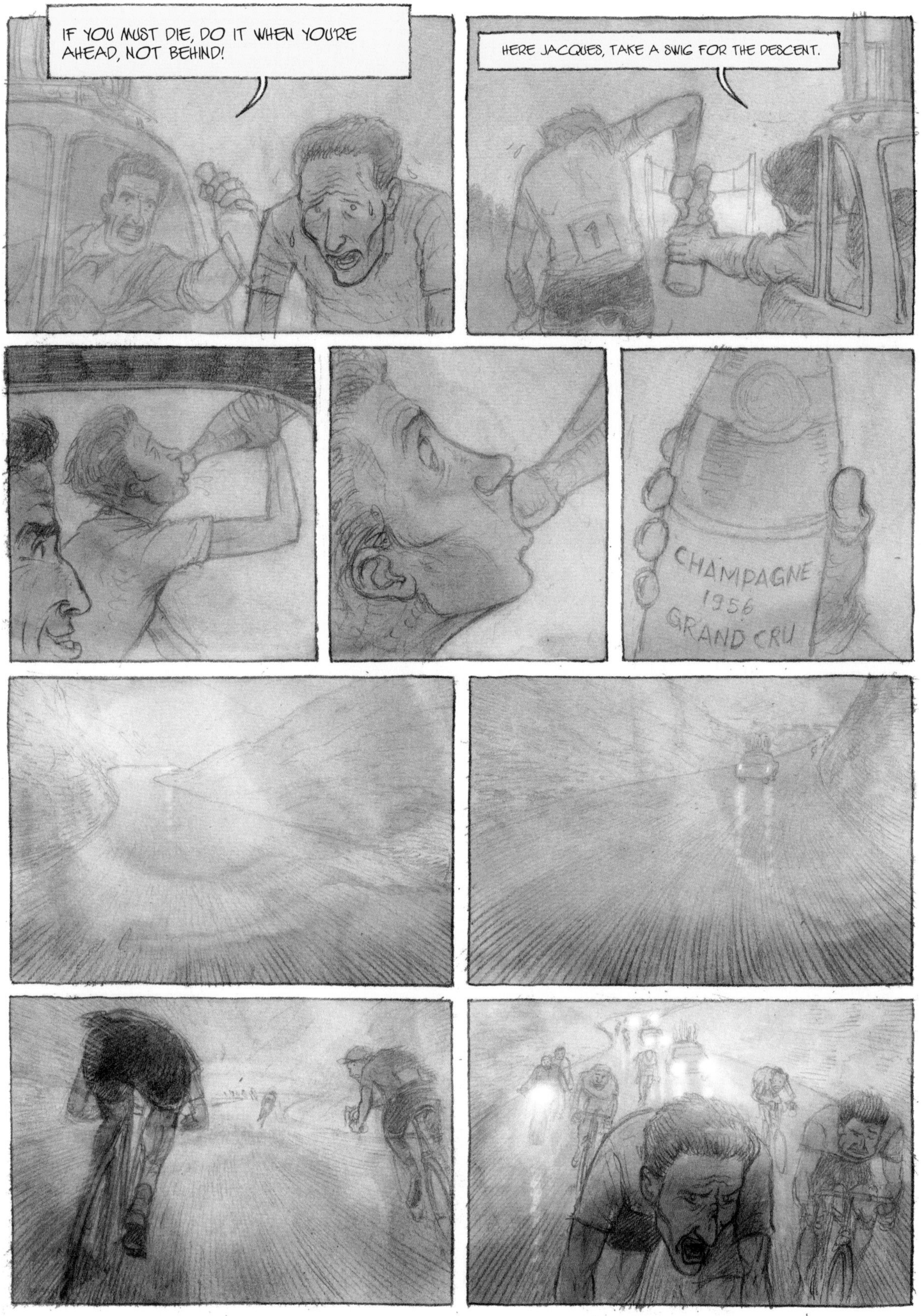
IF YOU MUST DIE, DO IT WHEN YOU'RE AHEAD, NOT BEHIND!
HERE JACQUES, TAKE A SWIG FOR THE DESCENT.
1
CHAMPAGNE 1956 GRAND CRU

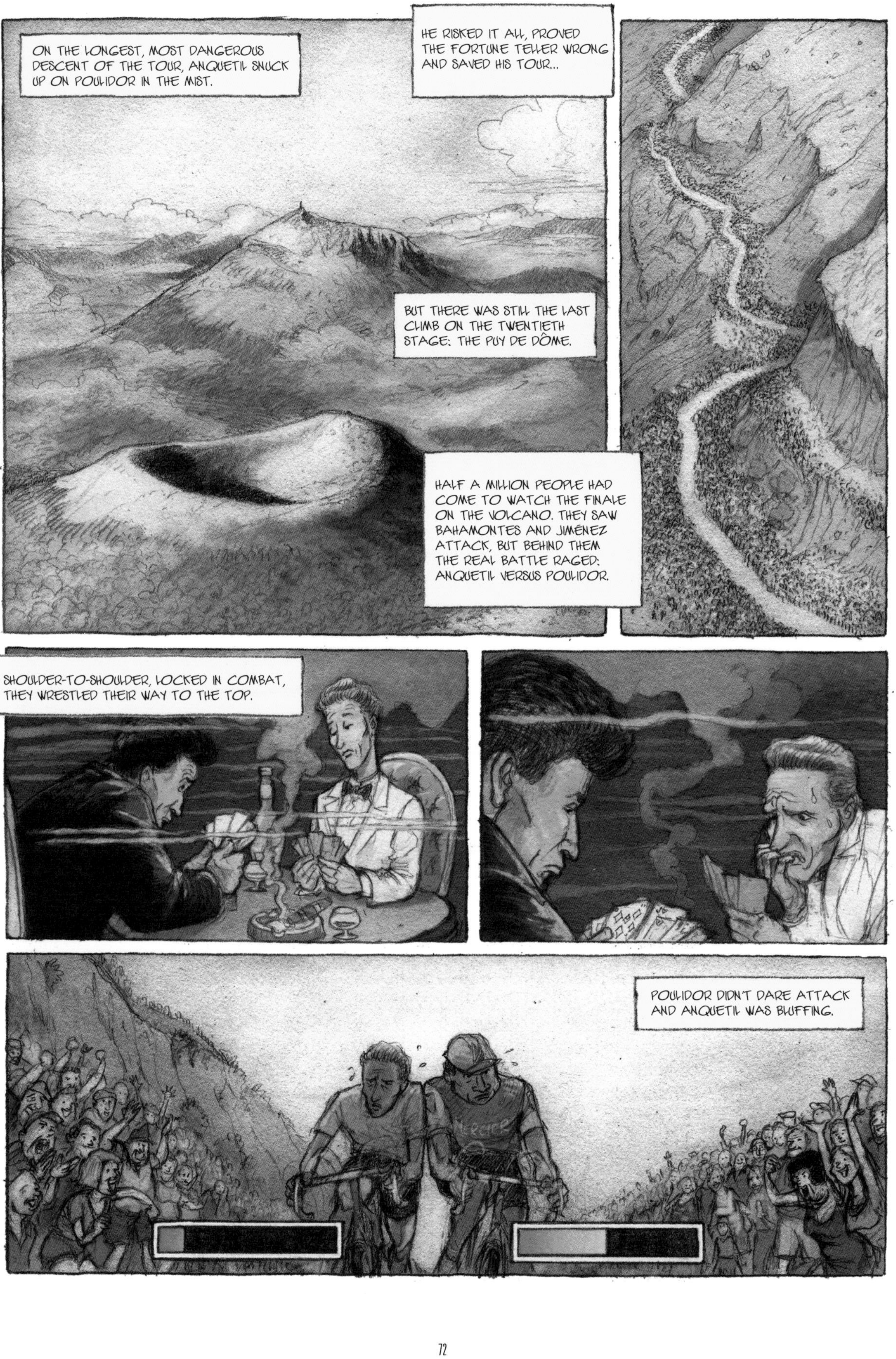
ON THE LONGEST, MOST DANGEROUS DESCENT OF THE TOUR, ANQUETIL SNUCK UP ON POULIDOR IN THE MIST.
HE RISKED IT ALL, PROVED THE FORTUNE TELLER WRONG AND SAVED HIS TOUR...
BUT THERE WAS STILL THE LAST CLIMB ON THE TWENTIETH STAGE: THE PUY DE DÔME.
HALF A MILLION PEOPLE HAD COME TO WATCH THE FINALE ON THE VOLCANO. THEY SAW BAHAMONTES AND JIMÉNEZ ATTACK, BUT BEHIND THEM THE REAL BATTLE RAGED: ANQUETIL VERSUS POULIDOR.
SHOULDER-TO-SHOULDER, LOCKED IN COMBAT, THEY WRESTLED THEIR WAY TO THE TOP.
POULIDOR DIDN'T DARE ATTACK AND ANQUETIL WAS BLUFFING.

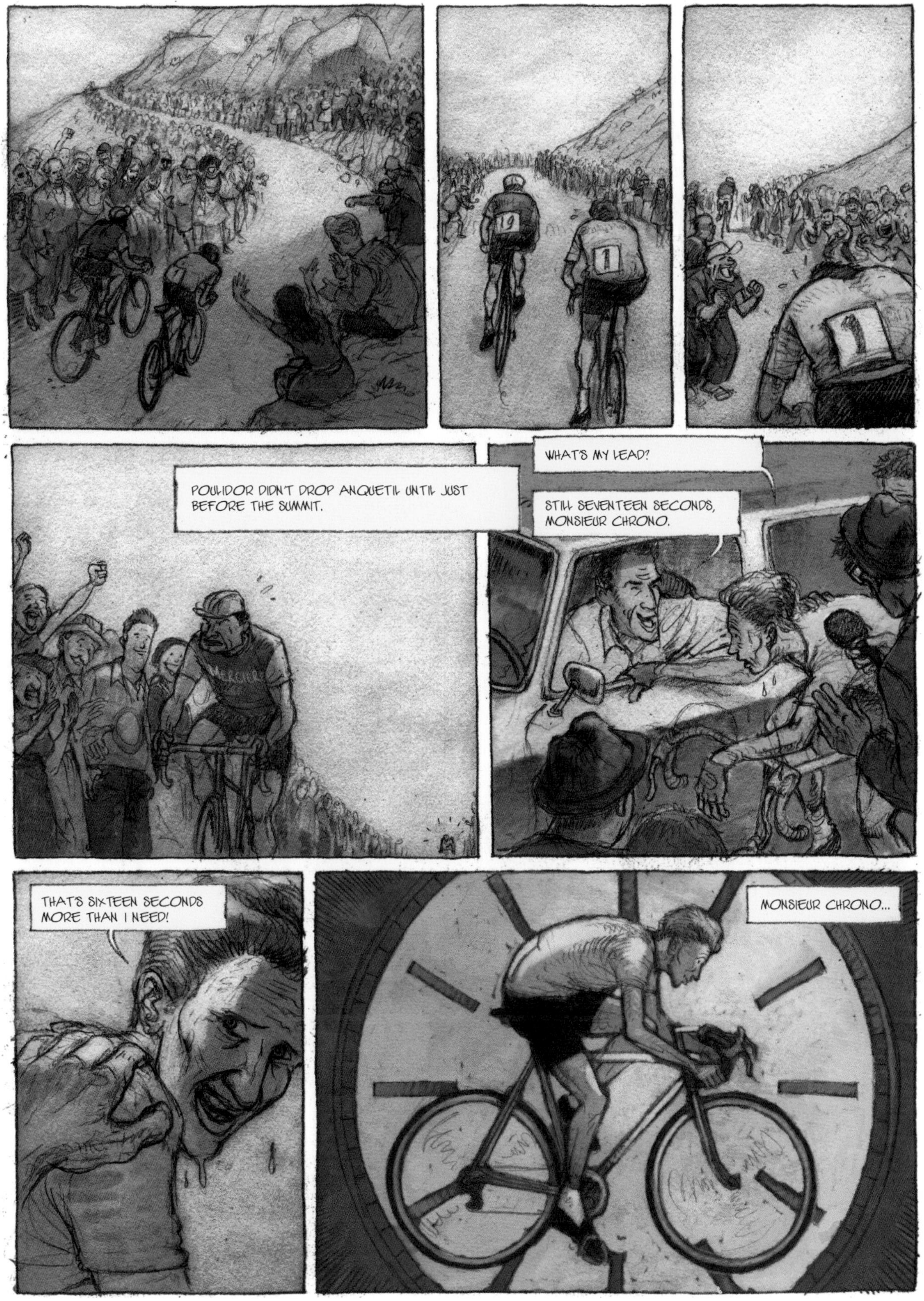
POULIDOR DIDN'T DROP ANQUETIL UNTIL JUST BEFORE THE SUMMIT.
WHAT'S MY LEAD?
STILL SEVENTEEN SECONDS, MONSIEUR CHRONO.
THAT'S SIXTEEN SECONDS MORE THAN I NEED!
MONSIEUR CHRONO...

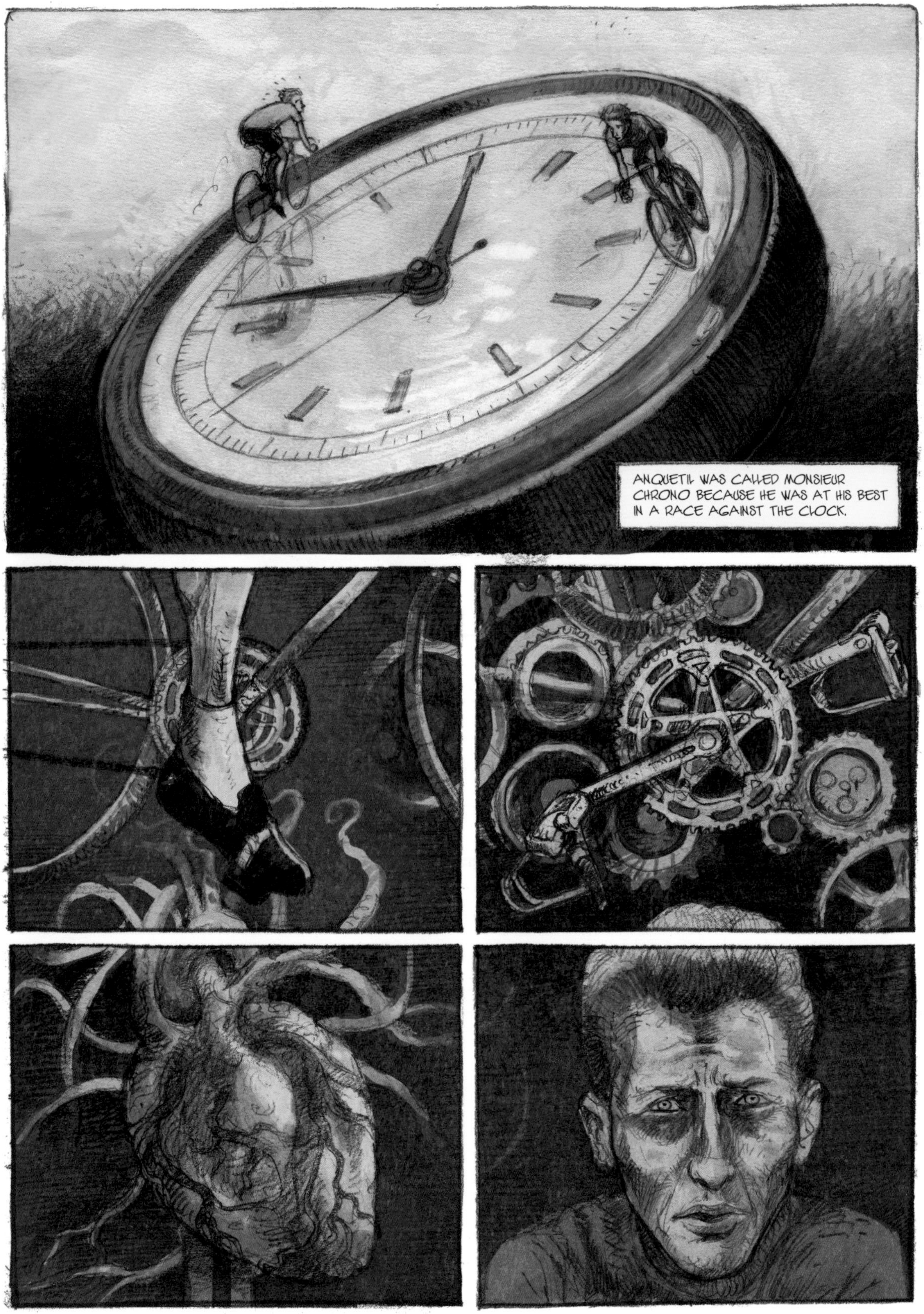
ANQUETIL WAS CALLED MONSIEUR CHRONO BECAUSE HE WAS AT HIS BEST IN A RACE AGAINST THE CLOCK.

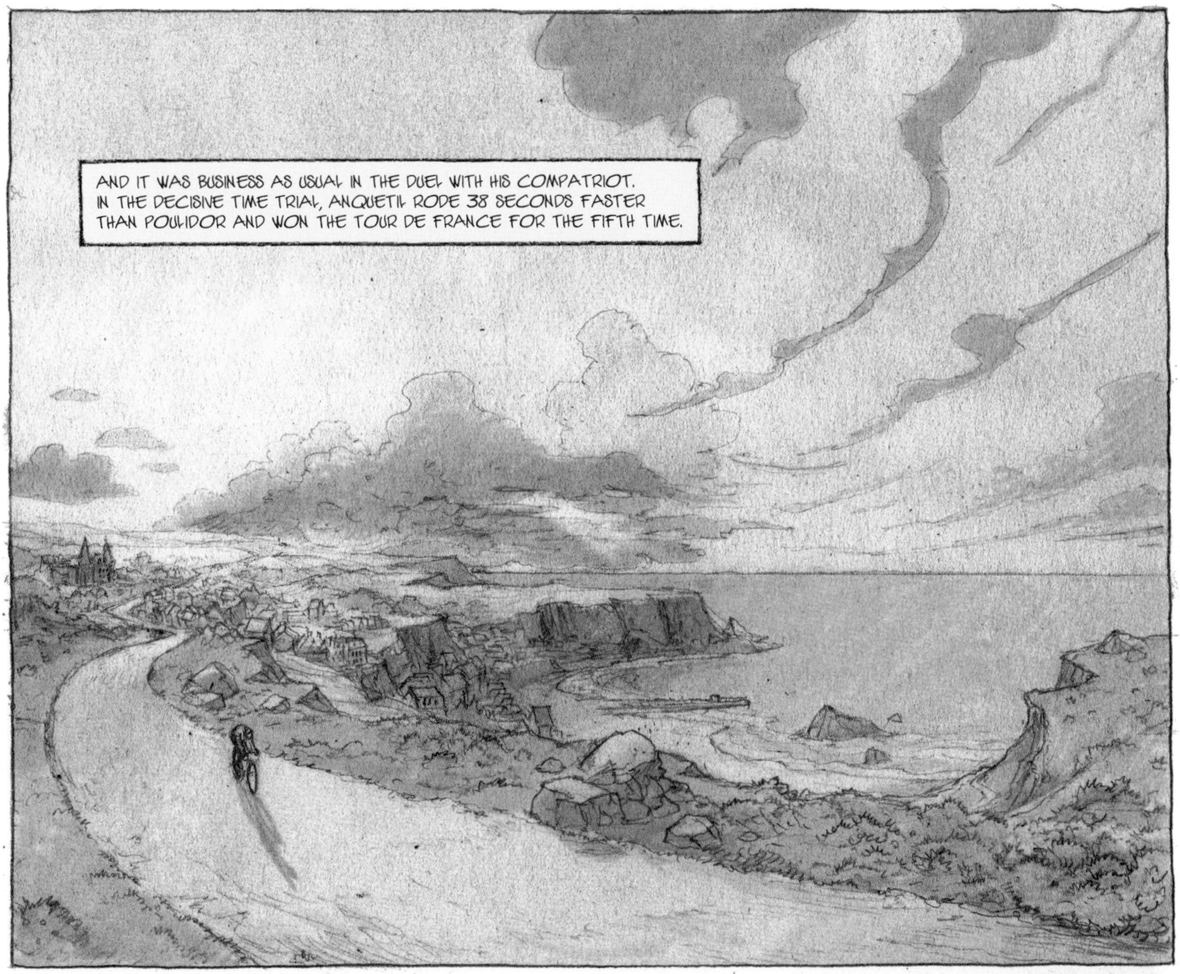
AND IT WAS BUSINESS AS USUAL IN THE DUEL WITH HIS COMPATRIOT. IN THE DECISIVE TIME TRIAL, ANQUETIL RODE 38 SECONDS FASTER THAN POULIDOR AND WON THE TOUR DE FRANCE FOR THE FIFTH TIME.

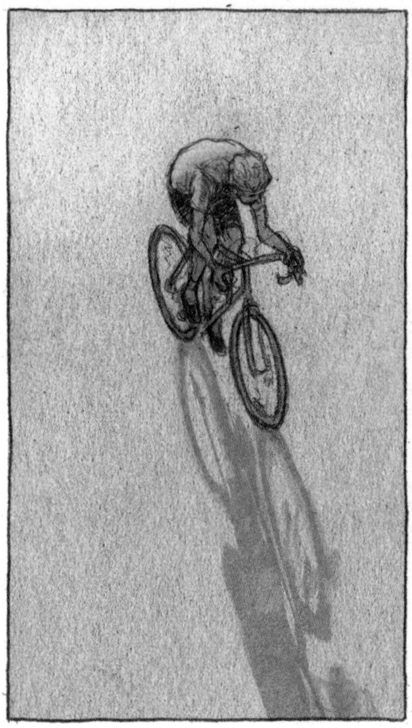

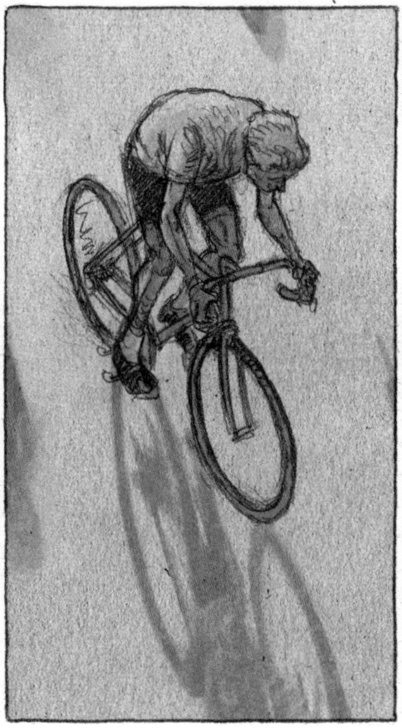

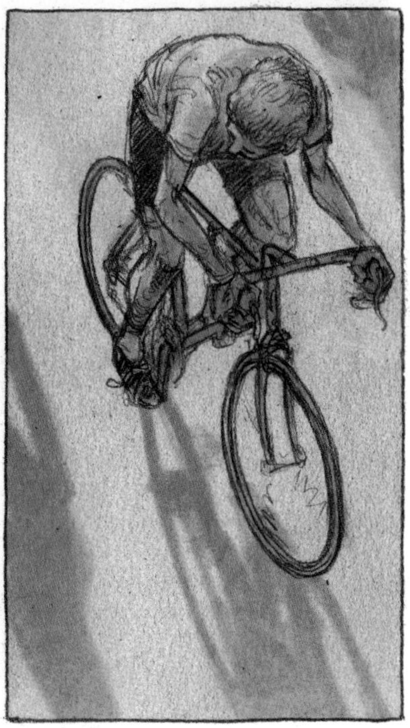

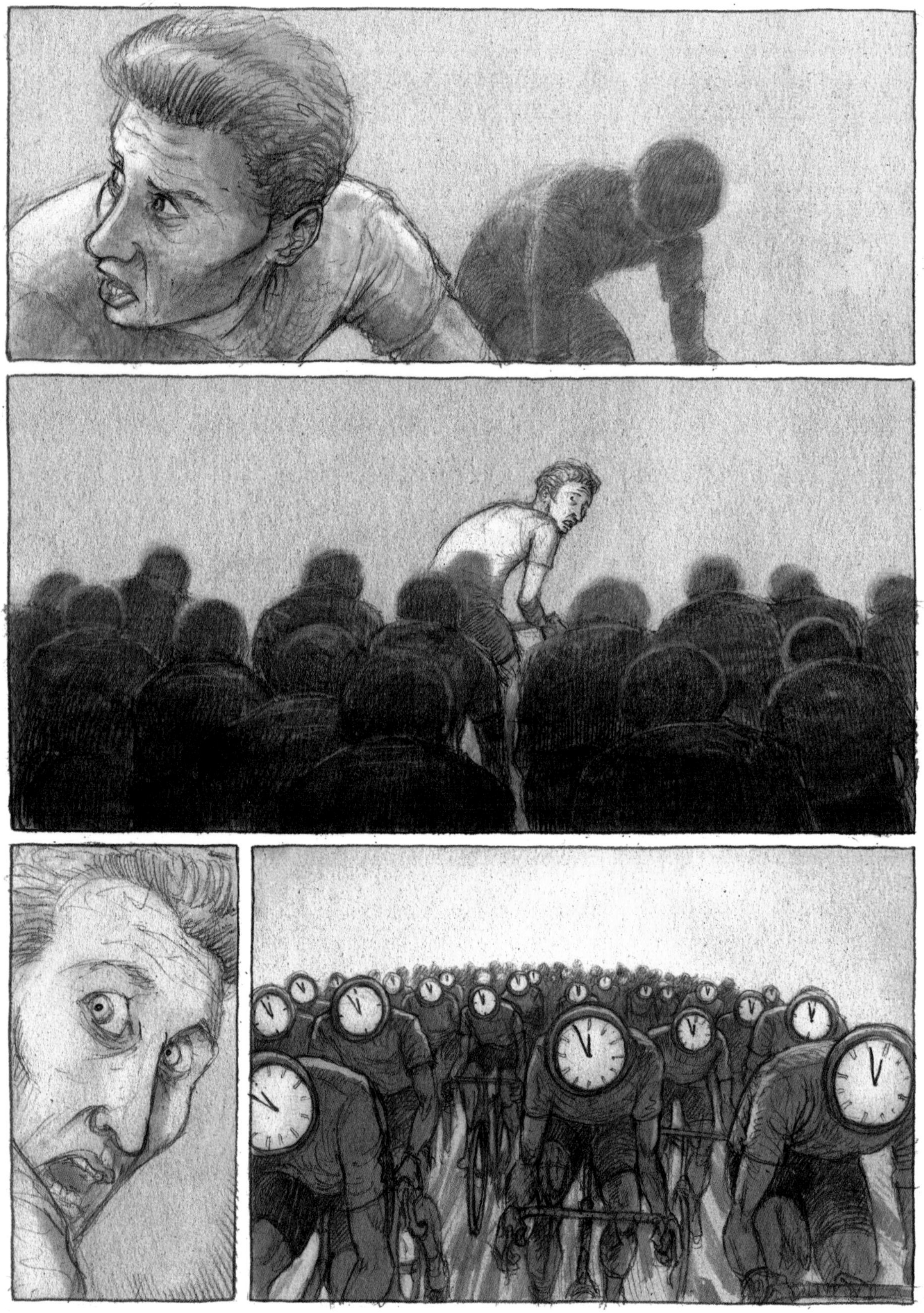

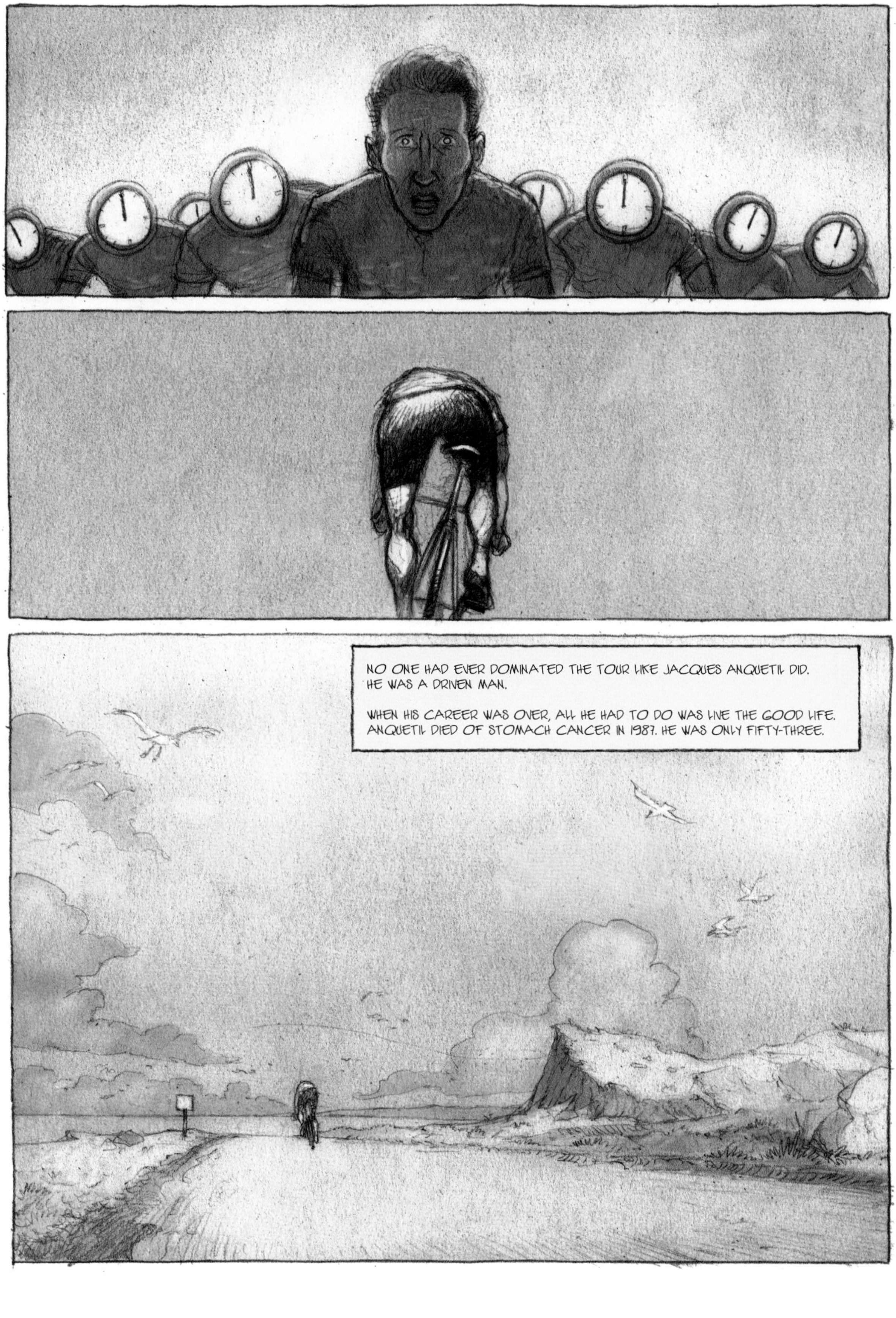
NO ONE HAD EVER DOMINATED THE TOUR LIKE JACQUES ANQUETIL DID. HE WAS A DRIVEN MAN.
WHEN HIS CAREER WAS OVER, ALL HE HAD TO DO WAS LIVE THE GOOD LIFE. ANQUETIL DIED OF STOMACH CANCER IN 1987. HE WAS ONLY FIFTY-THREE.

MONT VENTOUX

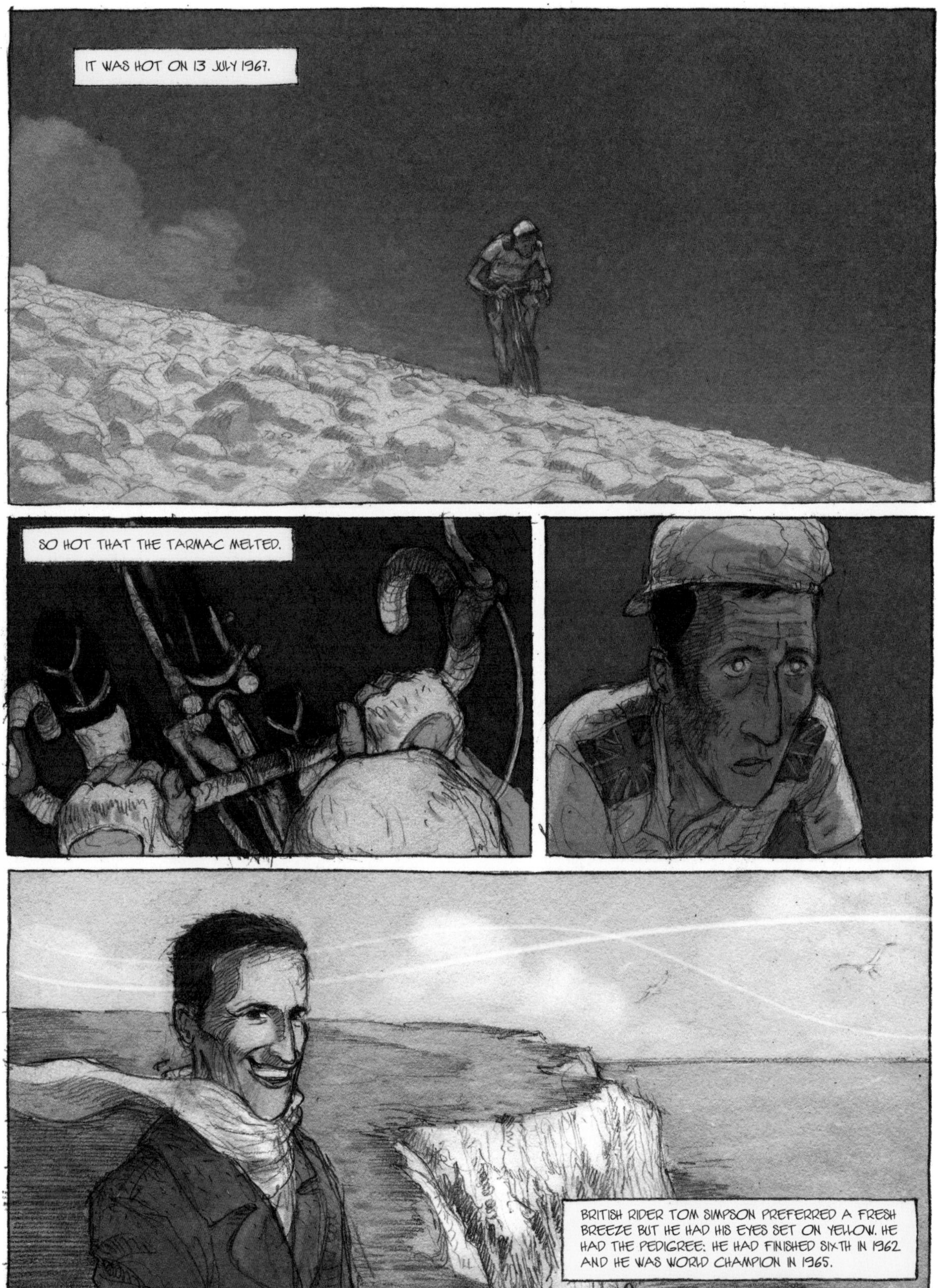
IT WAS HOT ON 13 JULY 1967.
SO HOT THAT THE TARMAC MELTED.
BRITISH RIDER TOM SIMPSON PREFERRED A FRESH BREEZE BUT HE HAD HIS EYES SET ON YELLOW. HE HAD THE PEDIGREE: HE HAD FINISHED SIXTH IN 1962 AND HE WAS WORLD CHAMPION IN 1965.

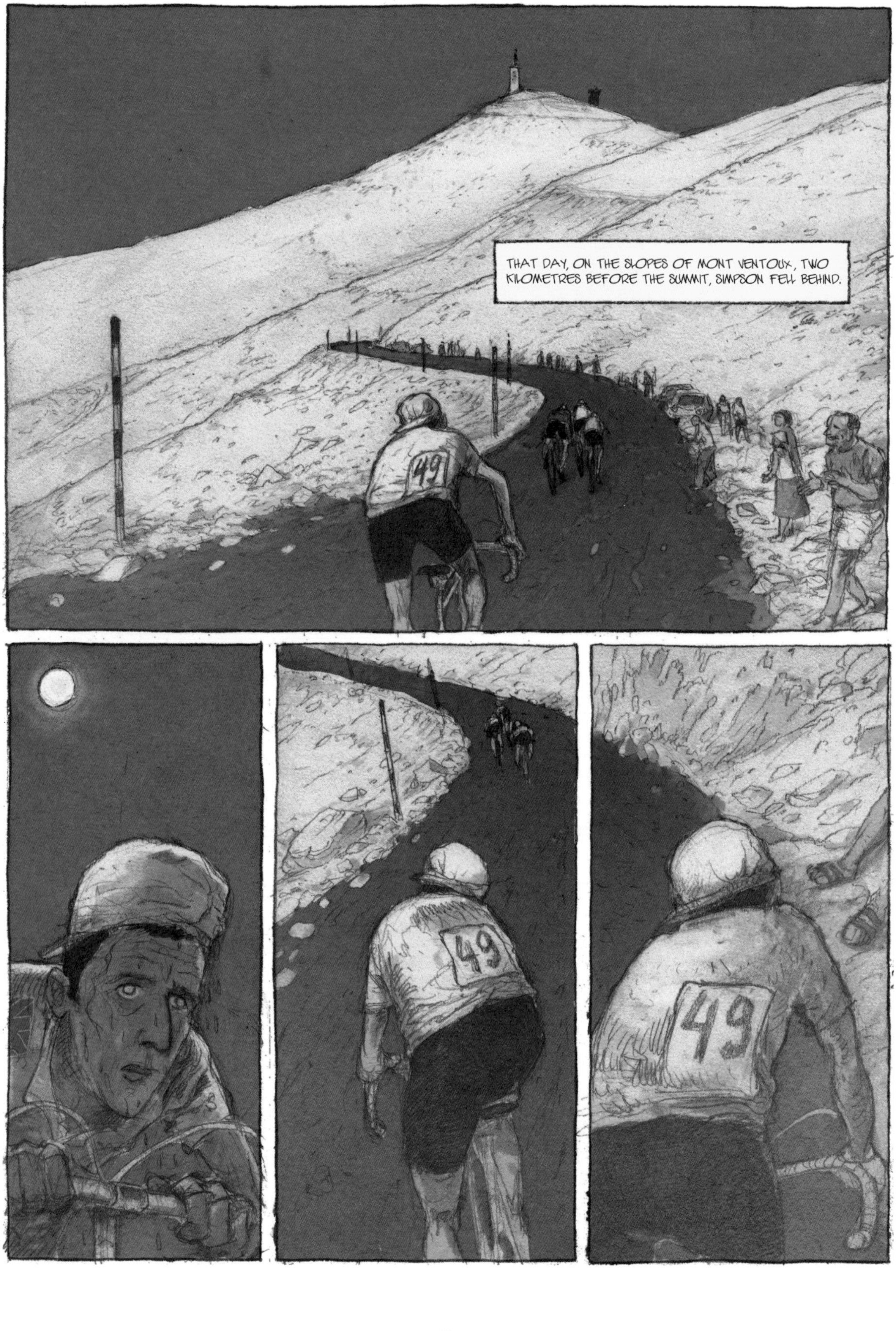
THAT DAY, ON THE SLOPES OF MONT VENTOUX, TWO KILOMETRES BEFORE THE SUMMIT, SIMPSON FELL BEHIND.
49
49
49

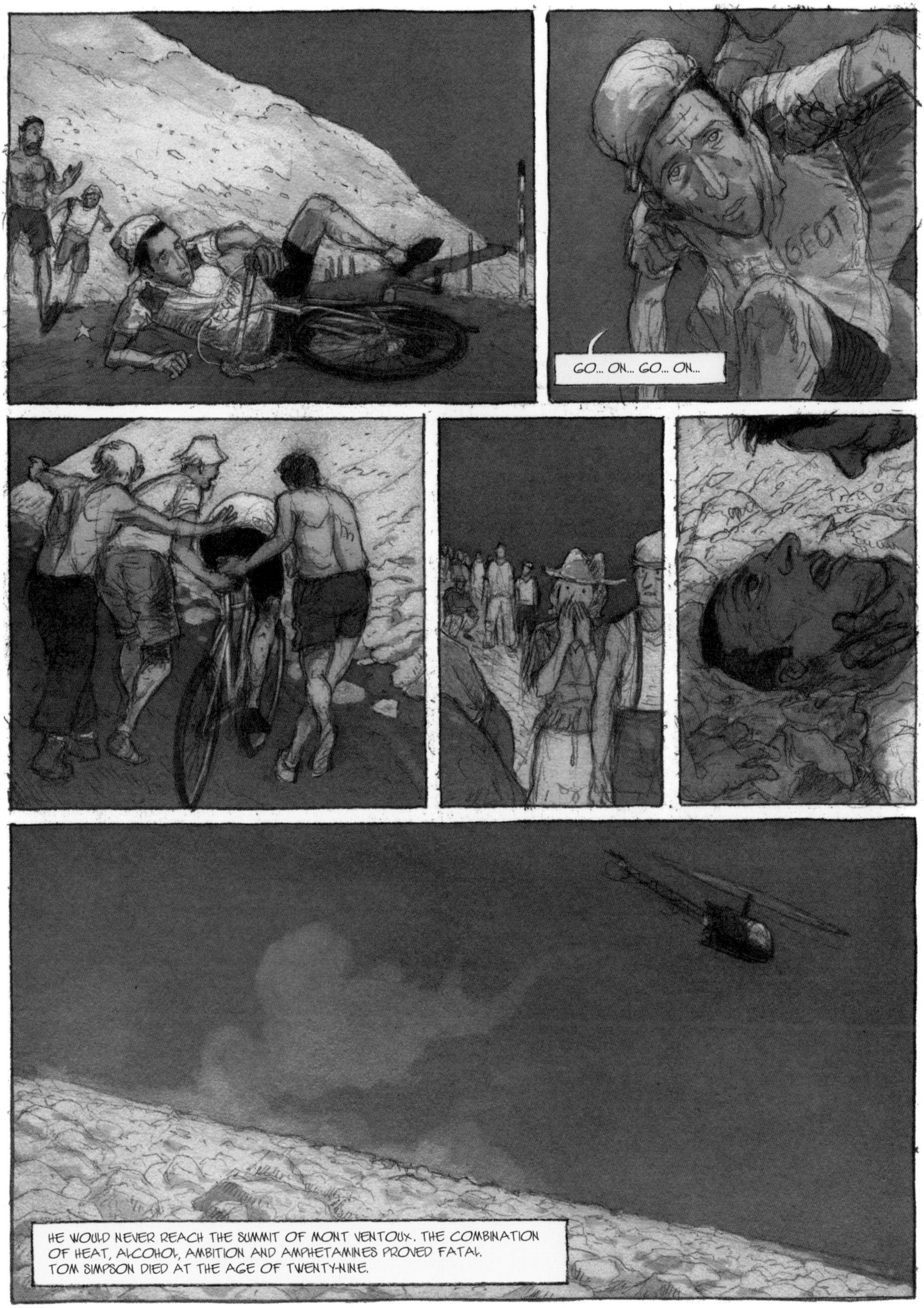
GO... ON... GO... ON...
HE WOULD NEVER REACH THE SUMMIT OF MONT VENTOUX. THE COMBINATION OF HEAT, ALCOHOL, AMBITION AND AMPHETAMINES PROVED FATAL. TOM SIMPSON DIED AT THE AGE OF TWENTY-NINE.

THE CANNIBAL

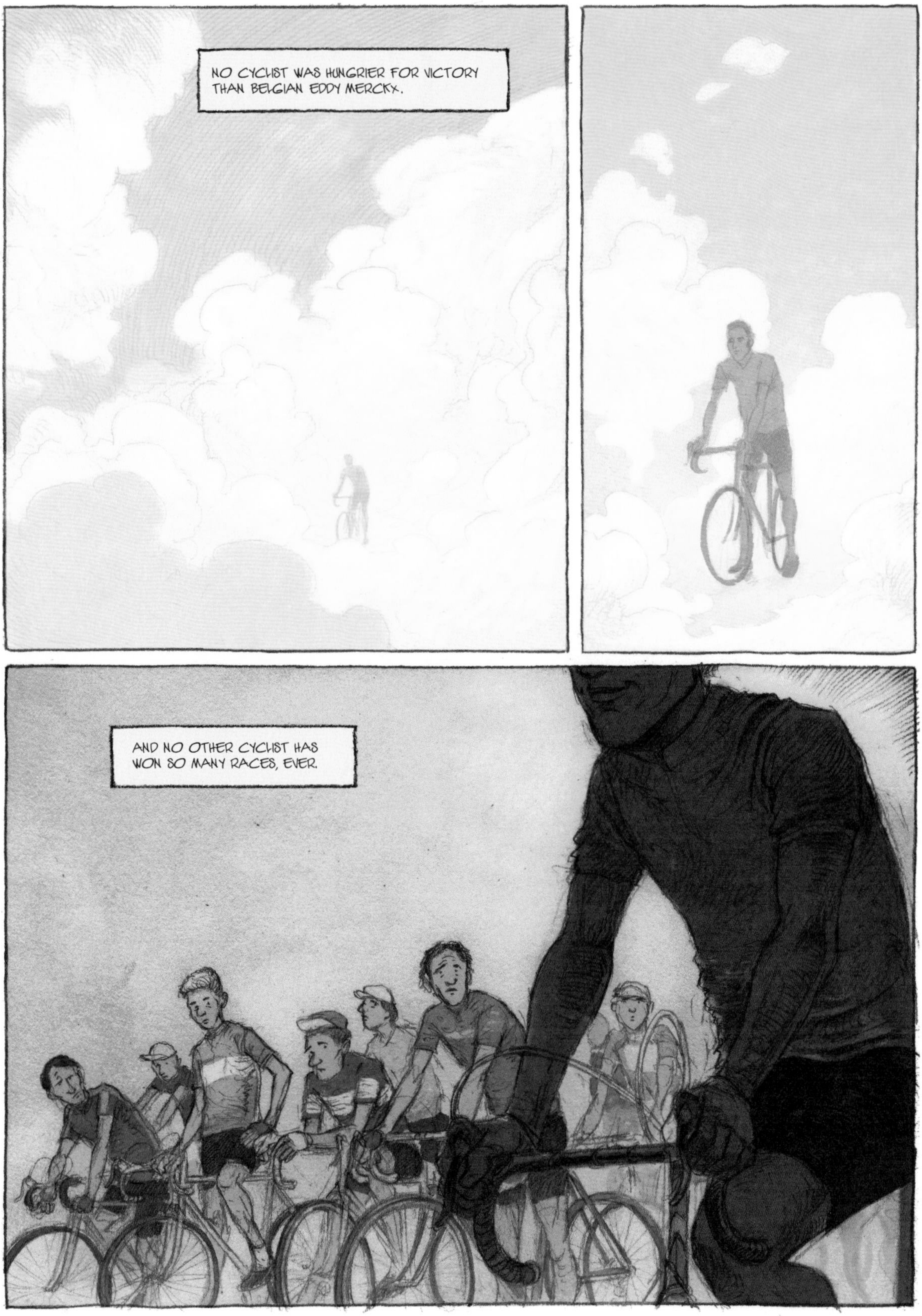
NO CYCLIST WAS HUNGRIER FOR VICTORY THAN BELGIAN EDDY MERCKX.
AND NO OTHER CYCLIST HAS WON SO MANY RACES, EVER.

MERCKX RODE THE TOUR FOR THE FIRST TIME IN 1969.

HE HAD ALREADY WON FOUR STAGES. HE'D BEEN WEARING THE YELLOW JERSEY FOR ALMOST TWO WEEKS AND HAD A BIG LEAD ON THE NEXT RIDER, FRENCHMAN ROGER PINGEON, THE 1967 WINNER OF THE TOUR.

SO HE COULD HAVE TAKEN THINGS A LITTLE EASIER DURING THE SEVENTEENTH STAGE, FROM LUCHON TO MOURENX.

POULIDOR AND PINGEON FELL BACK. ONLY MERCKX'S TEAMMATE AND FELLOW BELGIAN MARTIN VAN DEN BOSSCHE COULD KEEP UP.

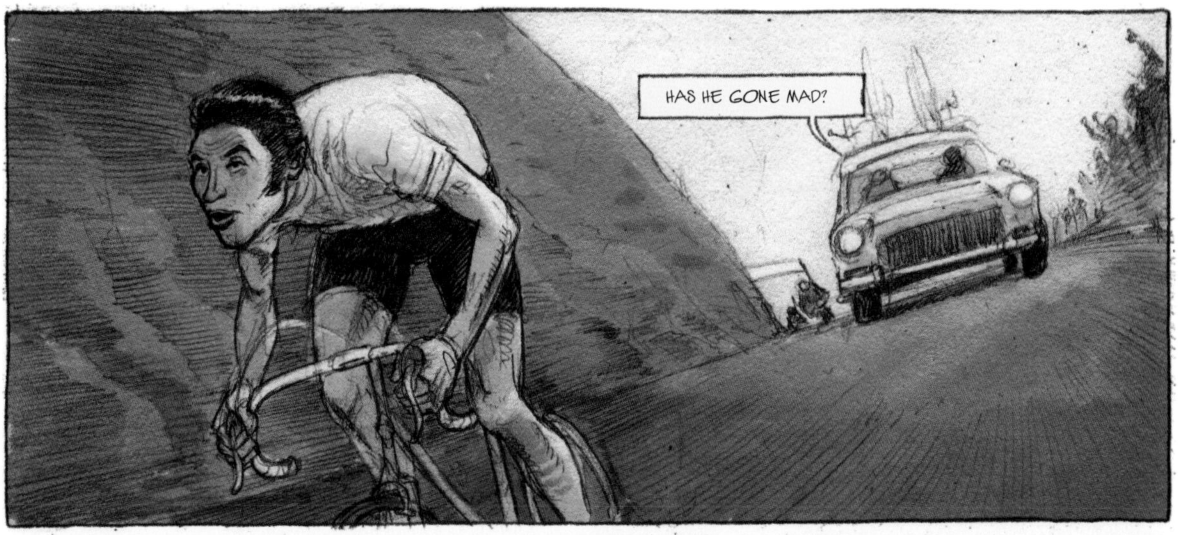
HAS HE GONE MAD?

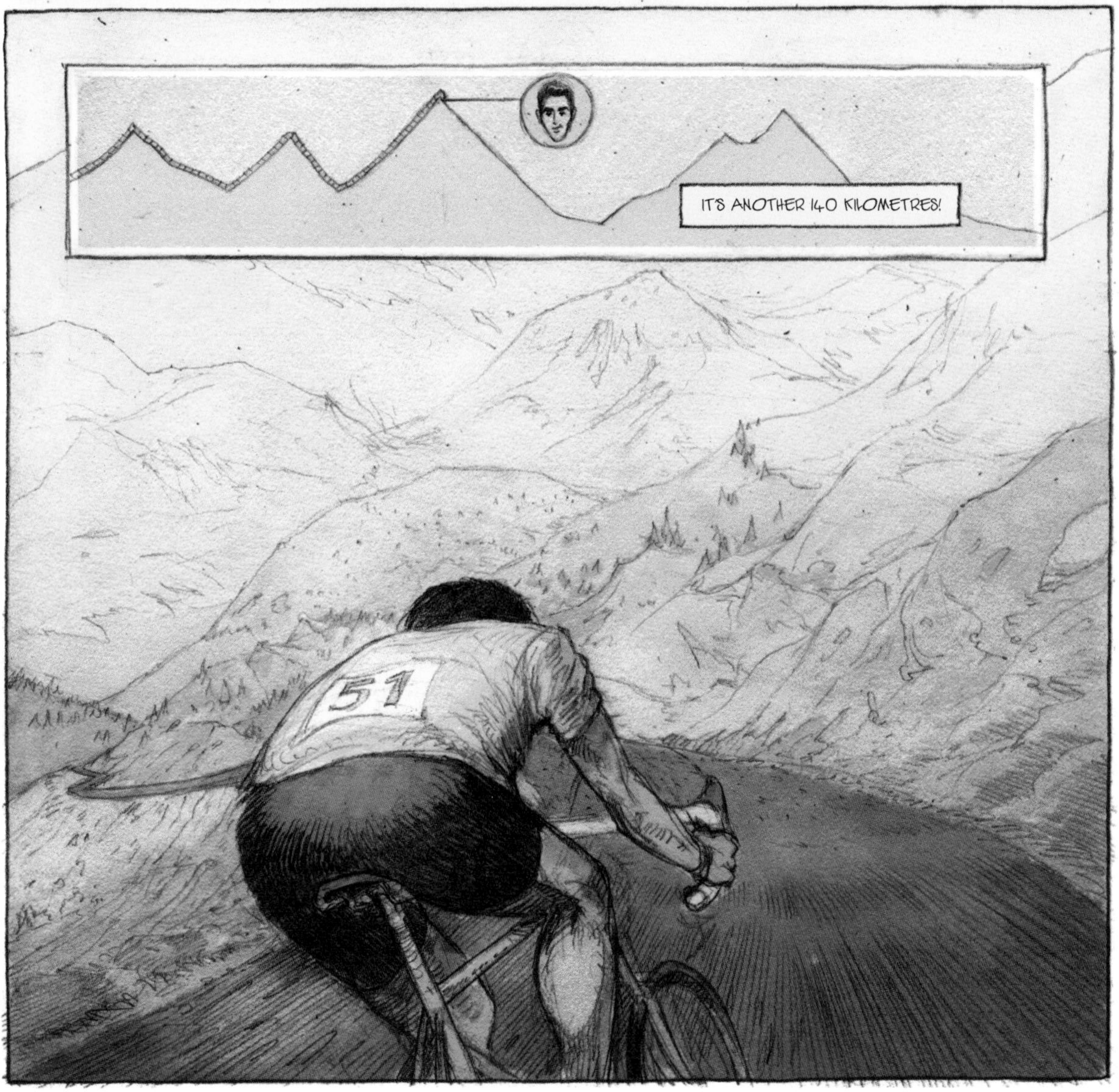
IT'S ANOTHER 140 KILOMETRES!

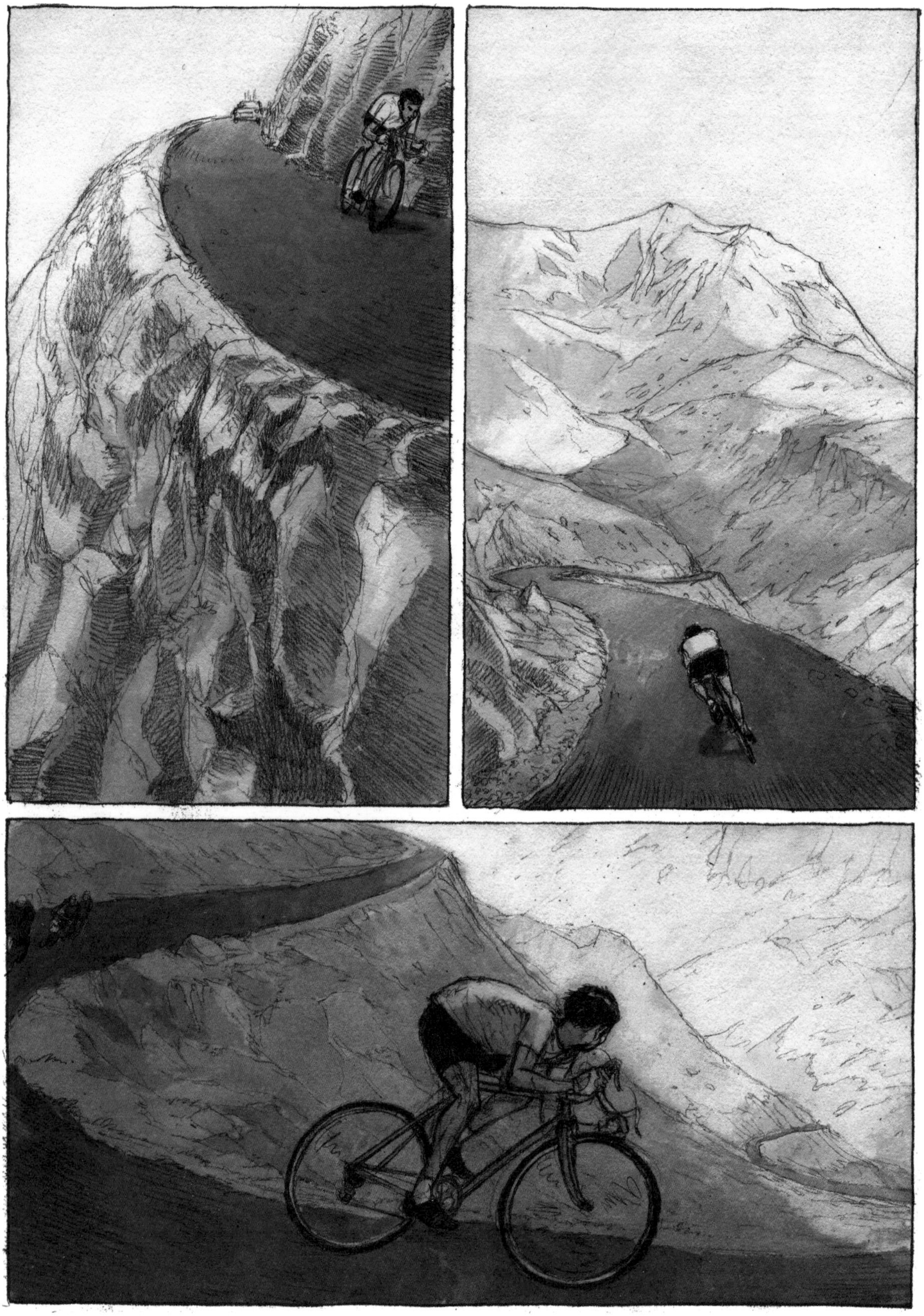

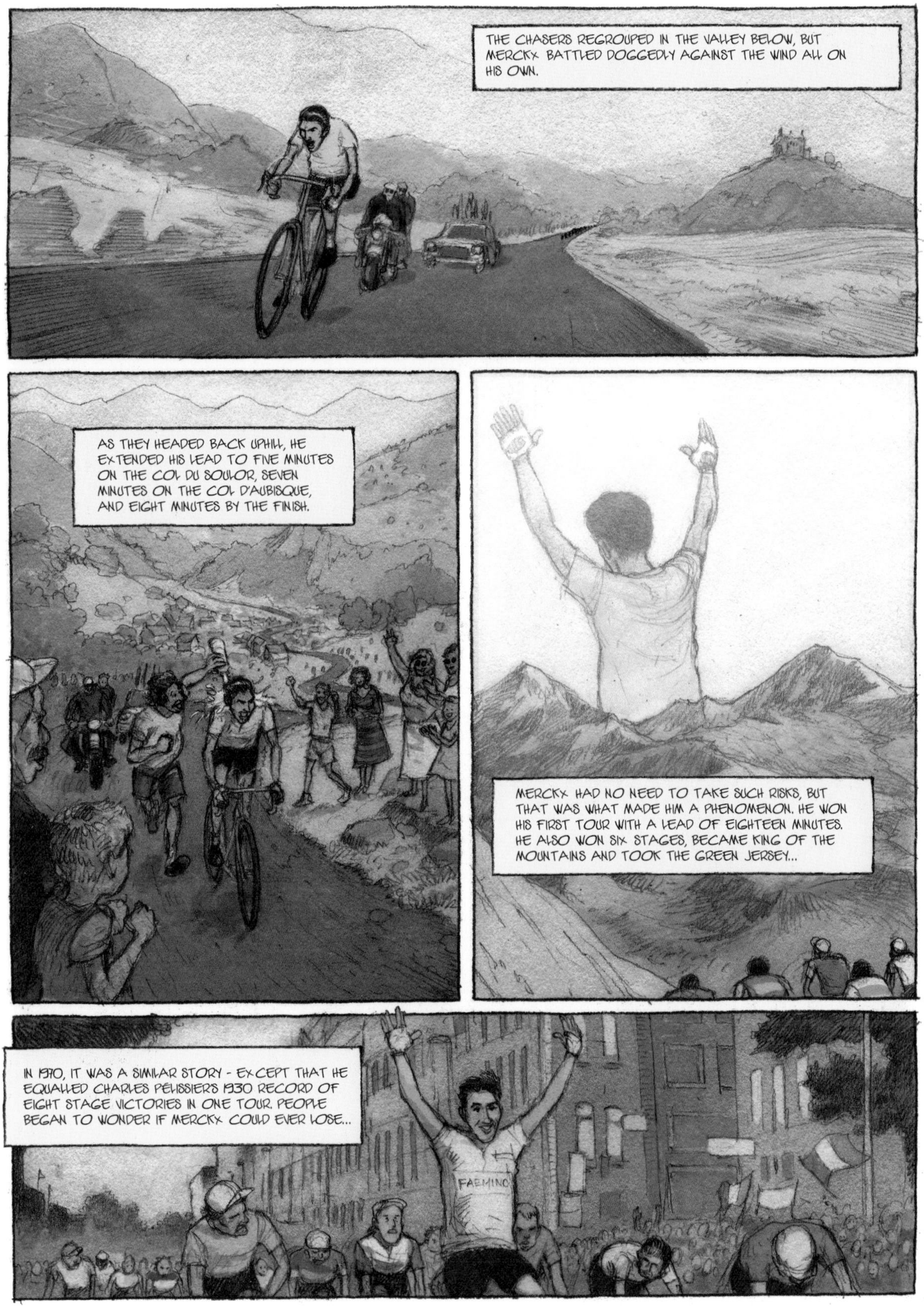
THE CHASERS REGROUPED IN THE VALLEY BELOW, BUT MERCKX BATTLED DOGGEDLY AGAINST THE WIND ALL ON HIS OWN.
AS THEY HEADED BACK UPHILL, HE EXTENDED HIS LEAD TO FIVE MINUTES ON THE COL DU SOULOR, SEVEN MINUTES ON THE COL D'AUBISQUE, AND EIGHT MINUTES BY THE FINISH.
MERCKX HAD NO NEED TO TAKE SUCH RISKS, BUT THAT WAS WHAT MADE HIM A PHENOMENON. HE WON HIS FIRST TOUR WITH A LEAD OF EIGHTEEN MINUTES. HE ALSO WON SIX STAGES, BECAME KING OF THE MOUNTAINS AND TOOK THE GREEN JERSEY...
IN 1970, IT WAS A SIMILAR STORY - EXCEPT THAT HE EQUALLED CHARLES PELISSIER'S 1930 RECORD OF EIGHT STAGE VICTORIES IN ONE TOUR. PEOPLE BEGAN TO WONDER IF MERCKX COULD EVER LOSE...
FAEMINO

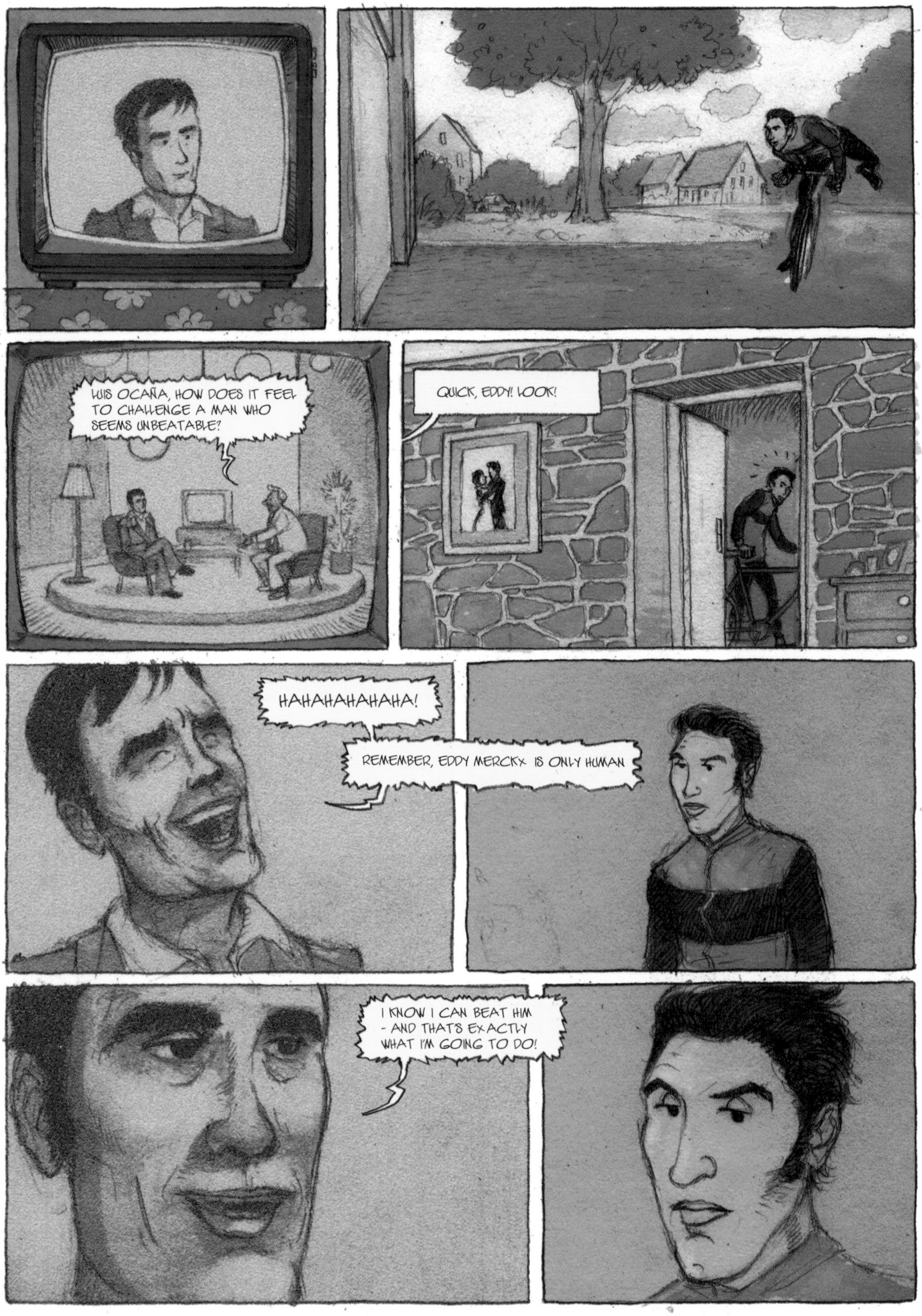
LUIS OCAÑA, HOW DOES IT FEEL TO CHALLENGE A MAN WHO SEEMS UNBEATABLE?
QUICK, EDDY! LOOK!
HAHAHAHAHAHA!
REMEMBER, EDDY MERCKX IS ONLY HUMAN
I KNOW I CAN BEAT HIM - AND THAT'S EXACTLY WHAT I'M GOING TO DO!

DURING STAGE ELEVEN OF THE 1971 TOUR, OCAÑA PROVED TRUE TO HIS WORD. HE BEAT MERCKX BY A MARGIN OF NINE MINUTES.

THE RESULT SEEMED CLEAR-CUT.

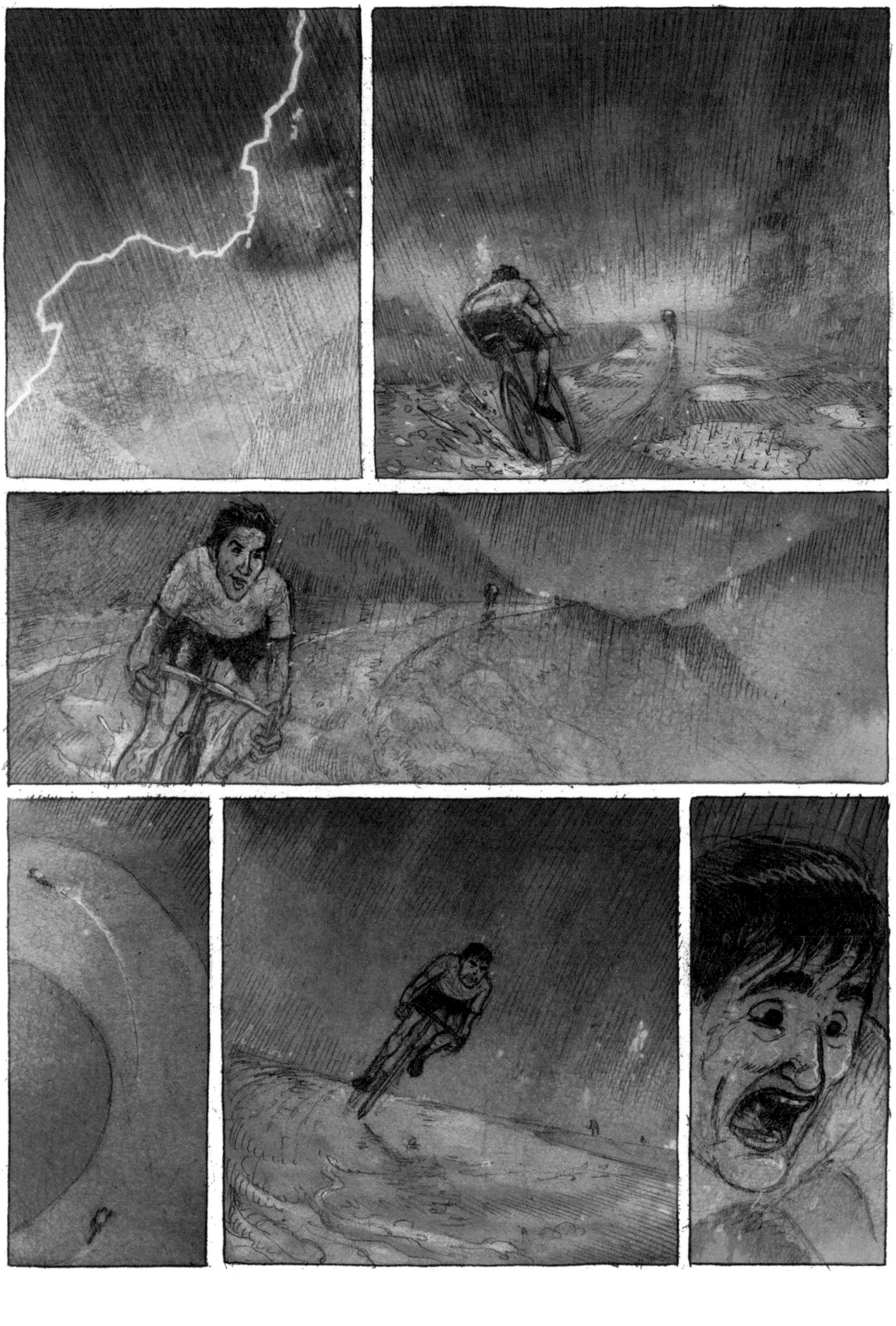

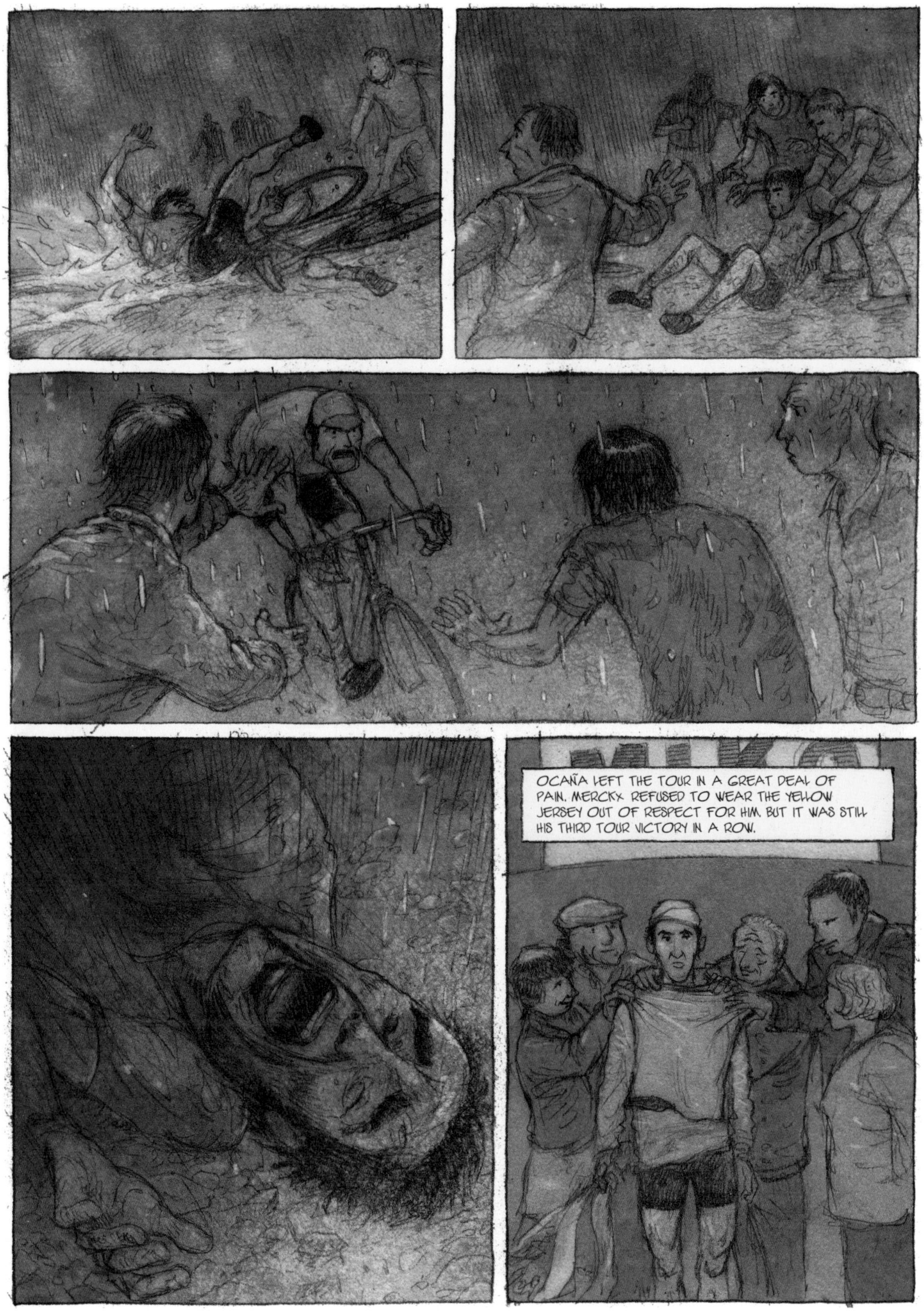
OCAÑA LEFT THE TOUR IN A GREAT DEAL OF PAIN. MERCKX REFUSED TO WEAR THE YELLOW JERSEY OUT OF RESPECT FOR HIM. BUT IT WAS STILL HIS THIRD TOUR VICTORY IN A ROW.

MERCKX COULDN'T STOP WINNING. HE WON NOT ONLY MOUNTAIN STAGES AND TIME TRIALS, BUT ALSO SPRINTS, OFTEN TO THE FRUSTRATION OF THE SPRINTERS, WHO THOUGHT HE WAS ENCROACHING ON THEIR TERRITORY.

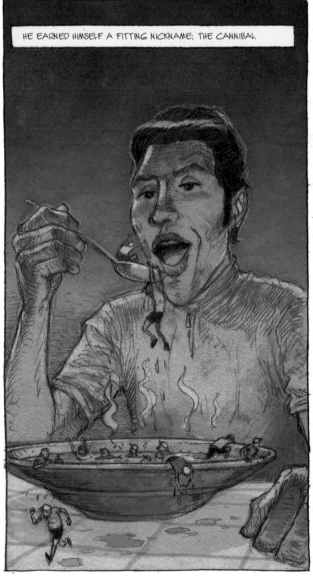

HE EARNED HIMSELF A FITTING NICKNAME: THE CANNIBAL.

IN 1972 AND 1974, MERCKX WON HIS FOURTH AND FIFTH VICTORIES. IN 1973, HE DID NOT TAKE PART, BECAUSE AFTER WINNING THE GIRO, HE ALSO WANTED TO RIDE THE VUELTA FOR ONCE. HE WON THAT RACE TOO.

ALTHOUGH INCREASING NUMBERS OF FANS WOULD HAVE PREFERRED HIM NOT TO RIDE, MERCKX LINED UP AT THE START OF THE 1975 TOUR.

THE ANTI-MERCKX MOOD WAS PALPABLE. CLOSE TO THE FINISH LINE OF THE FOURTEENTH STAGE, ON THE WAY UP THE PUY DE DÔME, A SPECTATOR PUNCHED MERCKX IN THE SIDE.

HE WAS ABLE TO CONTINUE, BUT HE RODE ON PAINKILLERS FROM THE TOUR DOCTOR.

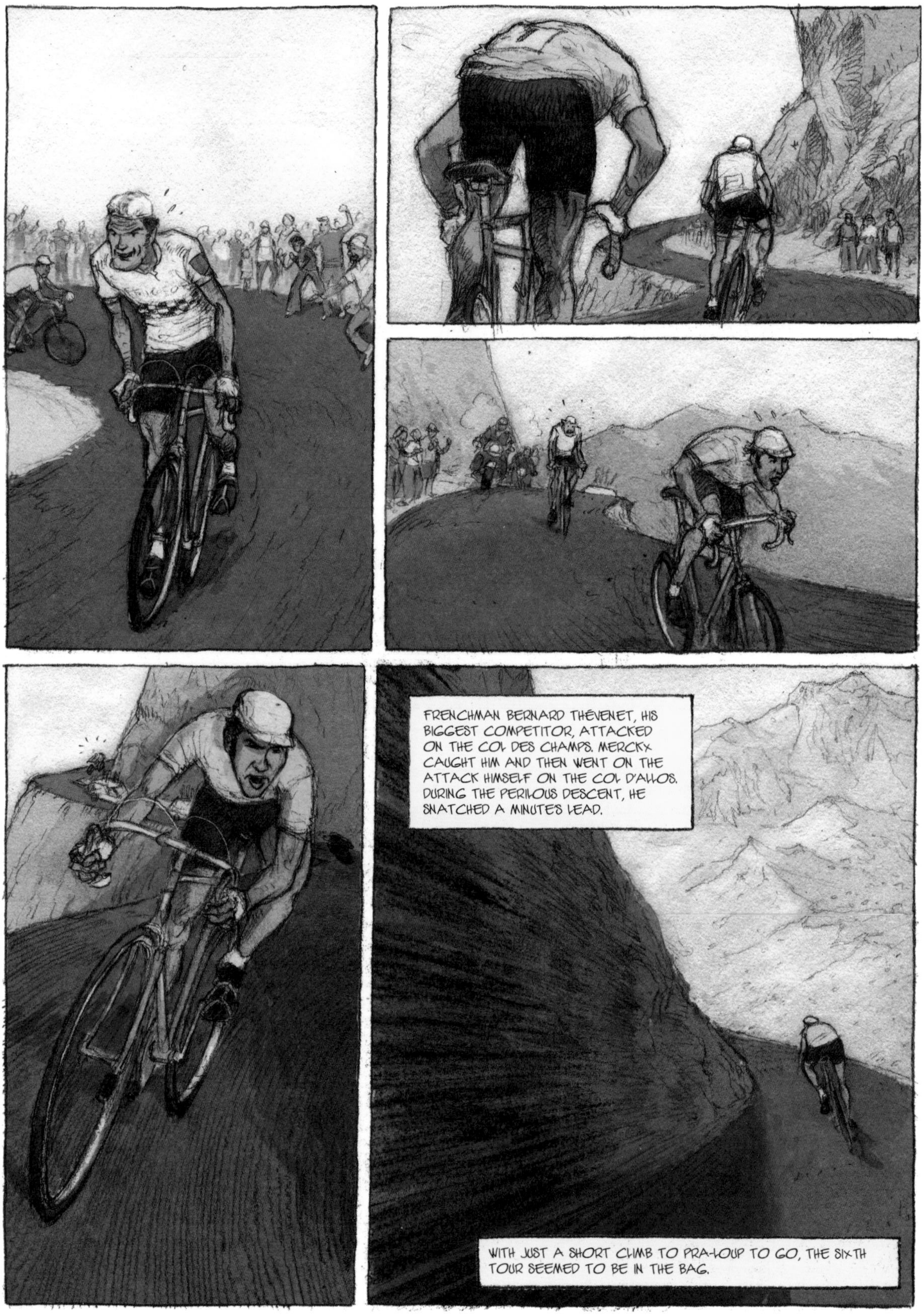

FRENCHMAN BERNARD THÉVENET, HIS BIGGEST COMPETITOR, ATTACKED ON THE COL DES CHAMPS. MERCKX CAUGHT HIM AND THEN WENT ON THE ATTACK HIMSELF ON THE COL D'ALLOS. DURING THE PERILOUS DESCENT, HE SNATCHED A MINUTE'S LEAD.
WITH JUST A SHORT CLIMB TO PRA-LOUP TO GO, THE SIXTH TOUR SEEMED TO BE IN THE BAG.

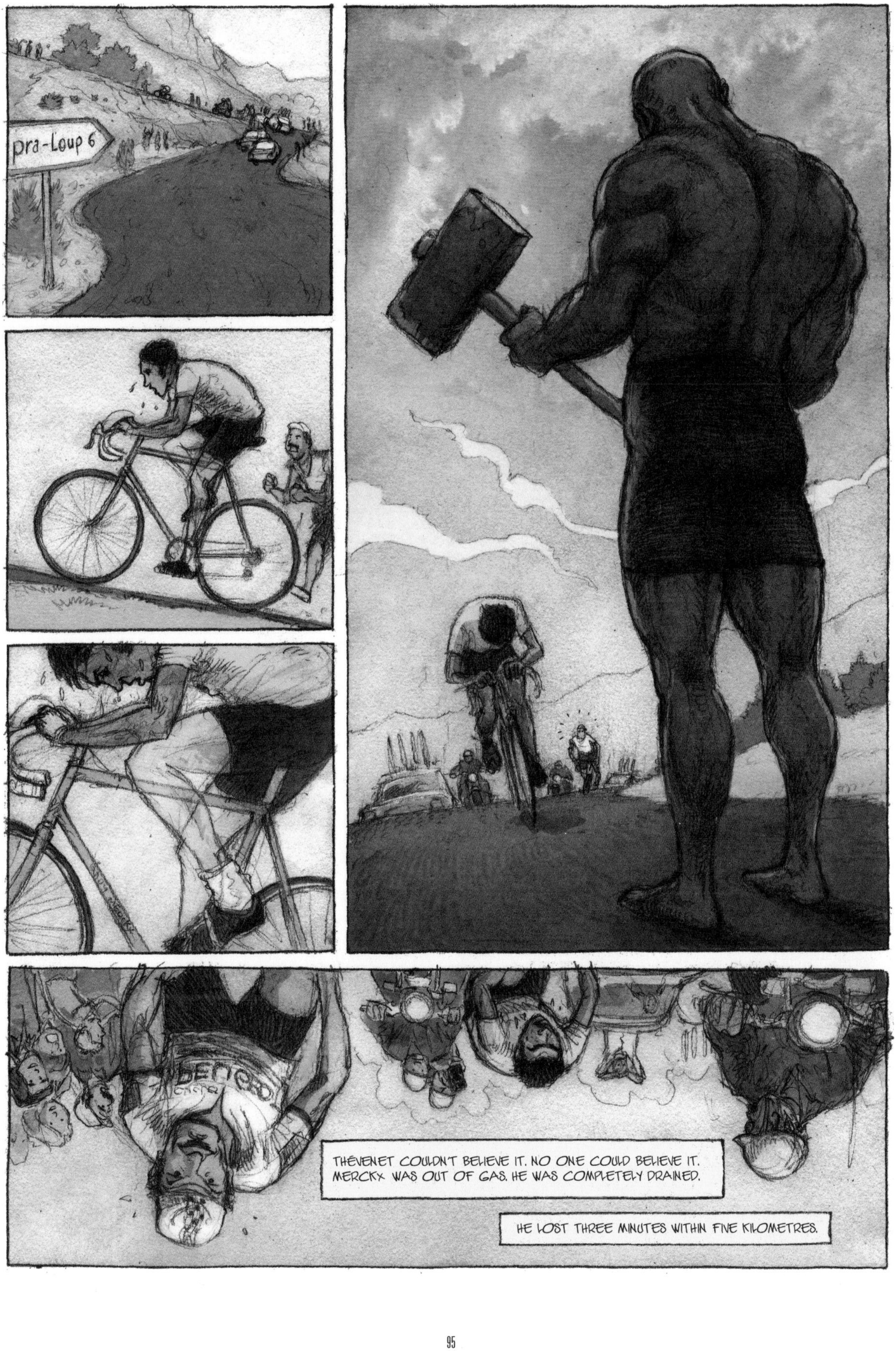
pra-Loup 6
THEVENET COULDN'T BELIEVE IT. NO ONE COULD BELIEVE IT.
MERCKX WAS OUT OF GAS. HE WAS COMPLETELY DRAINED.
HE LOST THREE MINUTES WITHIN FIVE KILOMETRES.

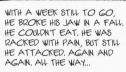
WITH A WEEK STILL TO GO, HE BROKE HIS JAW IN A FALL. HE COULDN'T EAT. HE WAS RACKED WITH PAIN, BUT STILL HE ATTACKED. AGAIN AND AGAIN. ALL THE WAY...

... TO PARIS.

TYPICAL MERCKX.

HE HAD ENSURED THEVENET WAS A WORTHY WINNER AND SECURED EXTRA PRIZE MONEY FOR HIS TEAMMATES. A TRULY GREAT CHAMPION IS GREAT IN VICTORY AND IN DEFEAT.

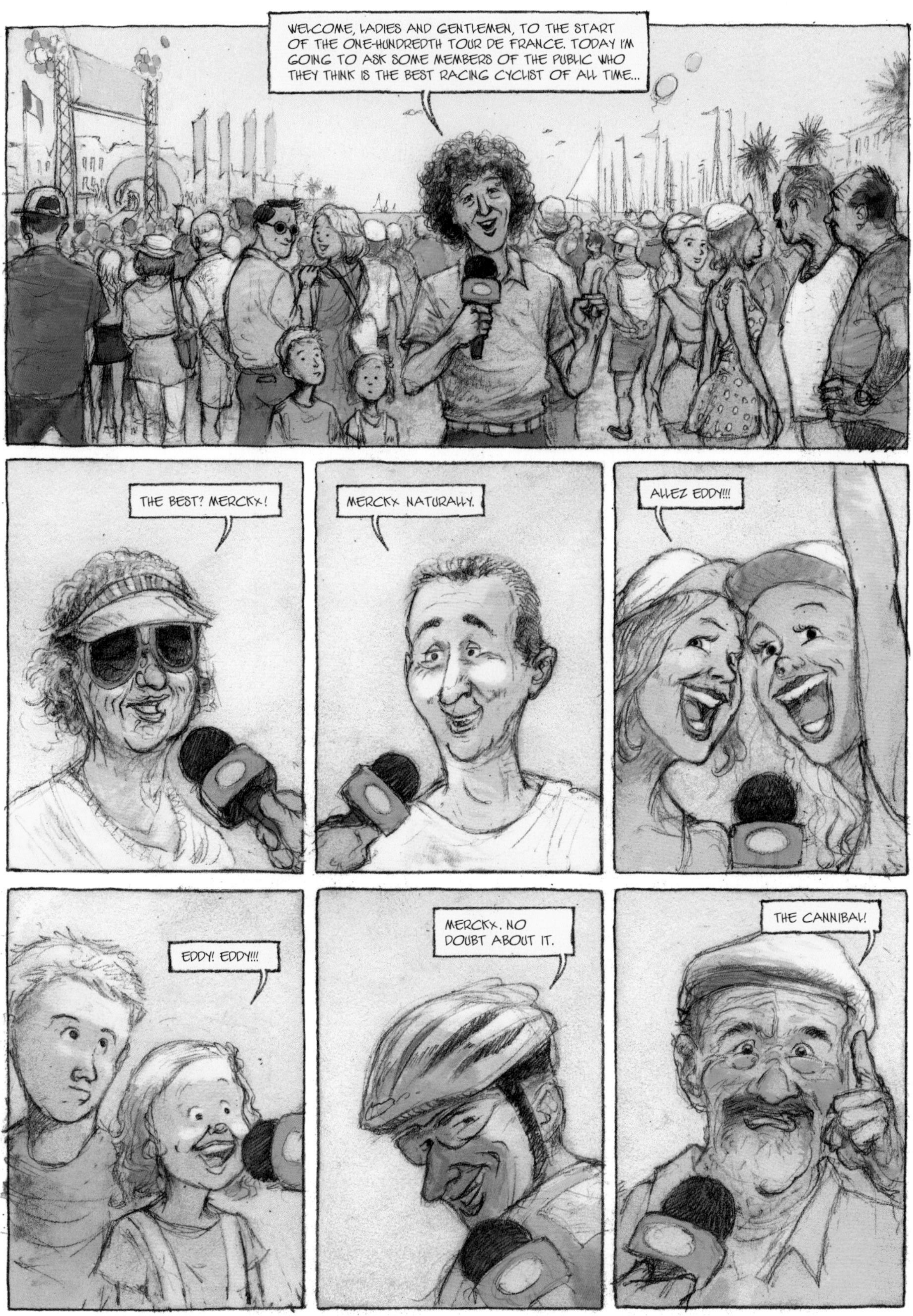
WELCOME, LADIES AND GENTLEMEN, TO THE START OF THE ONE-HUNDREDTH TOUR DE FRANCE. TODAY I'M GOING TO ASK SOME MEMBERS OF THE PUBLIC WHO THEY THINK IS THE BEST RACING CYCLIST OF ALL TIME...
THE BEST? MERCKX!
MERCKX NATURALLY.
ALLEZ EDDY!!!
EDDY! EDDY!!!
MERCKX. NO DOUBT ABOUT IT.
THE CANNIBAL!

CHAMPS-ÉLYSÉES

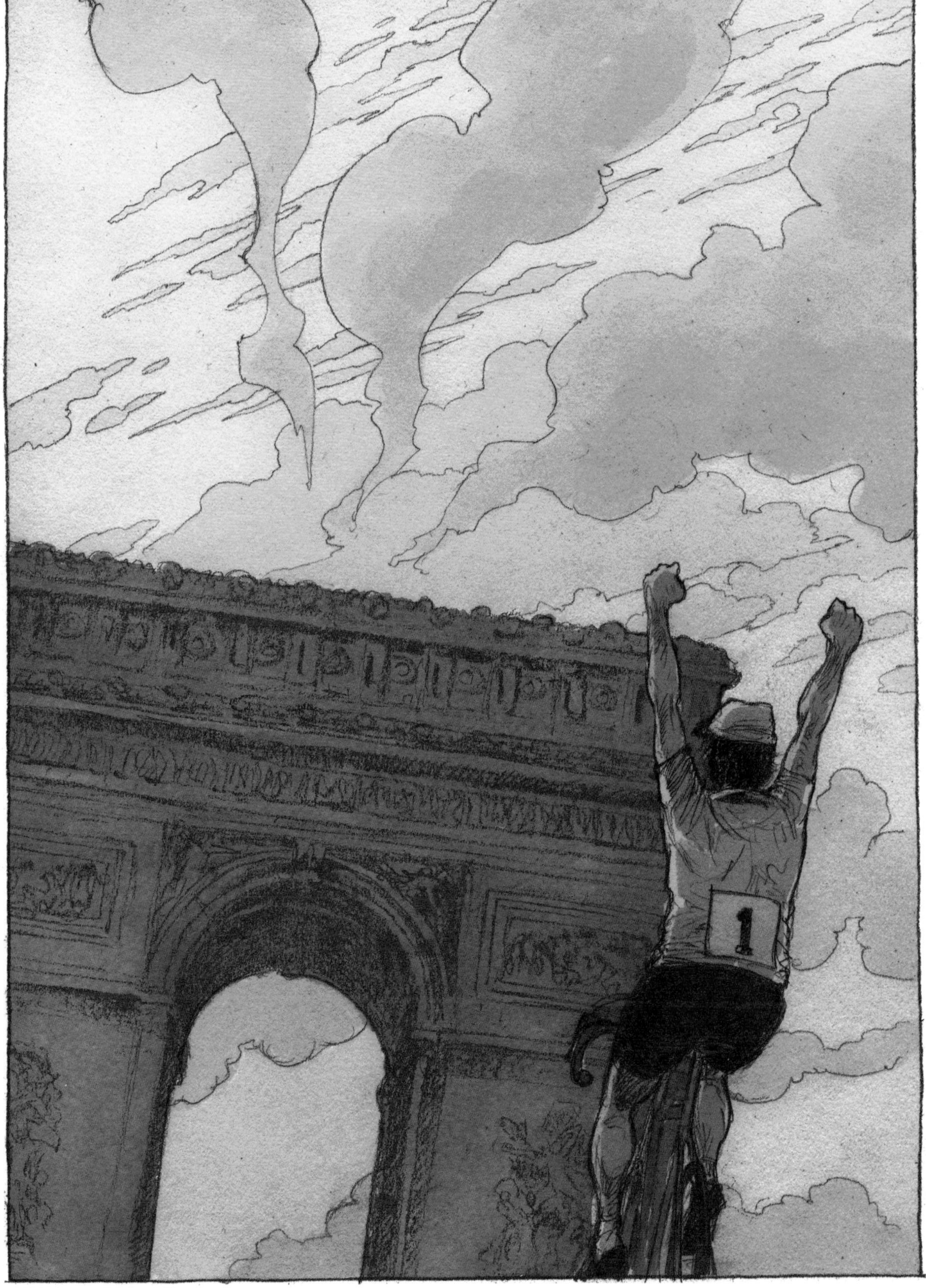
1

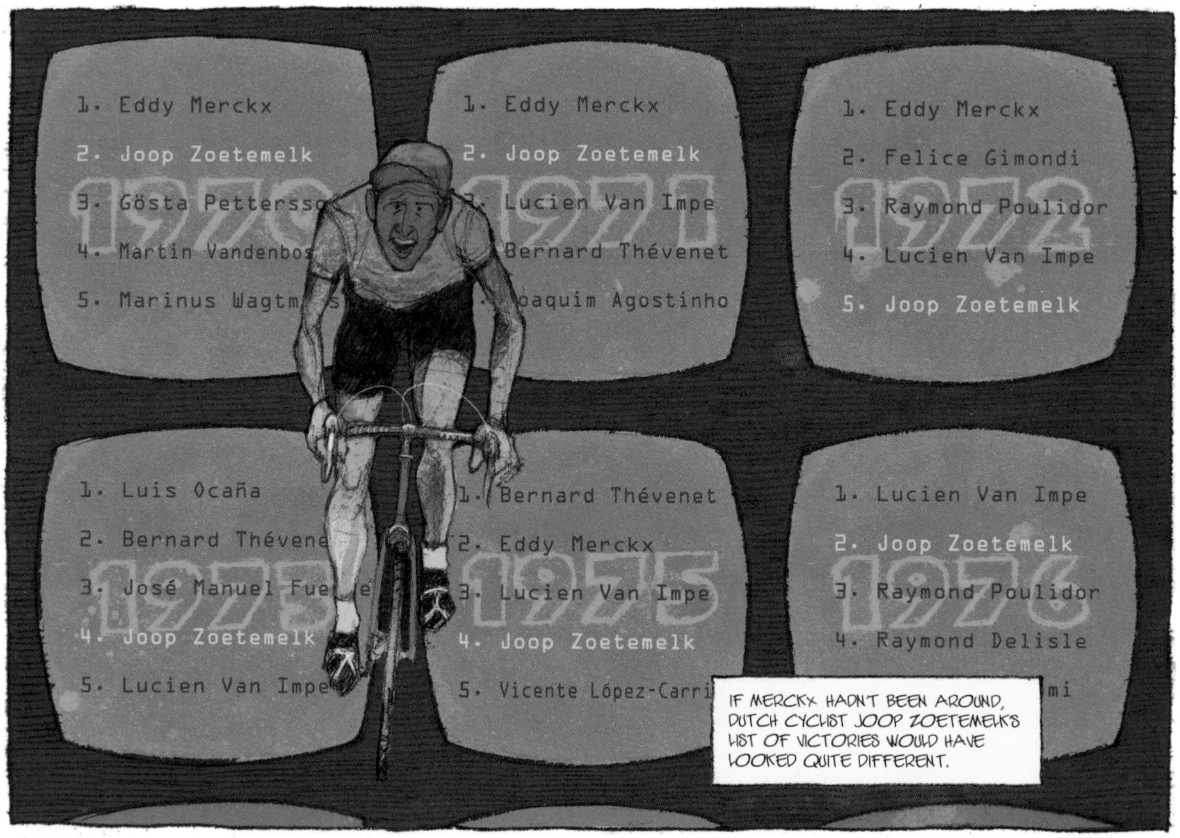
1. Eddy Merckx
2. Joop Zoetemelk
3. Gösta Petterss
4. Martin Vandenbos
5. Marinus Wagtm
1. Eddy Merckx
2. Joop Zoetemelk
Lucien Van Impe
Bernard Thévenet
oaquim Agostinho
1972
1. Eddy Merckx
2. Felice Gimondi
3. Raymond Poulidor
4. Lucien Van Impe
5. Joop Zoetemelk
1. Luis Ocaña
2. Bernard Théven
3. José Manuel Fue
4. Joop Zoetemelk
5. Lucien Van Impe
1975
1. Bernard Thévenet
2. Eddy Merckx
3. Lucien Van Impe
4. Joop Zoetemelk
5. Vicente López-Carri
1976
1. Lucien Van Impe
2. Joop Zoetemelk
3. Raymond Poulidor
4. Raymond Delisle
IF MERCKX HADN'T BEEN AROUND, DUTCH CYCLIST JOOP ZOETEMELK'S LIST OF VICTORIES WOULD HAVE LOOKED QUITE DIFFERENT.

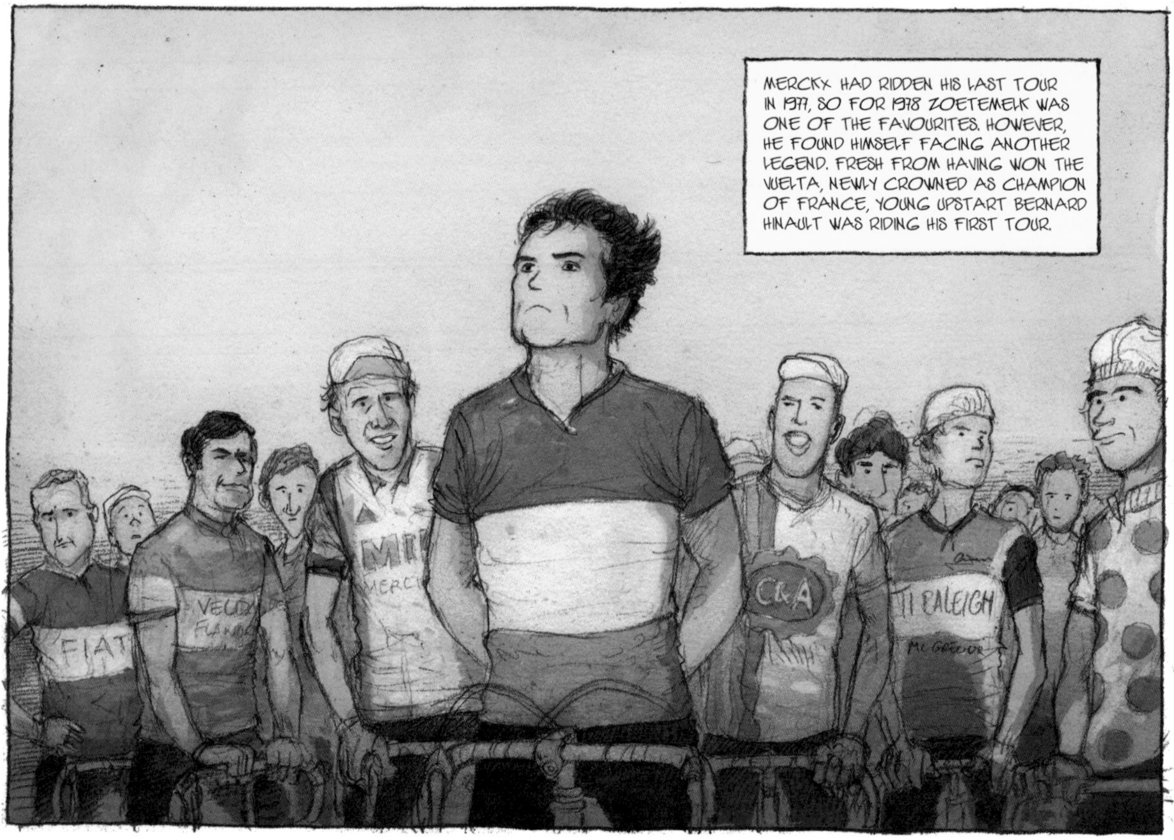
MERCKX HAD RIDDEN HIS LAST TOUR IN 1977, SO FOR 1978 ZOETEMELK WAS ONE OF THE FAVOURITES. HOWEVER, HE FOUND HIMSELF FACING ANOTHER LEGEND. FRESH FROM HAVING WON THE VUELTA, NEWLY CROWNED AS CHAMPION OF FRANCE, YOUNG UPSTART BERNARD HINAULT WAS RIDING HIS FIRST TOUR.
FIAT
C&A
TI RALEIGH

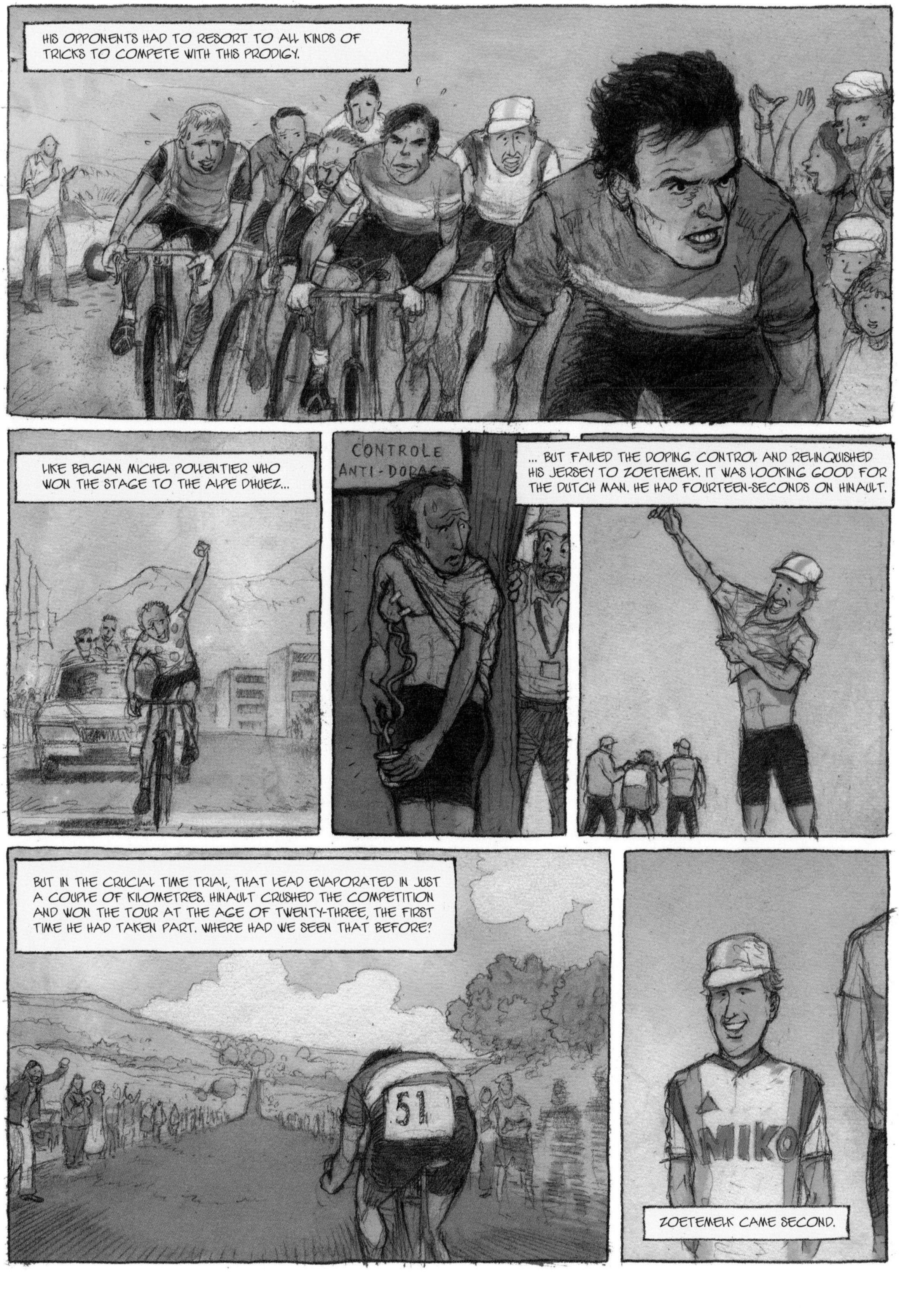
HIS OPPONENTS HAD TO RESORT TO ALL KINDS OF TRICKS TO COMPETE WITH THIS PRODIGY.
LIKE BELGIAN MICHEL POLLENTIER WHO WON THE STAGE TO THE ALPE D'HUEZ...
CONTROLE ANTI-DOPAGE
... BUT FAILED THE DOPING CONTROL AND RELINQUISHED HIS JERSEY TO ZOETEMELK. IT WAS LOOKING GOOD FOR THE DUTCH MAN. HE HAD FOURTEEN-SECONDS ON HINAULT.
BUT IN THE CRUCIAL TIME TRIAL, THAT LEAD EVAPORATED IN JUST A COUPLE OF KILOMETRES. HINAULT CRUSHED THE COMPETITION AND WON THE TOUR AT THE AGE OF TWENTY-THREE, THE FIRST TIME HE HAD TAKEN PART. WHERE HAD WE SEEN THAT BEFORE?
51
MIKO
ZOETEMELK CAME SECOND.

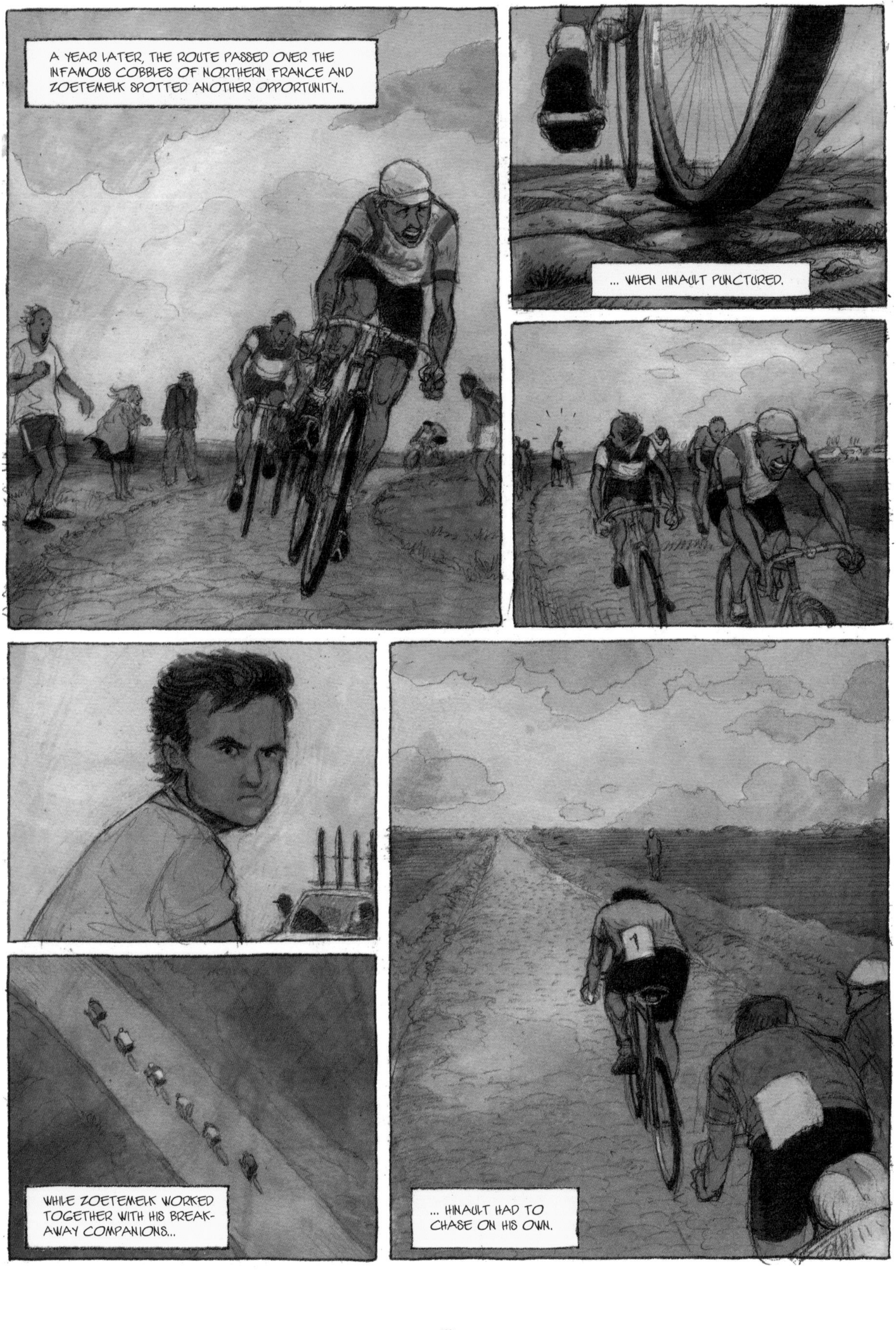
A YEAR LATER, THE ROUTE PASSED OVER THE INFAMOUS COBBLES OF NORTHERN FRANCE AND ZOETEMELK SPOTTED ANOTHER OPPORTUNITY...
... WHEN HINAULT PUNCTURED.
WHILE ZOETEMELK WORKED TOGETHER WITH HIS BREAK-AWAY COMPANIONS...
... HINAULT HAD TO CHASE ON HIS OWN.

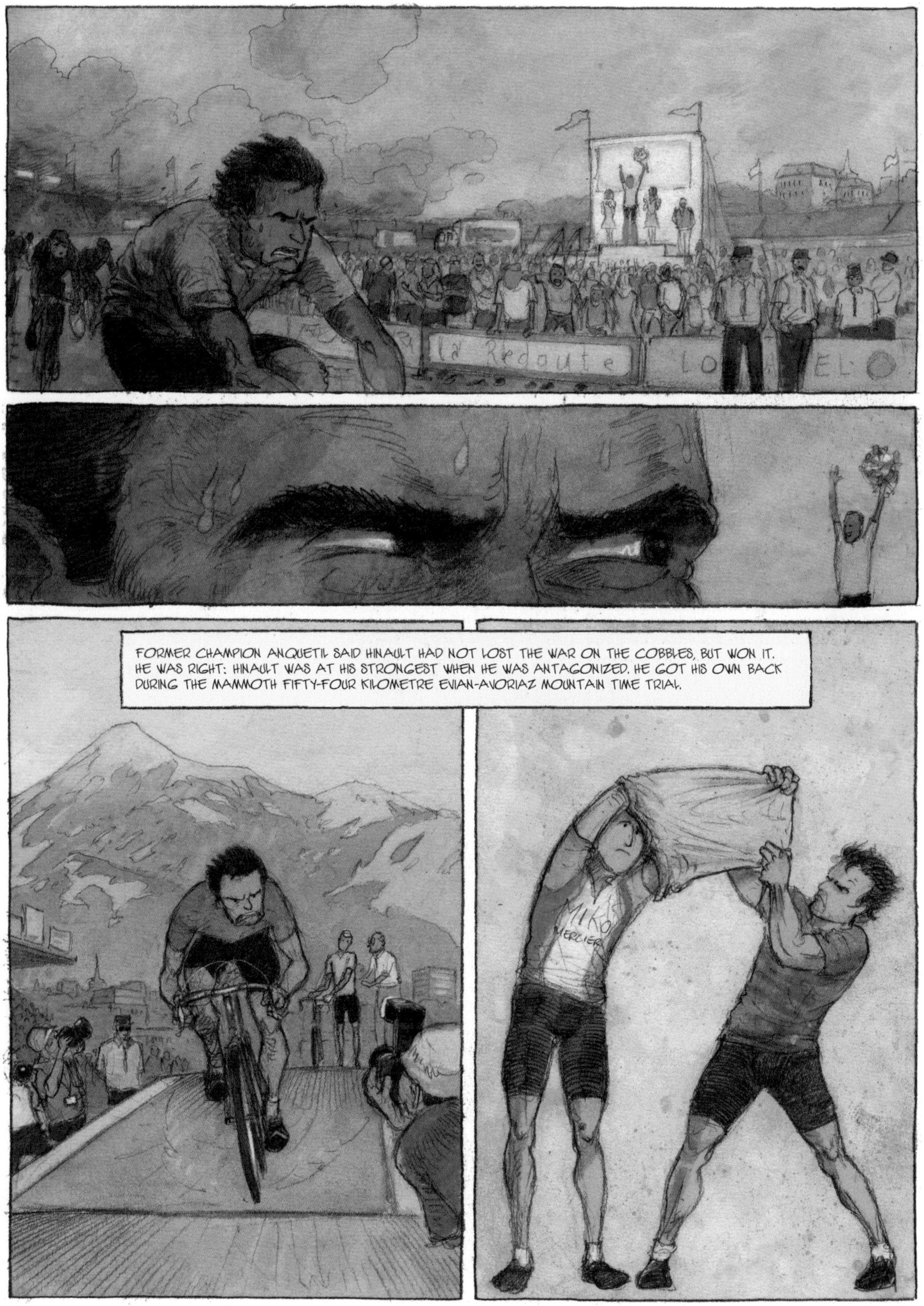
la Redoute
FORMER CHAMPION ANQUETIL SAID HINAULT HAD NOT LOST THE WAR ON THE COBBLES, BUT WON IT. HE WAS RIGHT: HINAULT WAS AT HIS STRONGEST WHEN HE WAS ANTAGONIZED. HE GOT HIS OWN BACK DURING THE MAMMOTH FIFTY-FOUR KILOMETRE EVIAN-AVORIAZ MOUNTAIN TIME TRIAL.

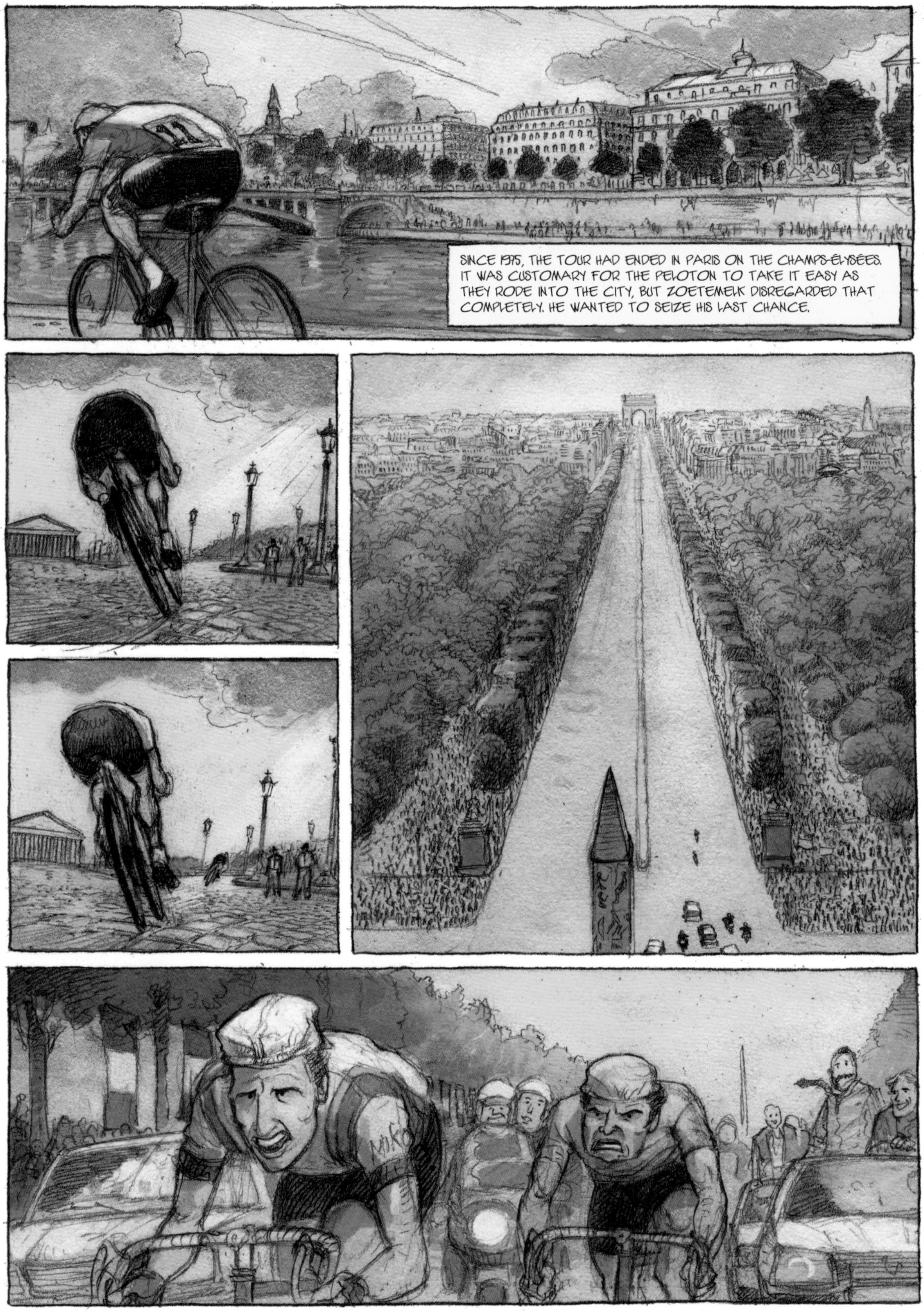
SINCE 1975, THE TOUR HAD ENDED IN PARIS ON THE CHAMPS-ÉLYSÉES. IT WAS CUSTOMARY FOR THE PELOTON TO TAKE IT EASY AS THEY RODE INTO THE CITY, BUT ZOETEMELK DISREGARDED THAT COMPLETELY. HE WANTED TO SEIZE HIS LAST CHANCE.

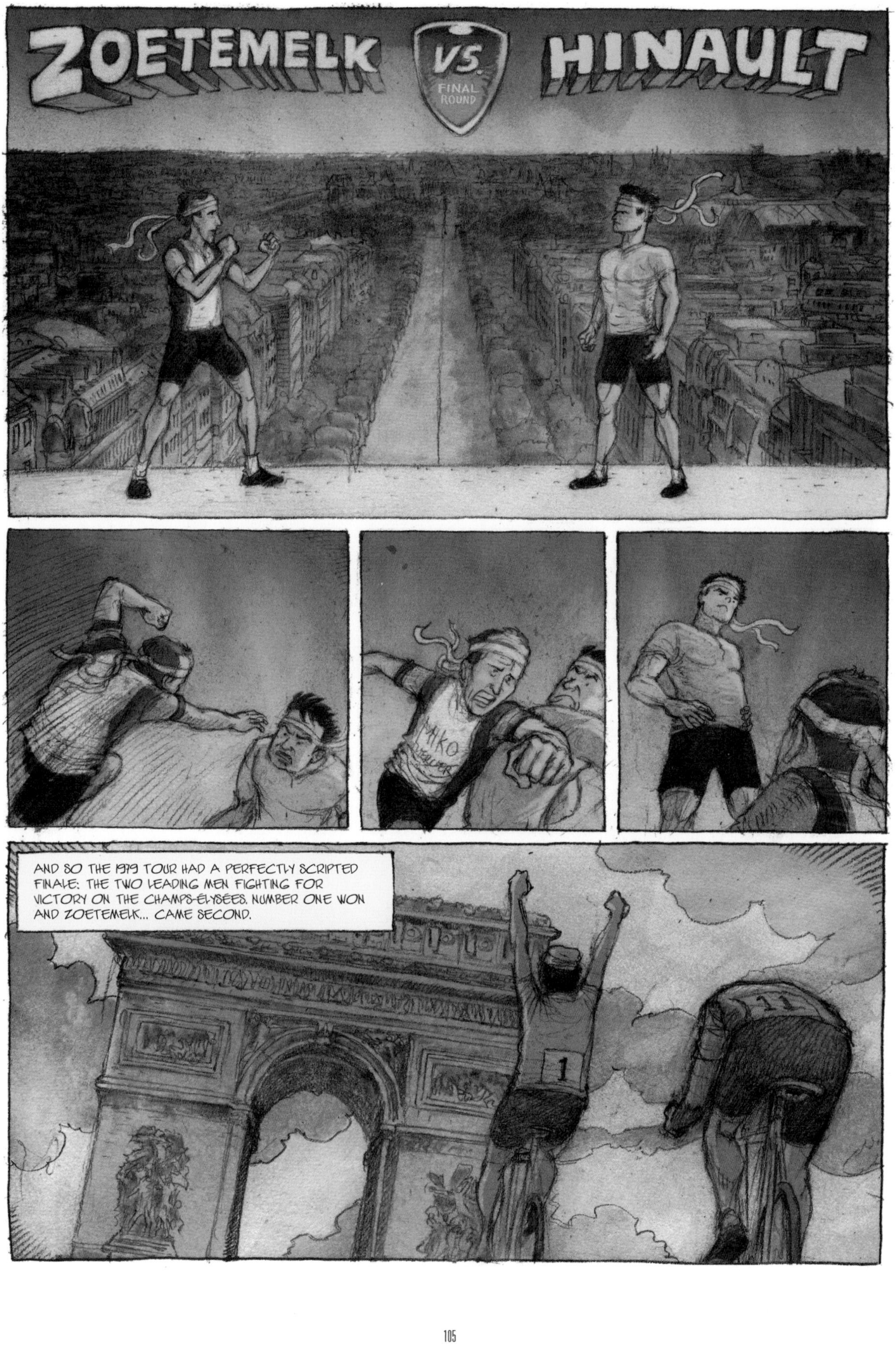
ZOETEMELK
VS.
FINAL ROUND
HINAULT
AND SO THE 1979 TOUR HAD A PERFECTLY SCRIPTED FINALE: THE TWO LEADING MEN FIGHTING FOR VICTORY ON THE CHAMPS-ÉLYSÉES. NUMBER ONE WON AND ZOETEMELK... CAME SECOND.
1
11

BUT HE DIDN'T LET ALL THOSE NEAR MISSES BOTHER HIM. IN FACT, IN 1980, HE GAVE IT ANOTHER SHOT.

AND WHAT HAPPENED? HINAULT ABANDONED THE TOUR WITH TENDINITIS.

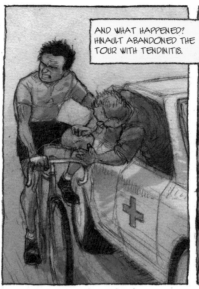

AT FIRST ZOETEMELK REFUSED TO DON THE YELLOW JERSEY...

AFTER A BIZARRE FALL CAUSED BY A TEAMMATE ZOETEMELK'S CHALLENGERS THOUGHT THEY WERE IN WITH A CHANCE ... BUT THIS TIME HE WASN'T TO BE DENIED.

AND SO, AT THE AGE OF THIRTY-THREE, HE WON HIS FIRST AND ONLY TOUR, TEN YEARS AFTER HAVING COME SECOND FOR THE FIRST TIME. ZOETEMELK RODE SIXTEEN TOURS AND NEVER GAVE UP ONCE. PERSISTENCE PAYS OFF.

1

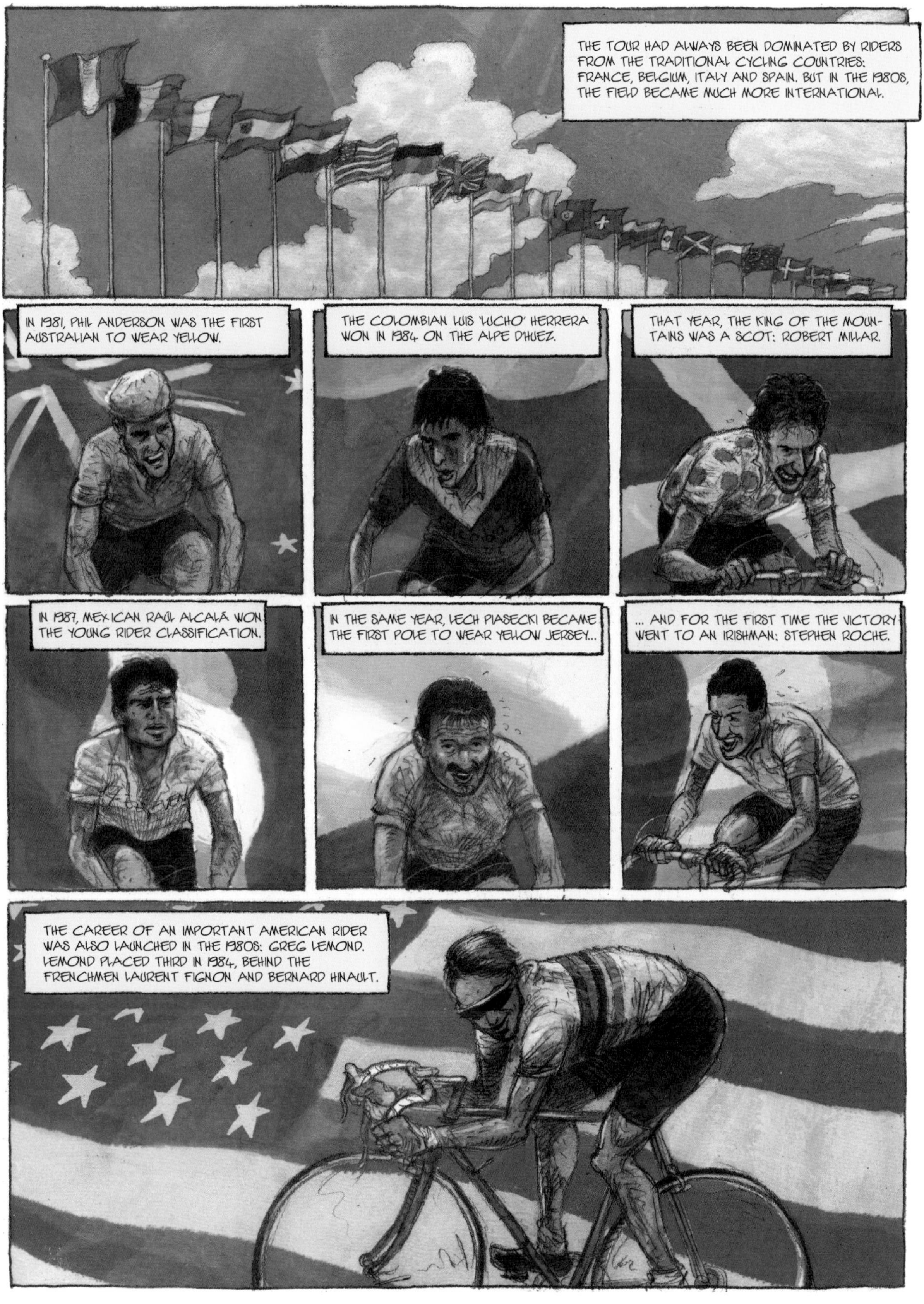
THE TOUR HAD ALWAYS BEEN DOMINATED BY RIDERS FROM THE TRADITIONAL CYCLING COUNTRIES: FRANCE, BELGIUM, ITALY AND SPAIN. BUT IN THE 1980S, THE FIELD BECAME MUCH MORE INTERNATIONAL.
IN 1981, PHIL ANDERSON WAS THE FIRST AUSTRALIAN TO WEAR YELLOW.
THE COLOMBIAN LUIS 'LUCHO' HERRERA WON IN 1984 ON THE ALPE D'HUEZ.
THAT YEAR, THE KING OF THE MOUNTAINS WAS A SCOT: ROBERT MILLAR.
IN 1987, MEXICAN RAÚL ALCALÁ WON THE YOUNG RIDER CLASSIFICATION.
IN THE SAME YEAR, LECH PIASECKI BECAME THE FIRST POLE TO WEAR YELLOW JERSEY...
... AND FOR THE FIRST TIME THE VICTORY WENT TO AN IRISHMAN: STEPHEN ROCHE.
THE CAREER OF AN IMPORTANT AMERICAN RIDER WAS ALSO LAUNCHED IN THE 1980S: GREG LEMOND. LEMOND PLACED THIRD IN 1984, BEHIND THE FRENCHMEN LAURENT FIGNON AND BERNARD HINAULT.

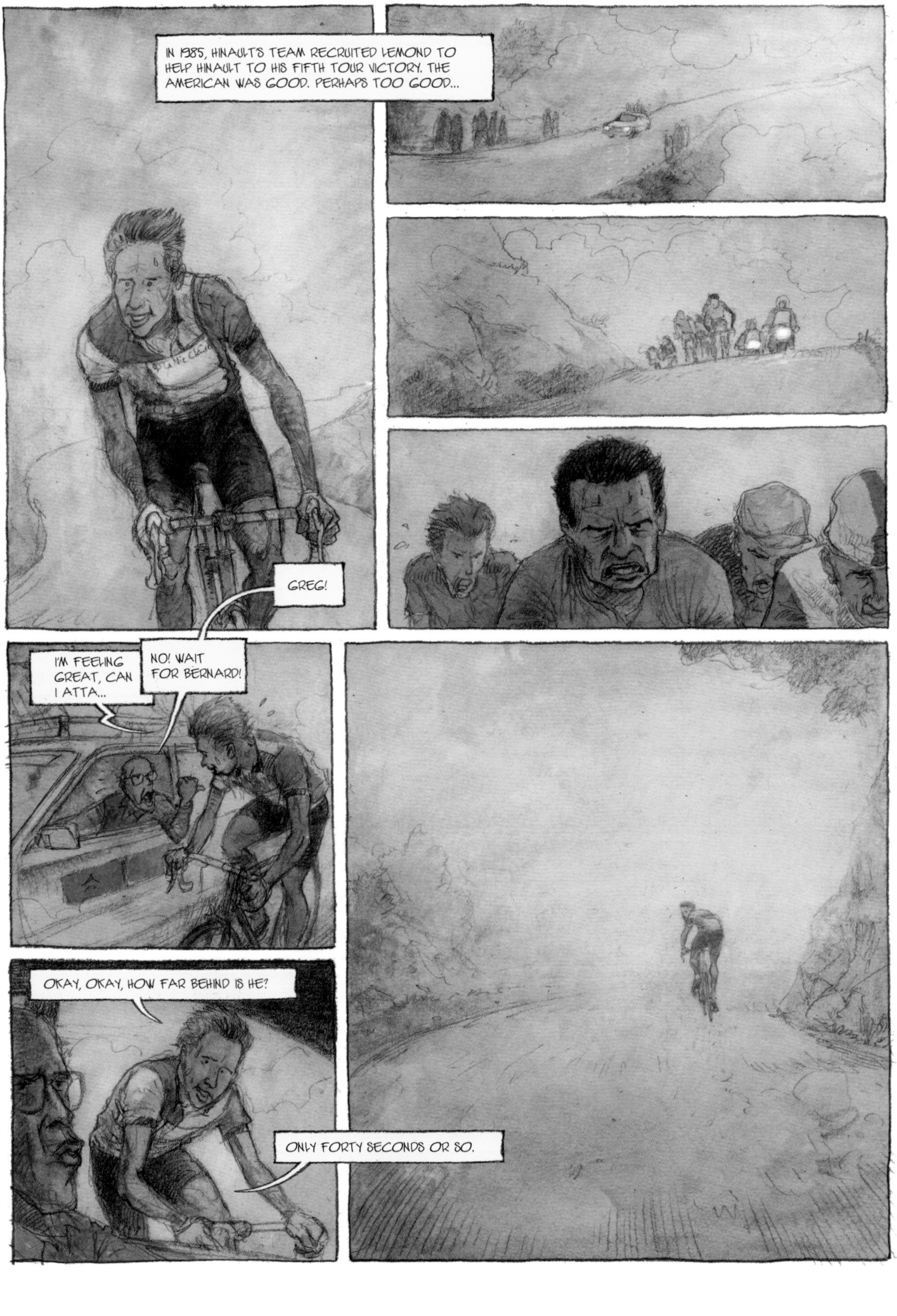
IN 1985, HINAULT'S TEAM RECRUITED LEMOND TO HELP HINAULT TO HIS FIFTH TOUR VICTORY. THE AMERICAN WAS GOOD. PERHAPS TOO GOOD...
GREG!
I'M FEELING GREAT, CAN I ATTA...
NO! WAIT FOR BERNARD!
OKAY, OKAY, HOW FAR BEHIND IS HE?
ONLY FORTY SECONDS OR SO.

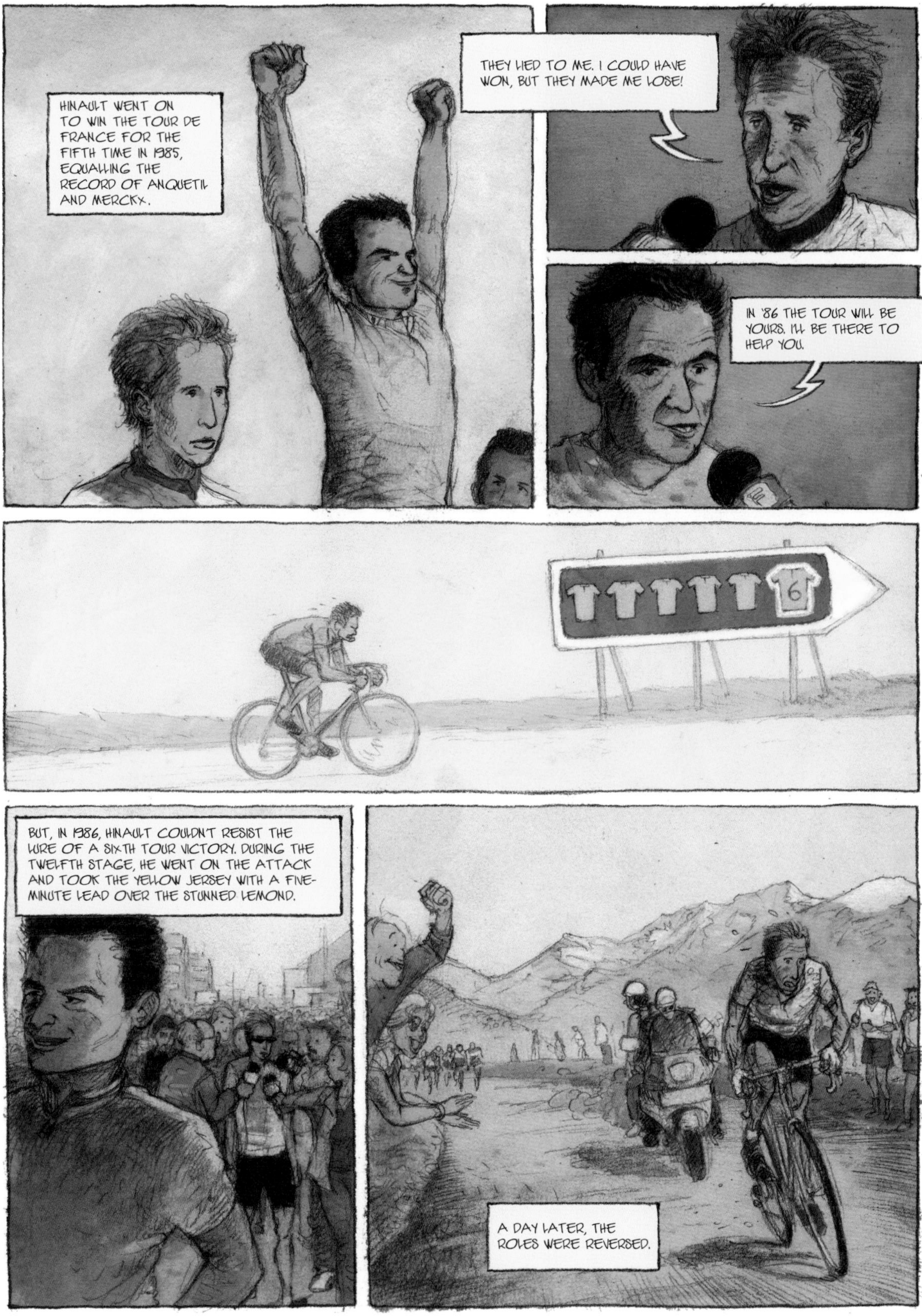
HINAULT WENT ON TO WIN THE TOUR DE FRANCE FOR THE FIFTH TIME IN 1985, EQUALLING THE RECORD OF ANQUETIL AND MERCKX.
THEY LIED TO ME. I COULD HAVE WON, BUT THEY MADE ME LOSE!
IN '86 THE TOUR WILL BE YOURS. I'LL BE THERE TO HELP YOU.
6
BUT, IN 1986, HINAULT COULDN'T RESIST THE LURE OF A SIXTH TOUR VICTORY. DURING THE TWELFTH STAGE, HE WENT ON THE ATTACK AND TOOK THE YELLOW JERSEY WITH A FIVE-MINUTE LEAD OVER THE STUNNED LEMOND.
A DAY LATER, THE ROLES WERE REVERSED.

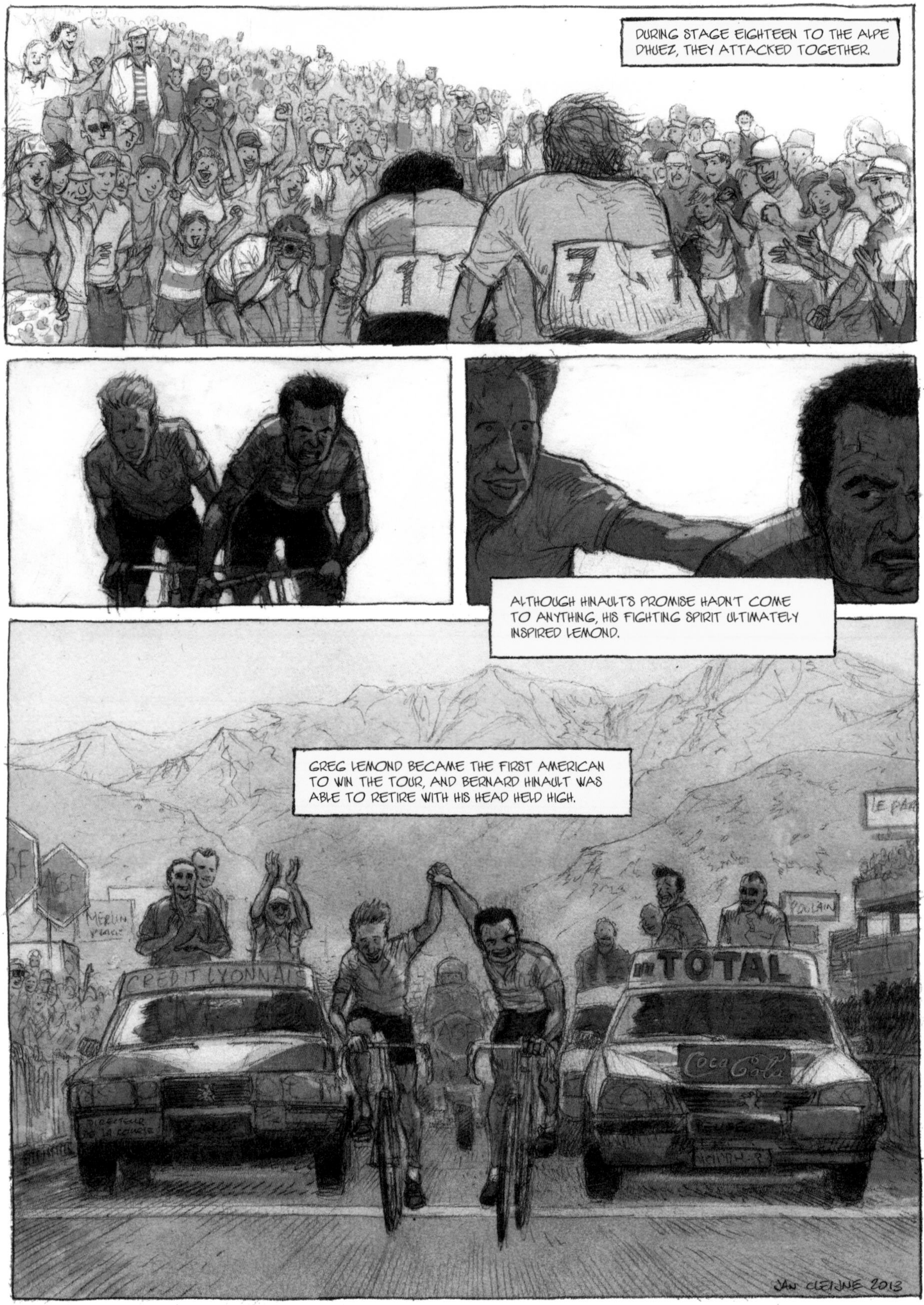
DURING STAGE EIGHTEEN TO THE ALPE D'HUEZ, THEY ATTACKED TOGETHER.
ALTHOUGH HINAULT'S PROMISE HADN'T COME TO ANYTHING, HIS FIGHTING SPIRIT ULTIMATELY INSPIRED LEMOND.
GREG LEMOND BECAME THE FIRST AMERICAN TO WIN THE TOUR, AND BERNARD HINAULT WAS ABLE TO RETIRE WITH HIS HEAD HELD HIGH.
CREDIT LYONNAIS
TOTAL
POULAIN
Coca Cola
JAN CLEIJNE 2013

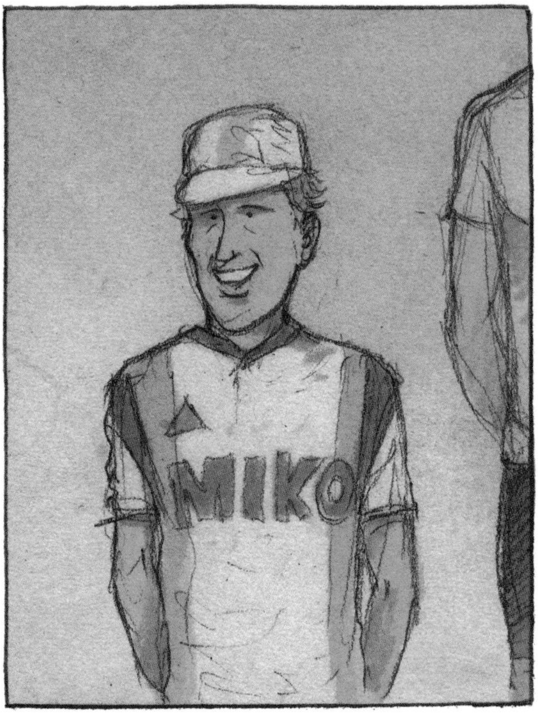
MIKO

9

TOP GEAR

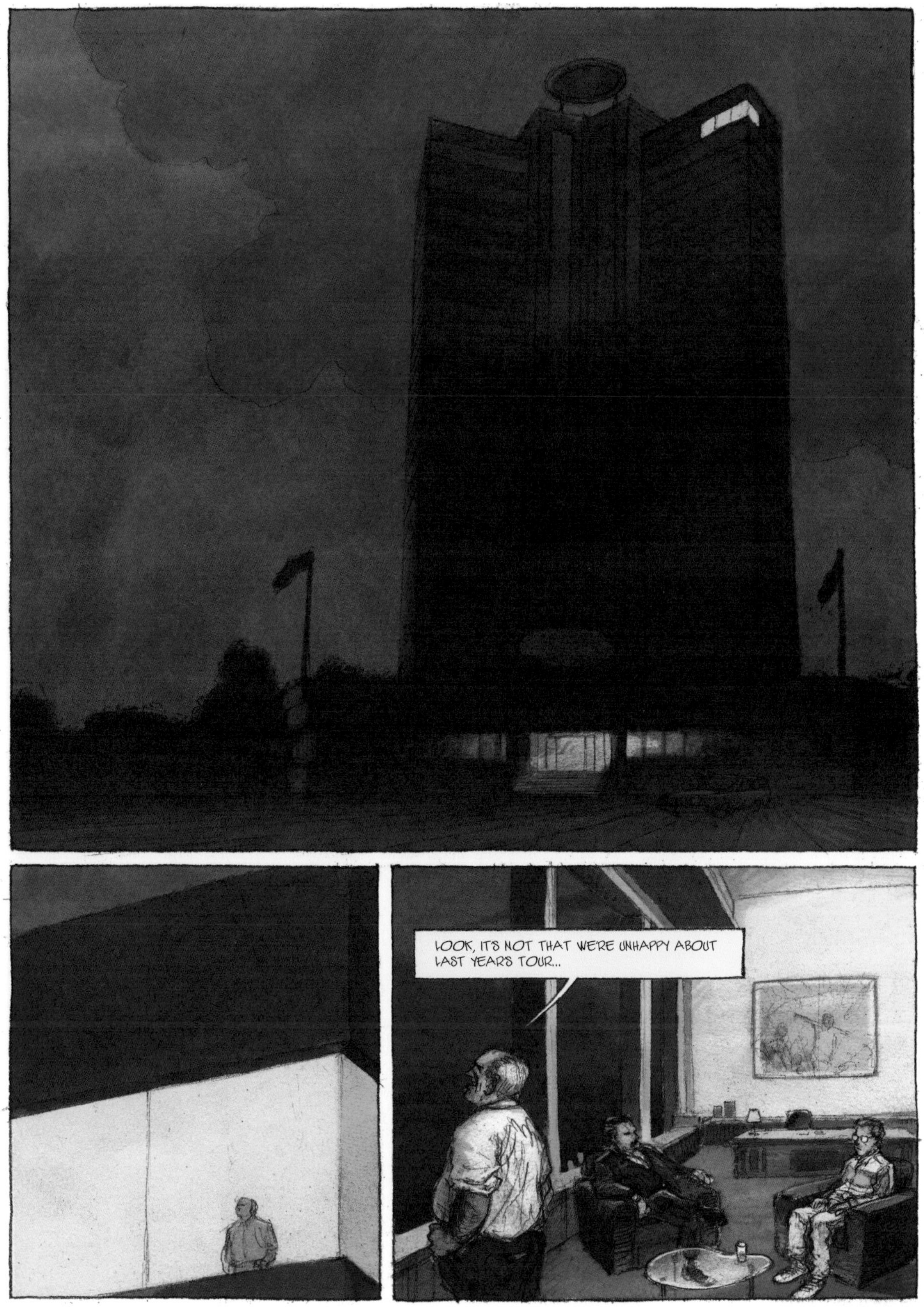

LOOK, IT'S NOT THAT WE'RE UNHAPPY ABOUT LAST YEAR'S TOUR...

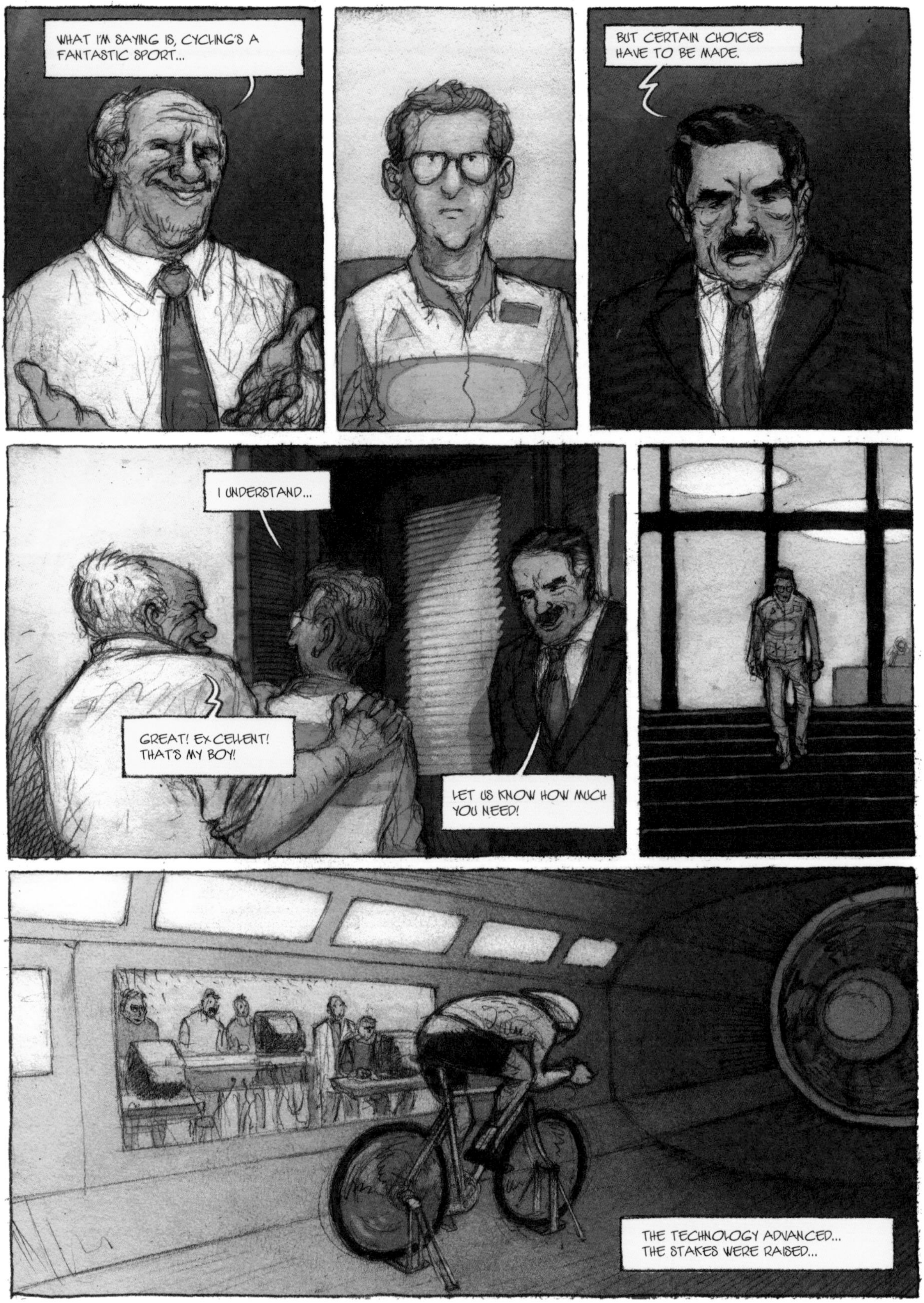
WHAT I'M SAYING IS, CYCLING'S A FANTASTIC SPORT...
BUT CERTAIN CHOICES HAVE TO BE MADE.
I UNDERSTAND...
GREAT! EXCELLENT! THAT'S MY BOY!
LET US KNOW HOW MUCH YOU NEED!
THE TECHNOLOGY ADVANCED... THE STAKES WERE RAISED...

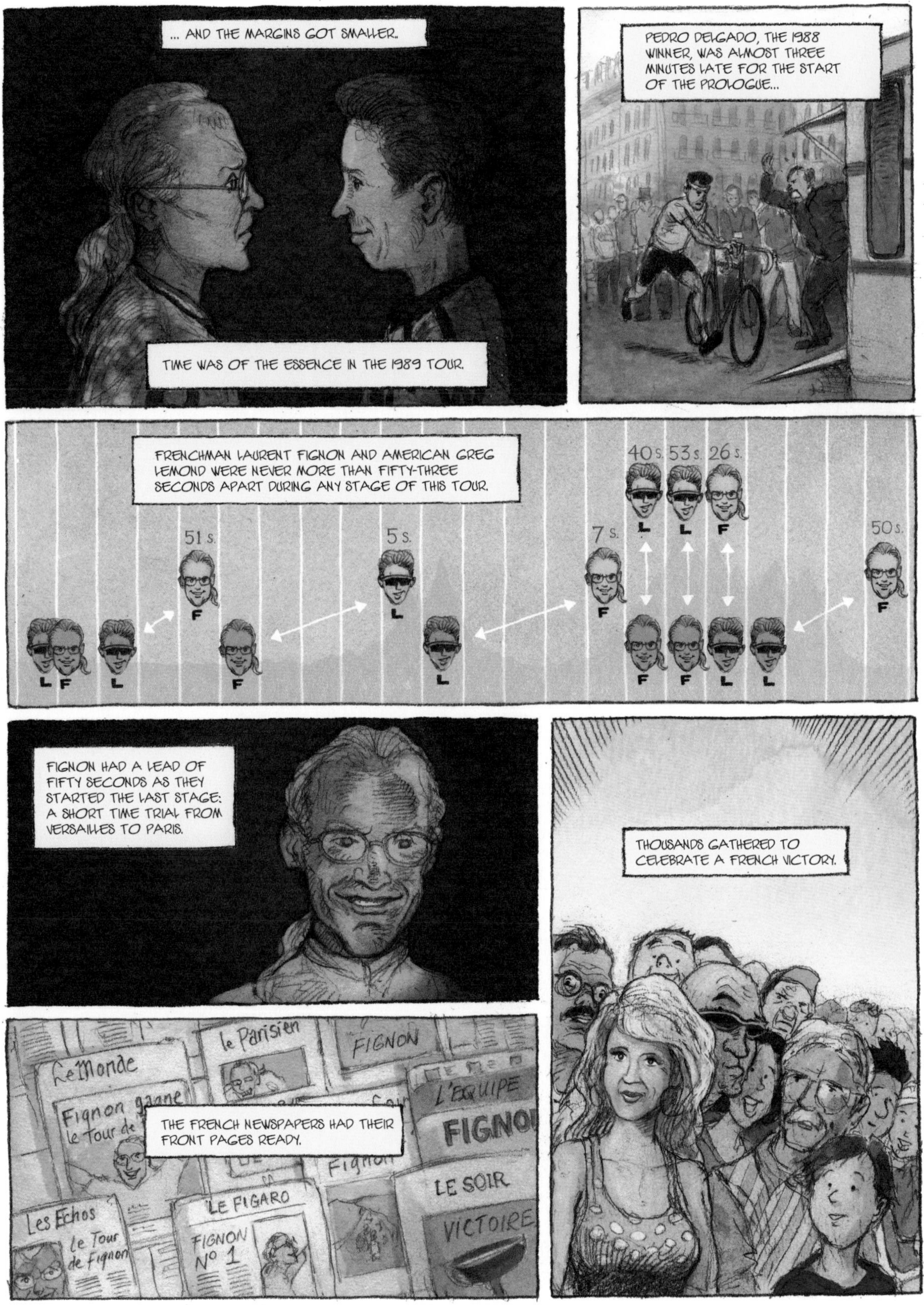
... AND THE MARGINS GOT SMALLER.
TIME WAS OF THE ESSENCE IN THE 1989 TOUR.
PEDRO DELGADO, THE 1988 WINNER, WAS ALMOST THREE MINUTES LATE FOR THE START OF THE PROLOGUE...
FRENCHMAN LAURENT FIGNON AND AMERICAN GREG LEMOND WERE NEVER MORE THAN FIFTY-THREE SECONDS APART DURING ANY STAGE OF THIS TOUR.
51 s.
5 s.
7 s.
40 s.
53 s.
26 s.
50 s.
FIGNON HAD A LEAD OF FIFTY SECONDS AS THEY STARTED THE LAST STAGE: A SHORT TIME TRIAL FROM VERSAILLES TO PARIS.
THOUSANDS GATHERED TO CELEBRATE A FRENCH VICTORY.
le Parisien
FIGNON
Le Monde
L'EQUIPE
THE FRENCH NEWSPAPERS HAD THEIR FRONT PAGES READY.
Fignon
LE SOIR
Les Echos
le Tour de Fignon
LE FIGARO
FIGNON N° 1
VICTOIRE

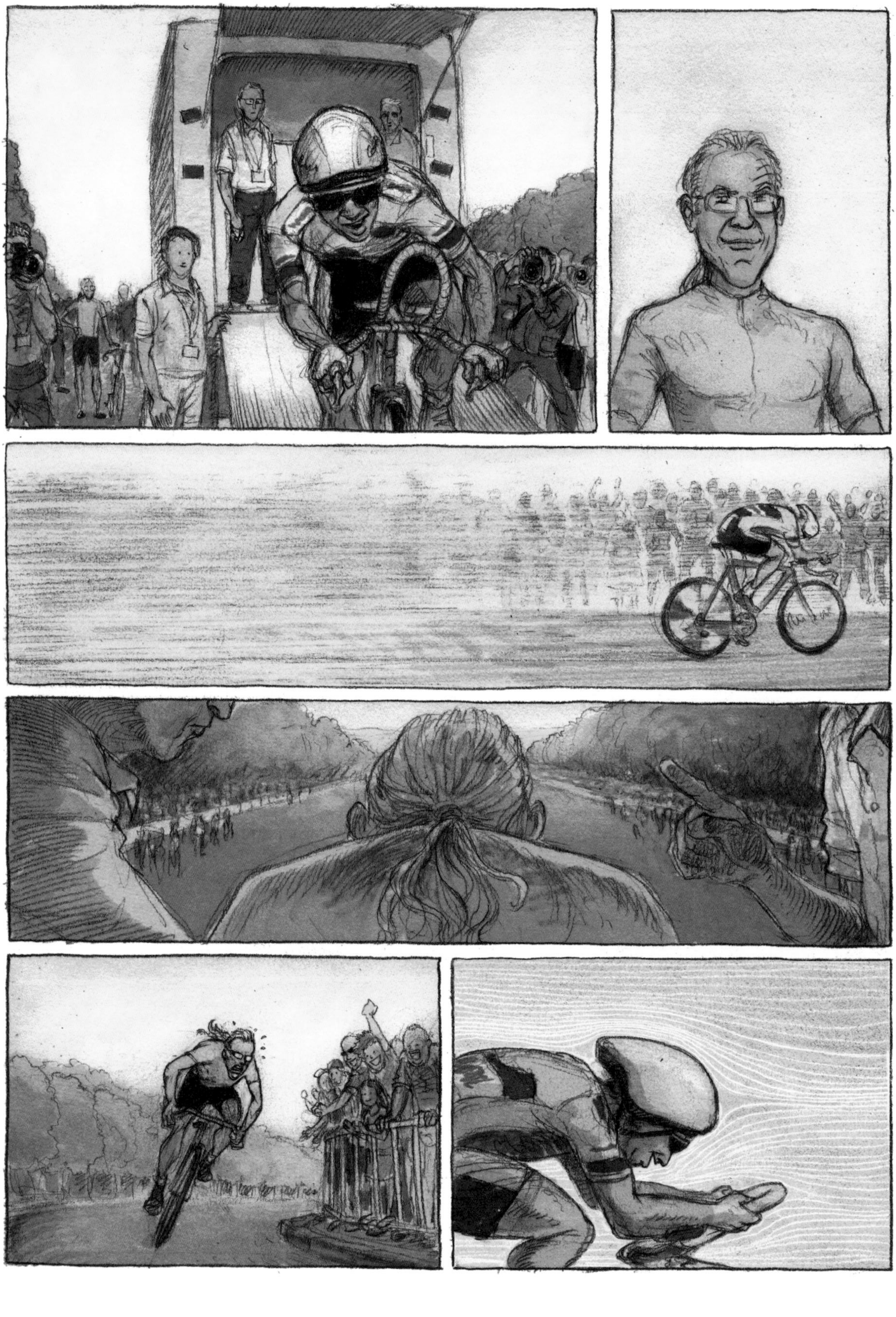

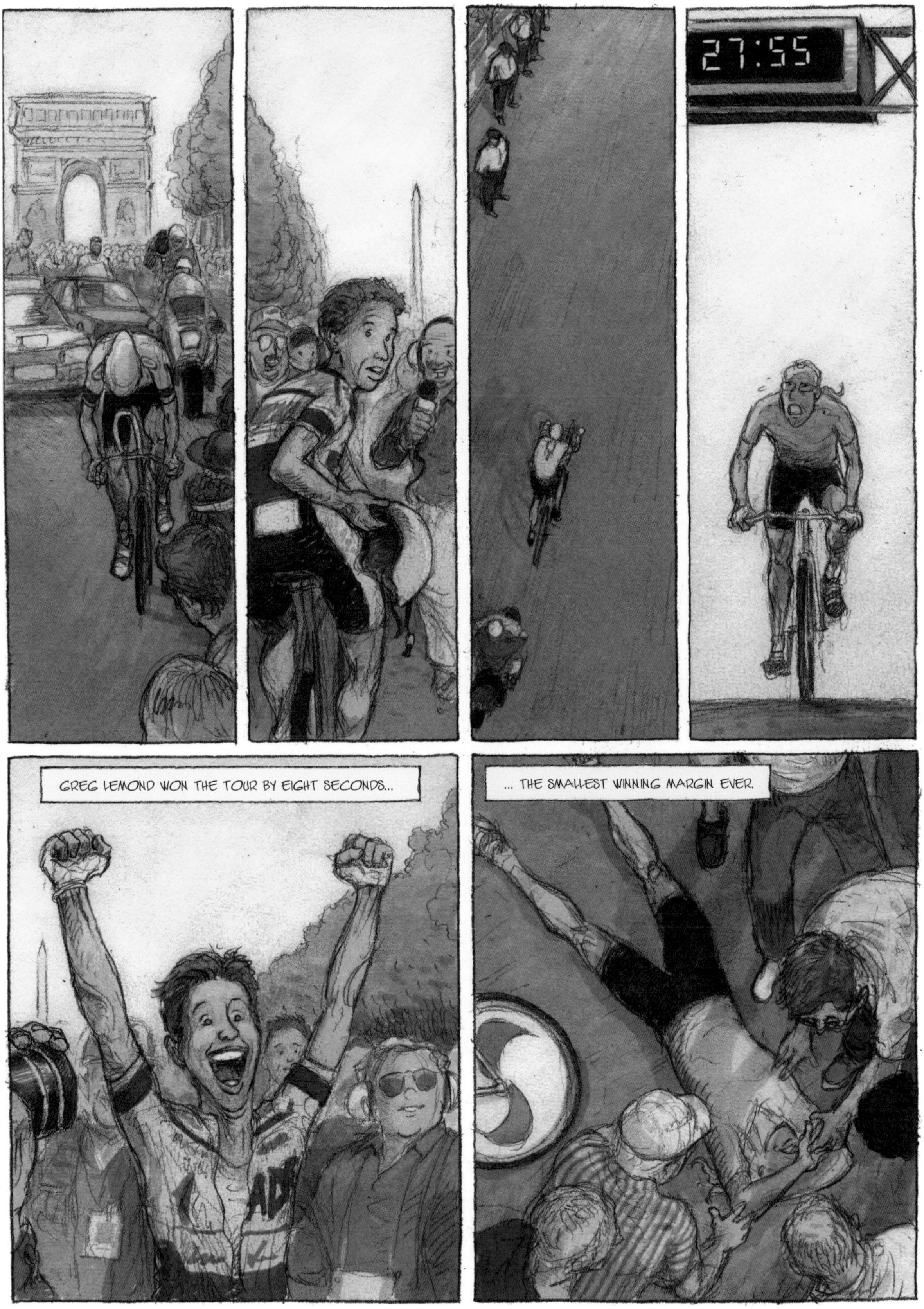
27:55
GREG LEMOND WON THE TOUR BY EIGHT SECONDS...
... THE SMALLEST WINNING MARGIN EVER.

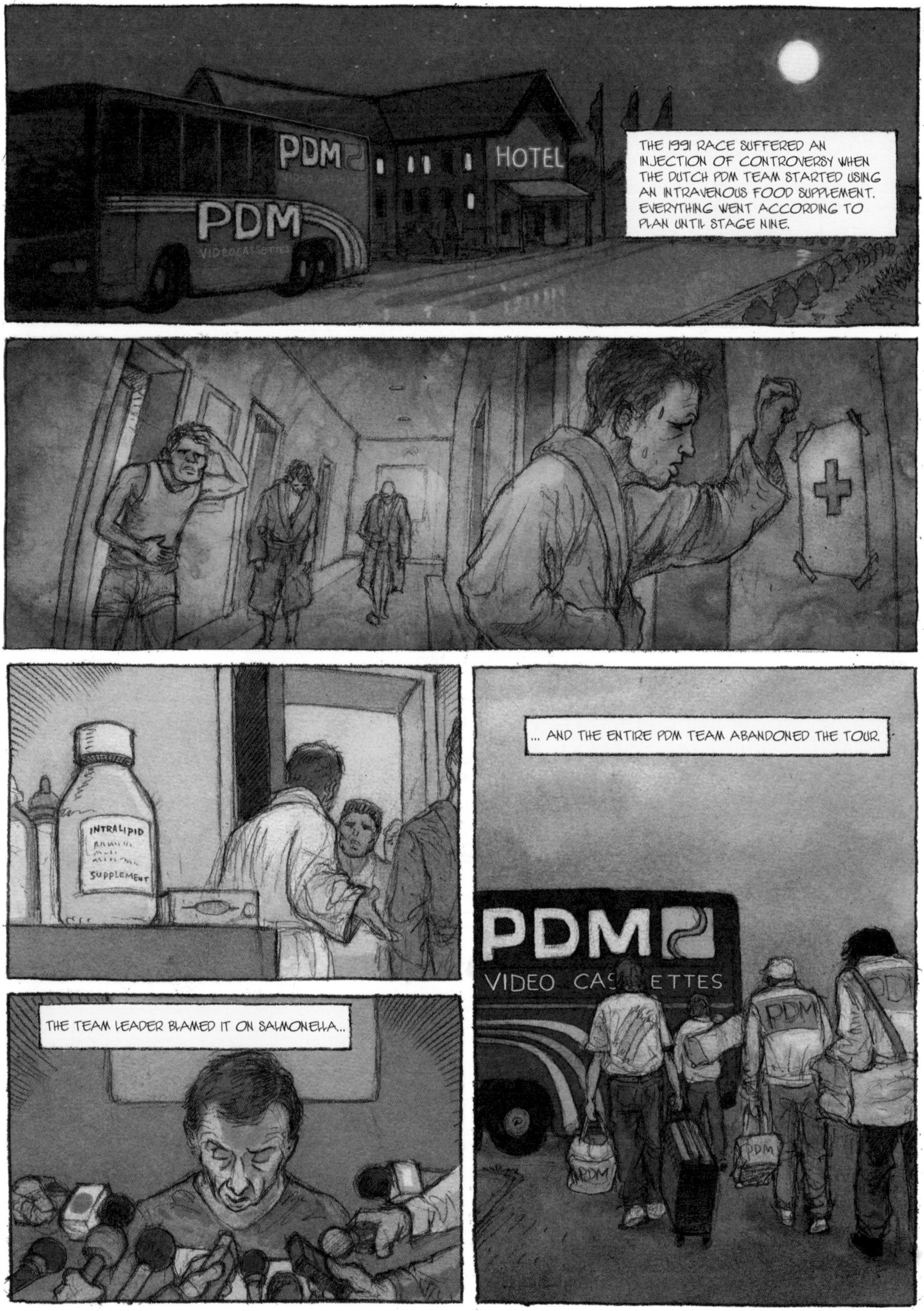

PDM
HOTEL
PDM
VIDEOCASSETTES
THE 1991 RACE SUFFERED AN INJECTION OF CONTROVERSY WHEN THE DUTCH PDM TEAM STARTED USING AN INTRAVENOUS FOOD SUPPLEMENT. EVERYTHING WENT ACCORDING TO PLAN UNTIL STAGE NINE.
INTRALIPID
SUPPLEMENT
THE TEAM LEADER BLAMED IT ON SALMONELLA...
... AND THE ENTIRE PDM TEAM ABANDONED THE TOUR.
PDM
PDM
PDM
PDM

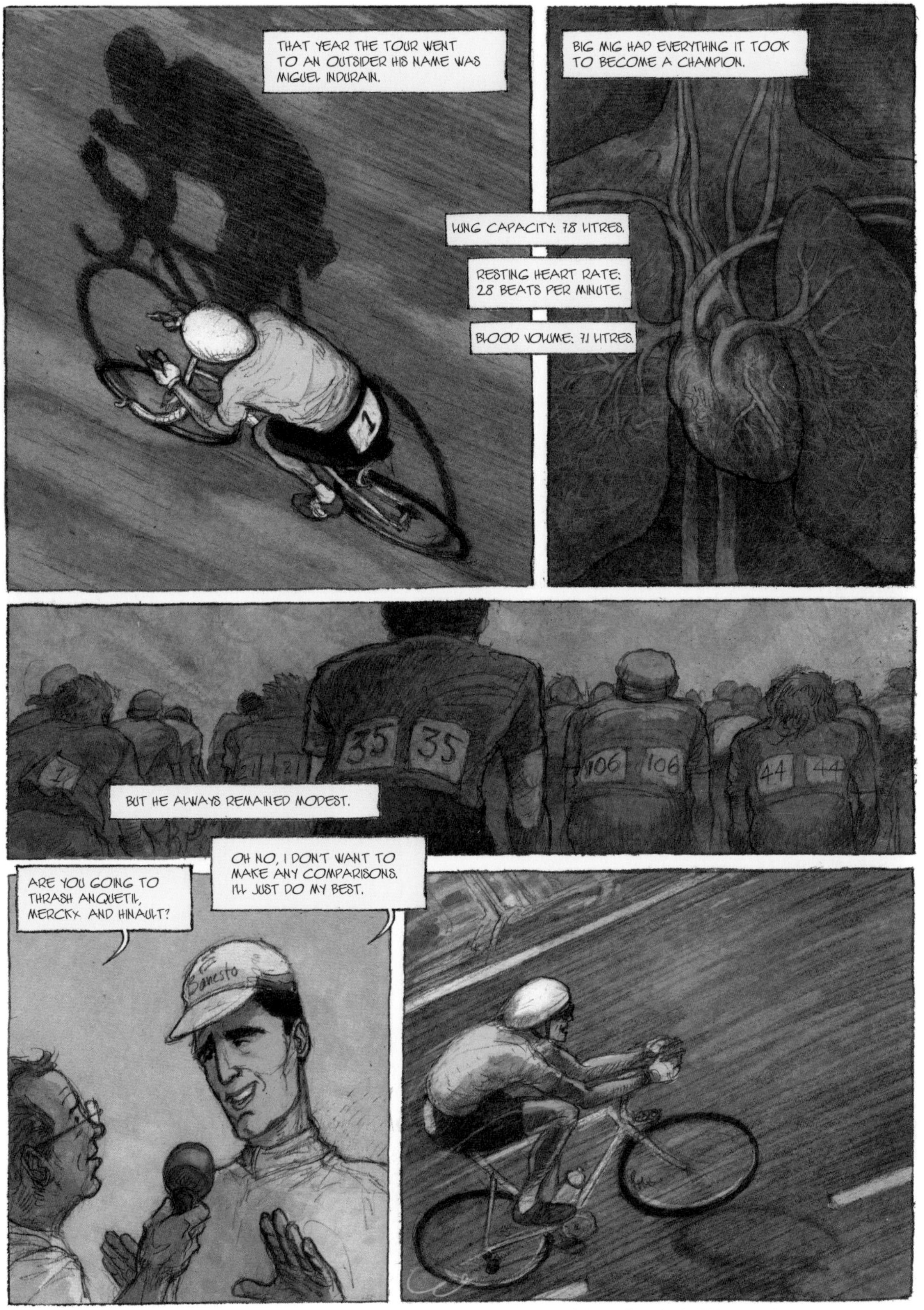
THAT YEAR THE TOUR WENT TO AN OUTSIDER HIS NAME WAS MIGUEL INDURAIN.
BIG MIG HAD EVERYTHING IT TOOK TO BECOME A CHAMPION.
LUNG CAPACITY: 7.8 LITRES.
RESTING HEART RATE: 28 BEATS PER MINUTE.
BLOOD VOLUME: 7.1 LITRES.
35
35
21
21
106
106
44
44
BUT HE ALWAYS REMAINED MODEST.
ARE YOU GOING TO THRASH ANQUETIL, MERCKX AND HINAULT?
OH NO, I DON'T WANT TO MAKE ANY COMPARISONS. I'LL JUST DO MY BEST.
Banesto

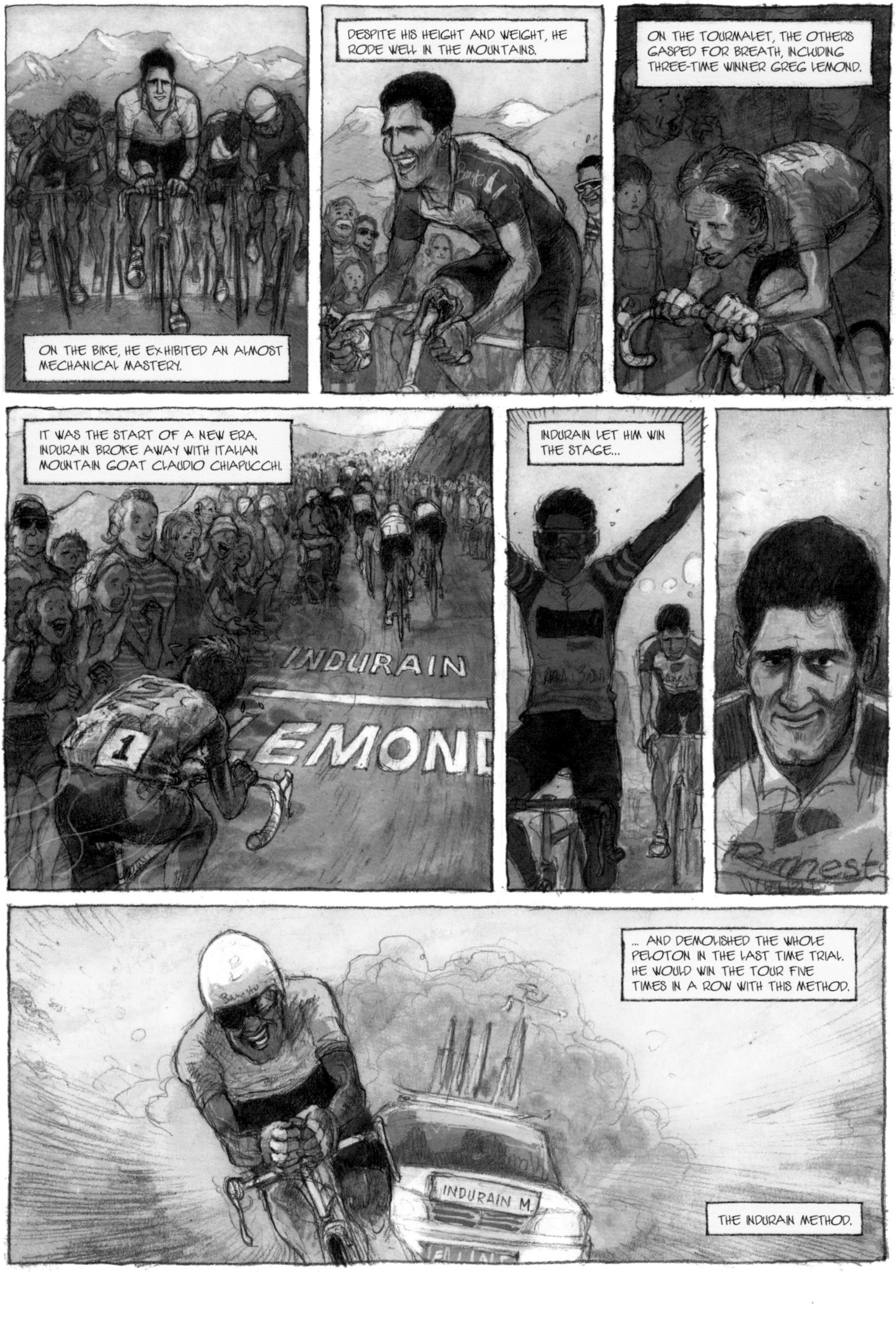
ON THE BIKE, HE EXHIBITED AN ALMOST MECHANICAL MASTERY.
DESPITE HIS HEIGHT AND WEIGHT, HE RODE WELL IN THE MOUNTAINS.
ON THE TOURMALET, THE OTHERS GASPED FOR BREATH, INCLUDING THREE-TIME WINNER GREG LEMOND.
IT WAS THE START OF A NEW ERA. INDURAIN BROKE AWAY WITH ITALIAN MOUNTAIN GOAT CLAUDIO CHIAPUCCHI.
INDURAIN
LEMOND
1
INDURAIN LET HIM WIN THE STAGE...
... AND DEMOLISHED THE WHOLE PELOTON IN THE LAST TIME TRIAL. HE WOULD WIN THE TOUR FIVE TIMES IN A ROW WITH THIS METHOD.
INDURAIN M.
THE INDURAIN METHOD.

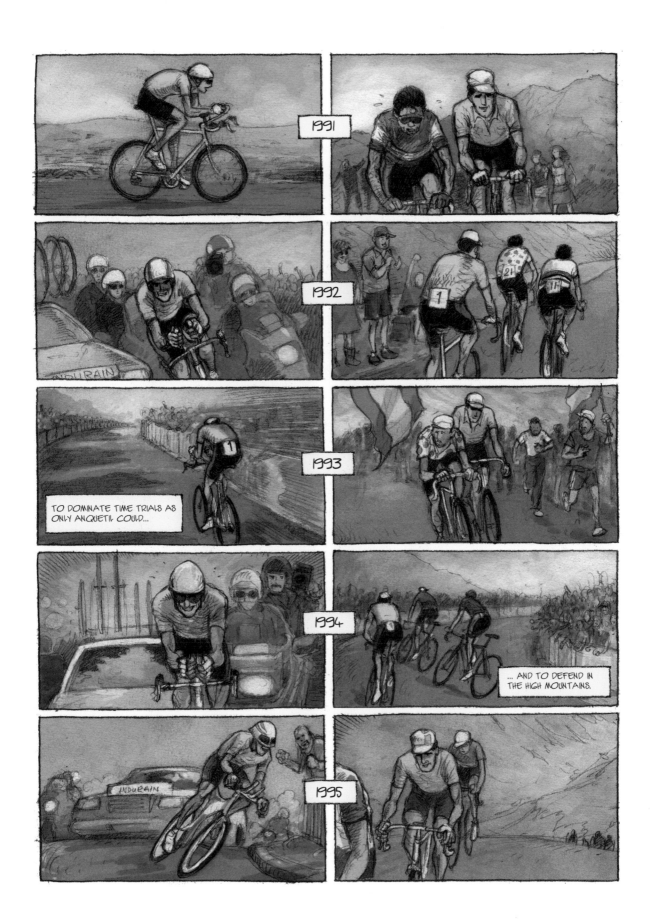

1991

1992

1993

TO DOMINATE TIME TRIALS AS ONLY ANQUETIL COULD...

1994

... AND TO DEFEND IN THE HIGH MOUNTAINS.

1995

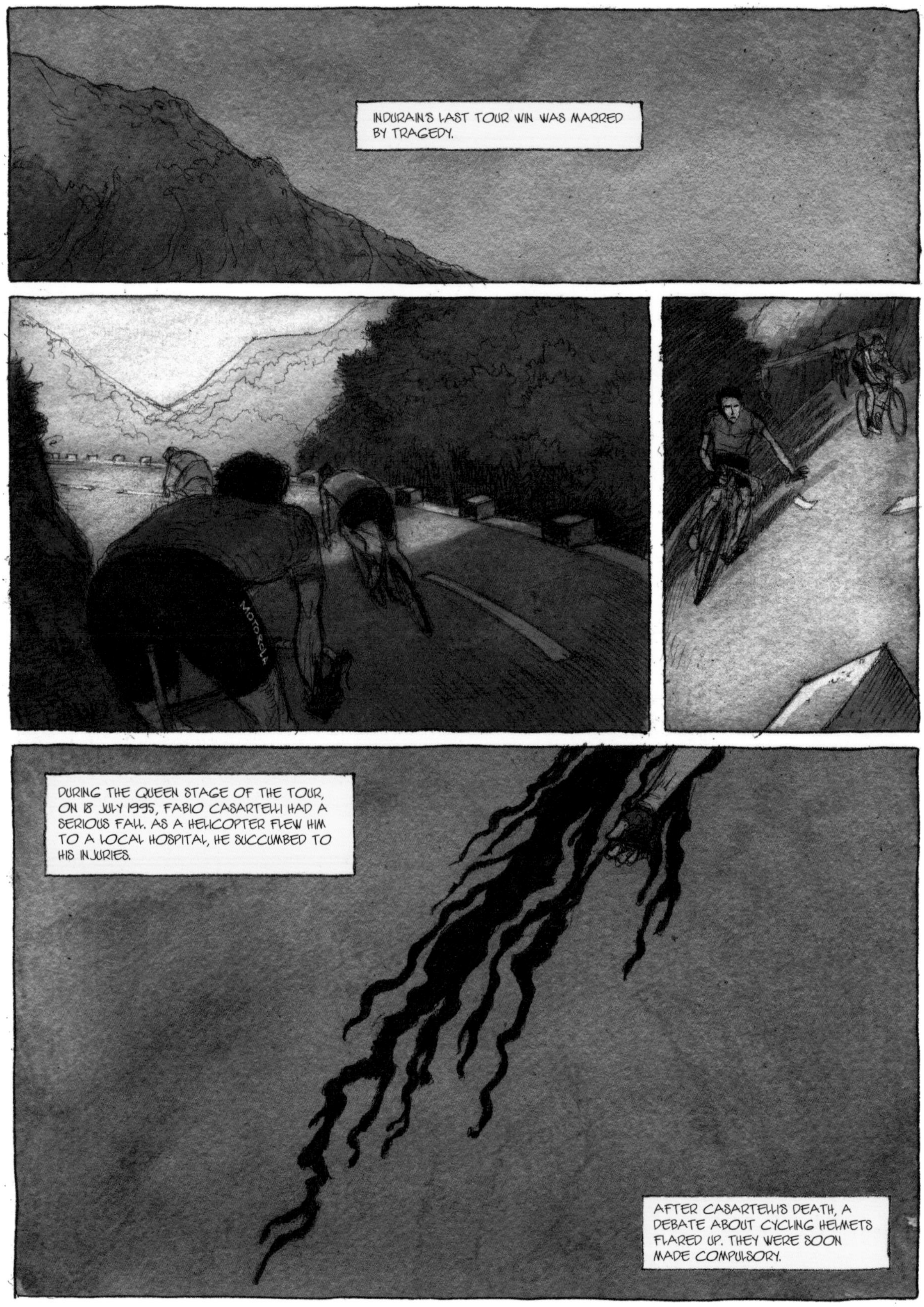
INDURAIN'S LAST TOUR WIN WAS MARRED BY TRAGEDY.
DURING THE QUEEN STAGE OF THE TOUR, ON 18 JULY 1995, FABIO CASARTELLI HAD A SERIOUS FALL. AS A HELICOPTER FLEW HIM TO A LOCAL HOSPITAL, HE SUCCUMBED TO HIS INJURIES.
AFTER CASARTELLI'S DEATH, A DEBATE ABOUT CYCLING HELMETS FLARED UP. THEY WERE SOON MADE COMPULSORY.

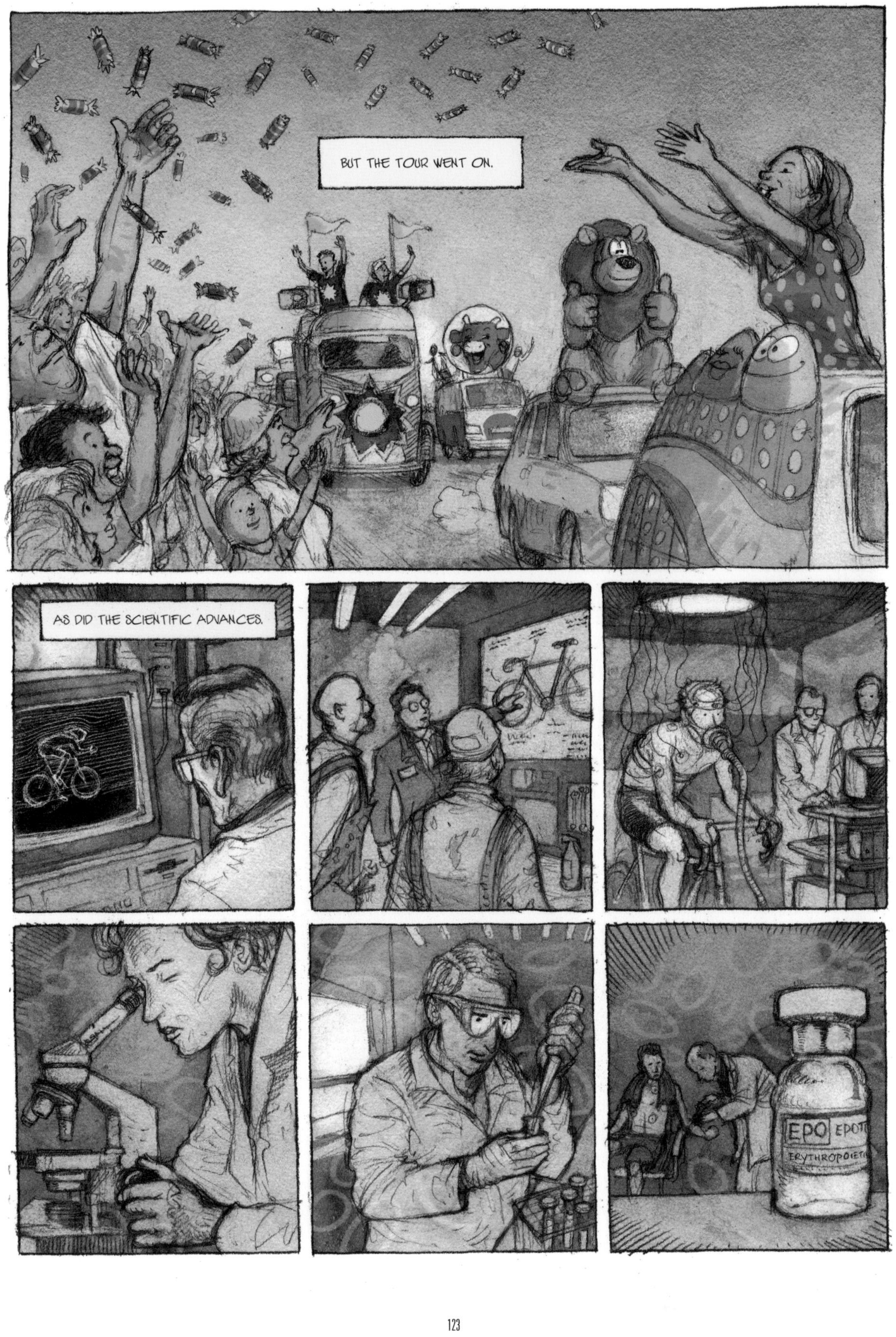
BUT THE TOUR WENT ON.
AS DID THE SCIENTIFIC ADVANCES.
EPO

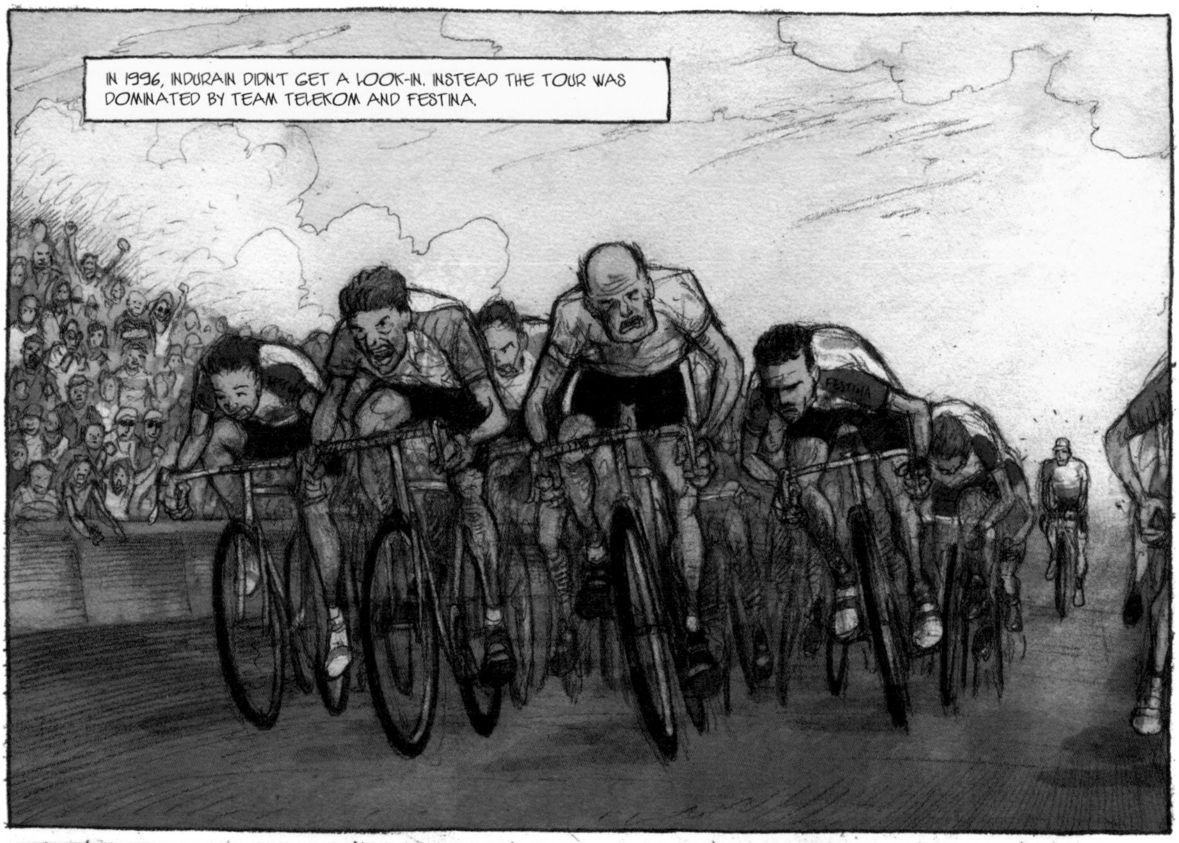
IN 1996, INDURAIN DIDN'T GET A LOOK-IN. INSTEAD THE TOUR WAS DOMINATED BY TEAM TELEKOM AND FESTINA.
FESTINA

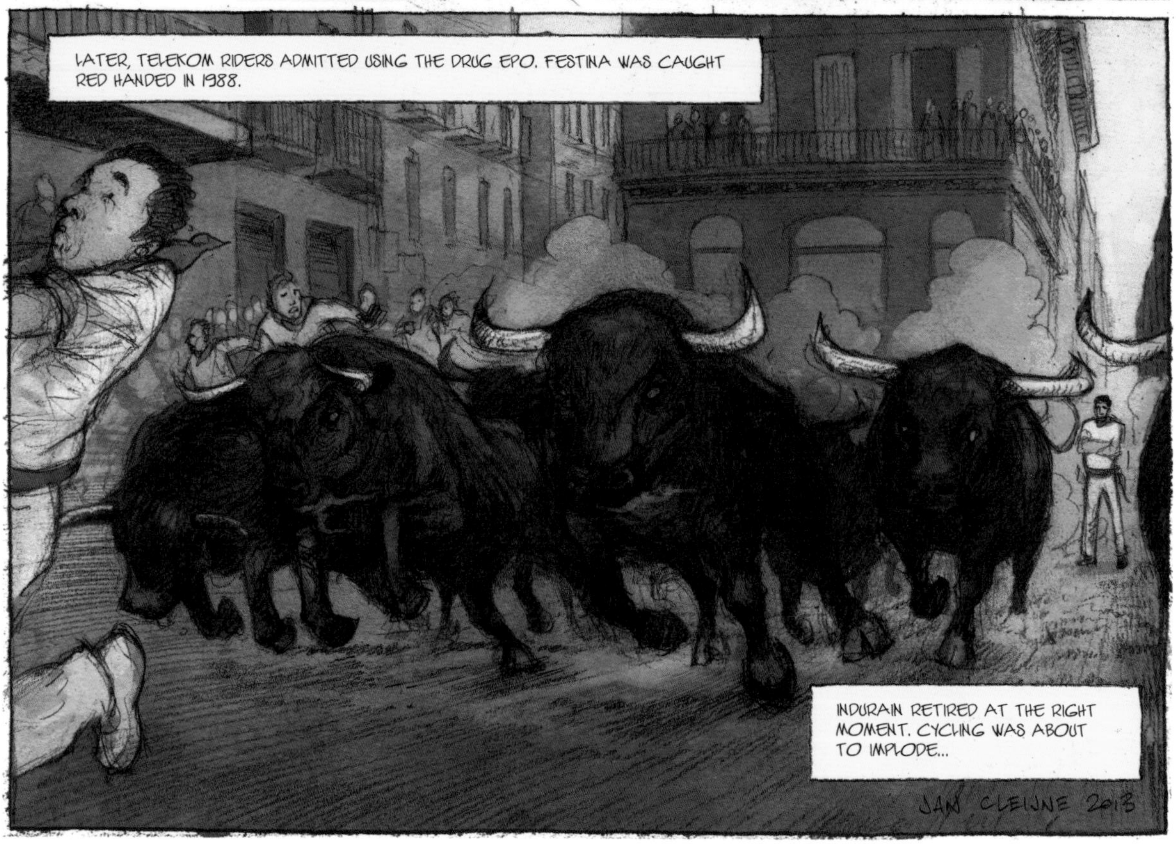
LATER, TELEKOM RIDERS ADMITTED USING THE DRUG EPO. FESTINA WAS CAUGHT RED HANDED IN 1988.
INDURAIN RETIRED AT THE RIGHT MOMENT. CYCLING WAS ABOUT TO IMPLODE...
JAN CLEIJNE 2013

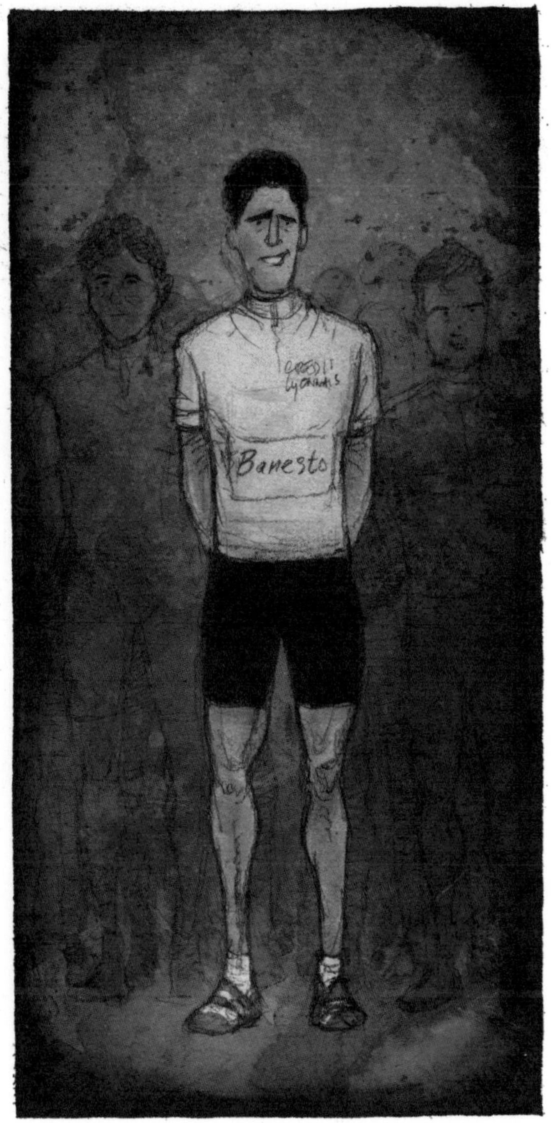
Banesto

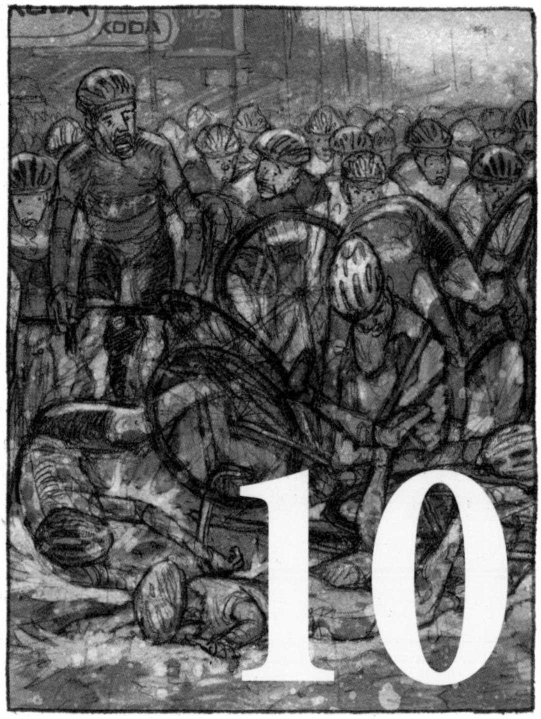
KODA

10

AFTER THE FALL

1998 CHANGED EVERYTHING.

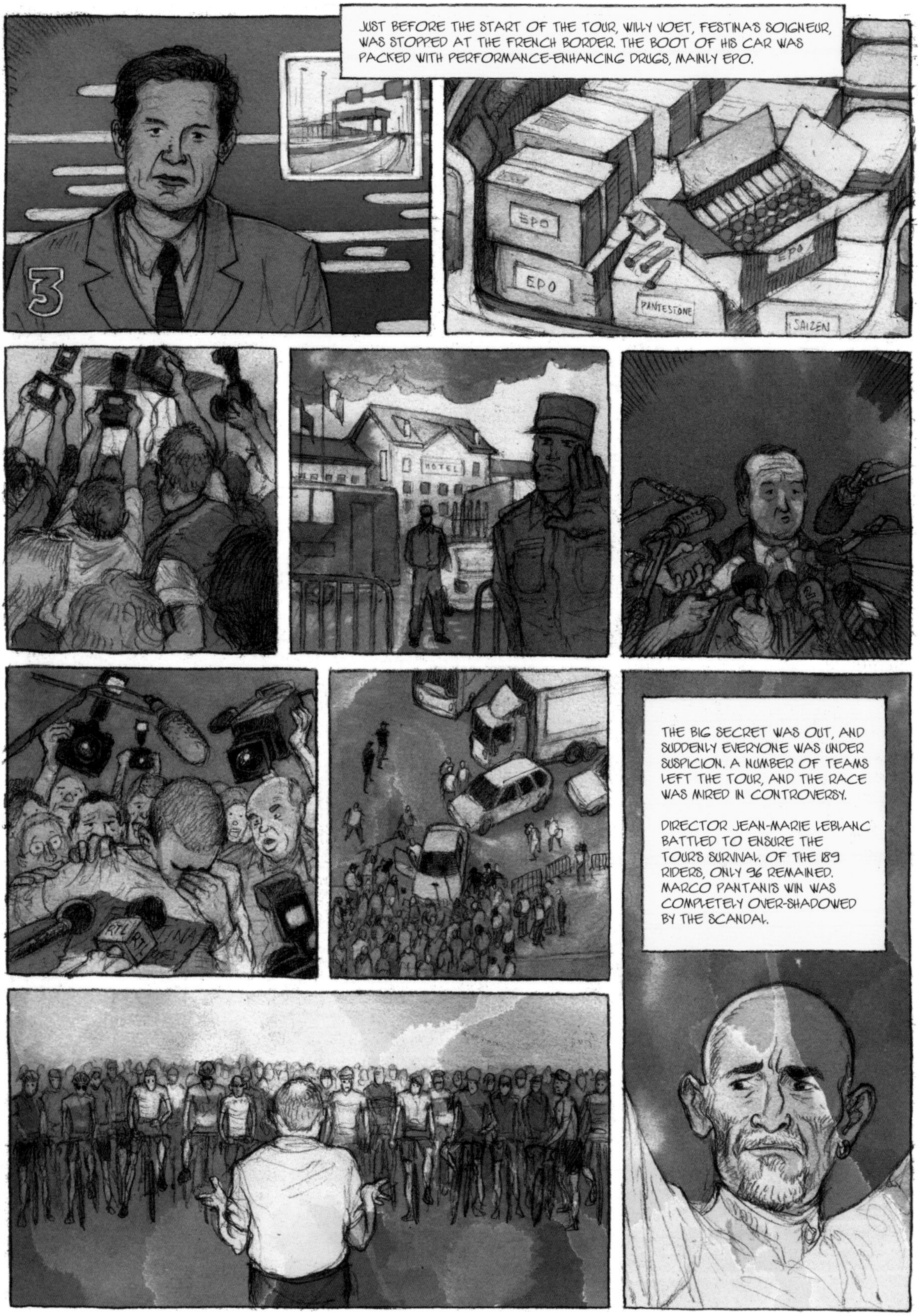
JUST BEFORE THE START OF THE TOUR, WILLY VOET, FESTINA'S SOIGNEUR, WAS STOPPED AT THE FRENCH BORDER. THE BOOT OF HIS CAR WAS PACKED WITH PERFORMANCE-ENHANCING DRUGS, MAINLY EPO.
3
EPO
EPO
EPO
PANTESTONE
SAIZEN
HOTEL
THE BIG SECRET WAS OUT, AND SUDDENLY EVERYONE WAS UNDER SUSPICION. A NUMBER OF TEAMS LEFT THE TOUR, AND THE RACE WAS MIRED IN CONTROVERSY.
DIRECTOR JEAN-MARIE LEBLANC BATTLED TO ENSURE THE TOUR'S SURVIVAL. OF THE 189 RIDERS, ONLY 96 REMAINED. MARCO PANTANI'S WIN WAS COMPLETELY OVER-SHADOWED BY THE SCANDAL.

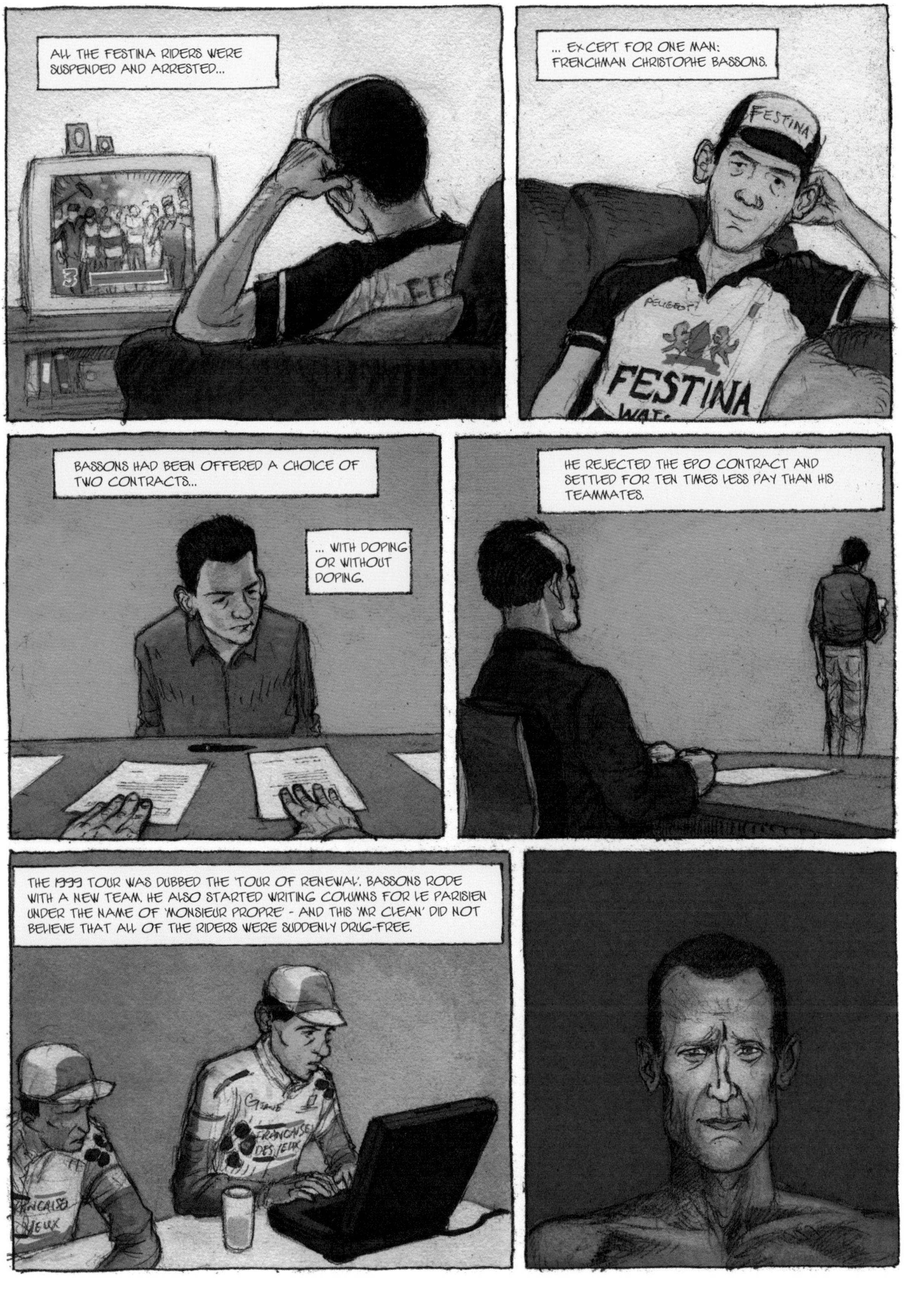
ALL THE FESTINA RIDERS WERE SUSPENDED AND ARRESTED...
FES
... EXCEPT FOR ONE MAN: FRENCHMAN CHRISTOPHE BASSONS.
FESTINA
PEUGEOT
FESTINA
BASSONS HAD BEEN OFFERED A CHOICE OF TWO CONTRACTS...
... WITH DOPING OR WITHOUT DOPING.
HE REJECTED THE EPO CONTRACT AND SETTLED FOR TEN TIMES LESS PAY THAN HIS TEAMMATES.
THE 1999 TOUR WAS DUBBED THE 'TOUR OF RENEWAL'. BASSONS RODE WITH A NEW TEAM. HE ALSO STARTED WRITING COLUMNS FOR LE PARISIEN UNDER THE NAME OF 'MONSIEUR PROPRE' - AND THIS 'MR CLEAN' DID NOT BELIEVE THAT ALL OF THE RIDERS WERE SUDDENLY DRUG-FREE.
FRANCAISE DES JEUX

THE AMERICAN LANCE ARMSTRONG ALSO RODE IN THAT TOUR, FOLLOWING HIS MIRACULOUS ESCAPE FROM DEATH. IT WAS THE COMEBACK OF THE CENTURY.

HE WON THE PROLOGUE...

... THE FIRST TIME TRIAL...

... AND THE FIRST MOUNTAIN STAGE...

BASSONS, HOWEVER, BELIEVED THAT THIS ACHIEVEMENT HAD LITTLE TO DO WITH THE NEW CYCLING ERA.

... BY A LONG WAY.

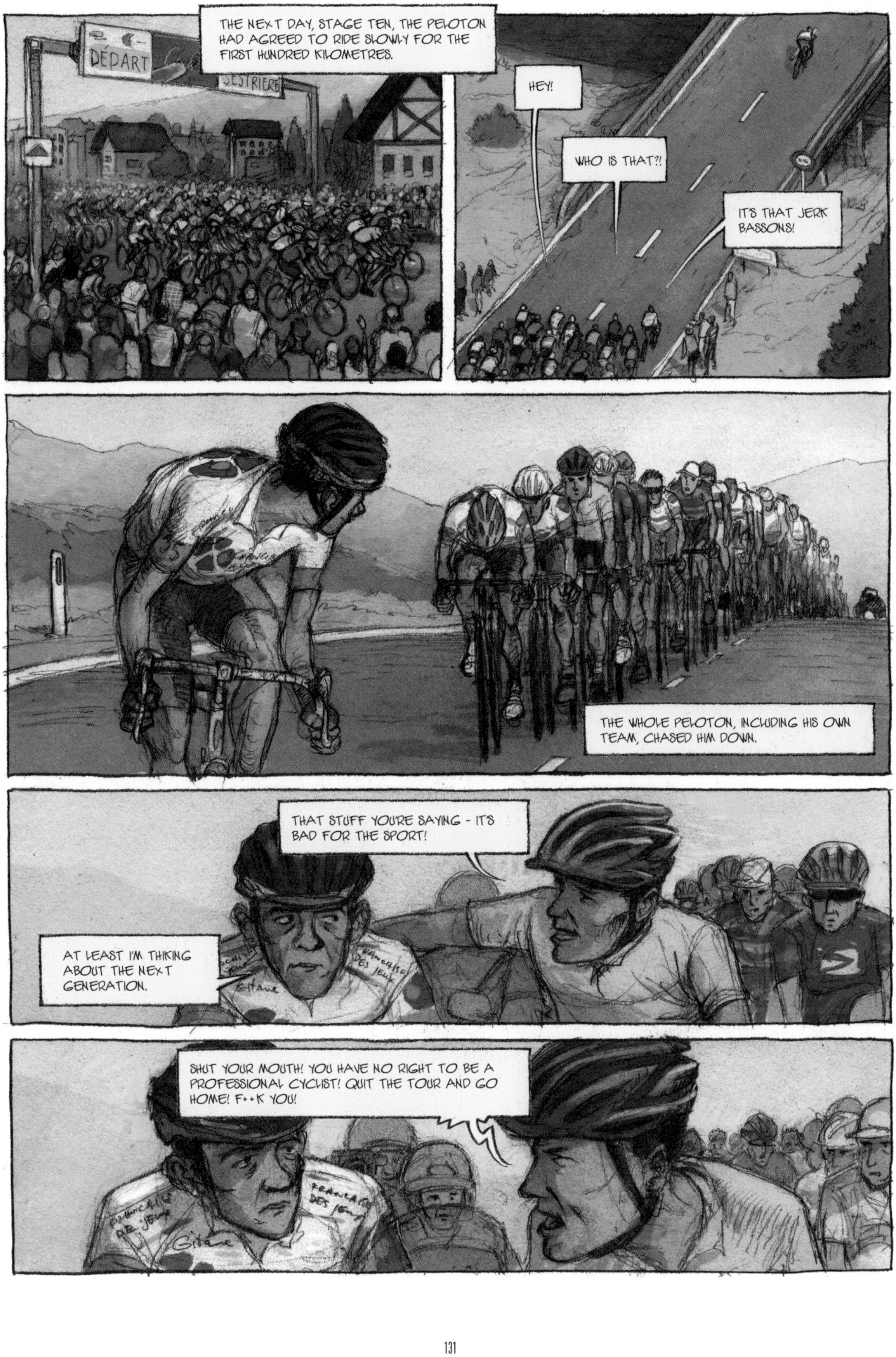
THE NEXT DAY, STAGE TEN, THE PELOTON HAD AGREED TO RIDE SLOWLY FOR THE FIRST HUNDRED KILOMETRES.
DÉPART
SESTRIERE
HEY!
WHO IS THAT?!
IT'S THAT JERK BASSONS!
THE WHOLE PELOTON, INCLUDING HIS OWN TEAM, CHASED HIM DOWN.
THAT STUFF YOU'RE SAYING - IT'S BAD FOR THE SPORT!
AT LEAST I'M THIKING ABOUT THE NEXT GENERATION.
SHUT YOUR MOUTH! YOU HAVE NO RIGHT TO BE A PROFESSIONAL CYCLIST! QUIT THE TOUR AND GO HOME! F++K YOU!

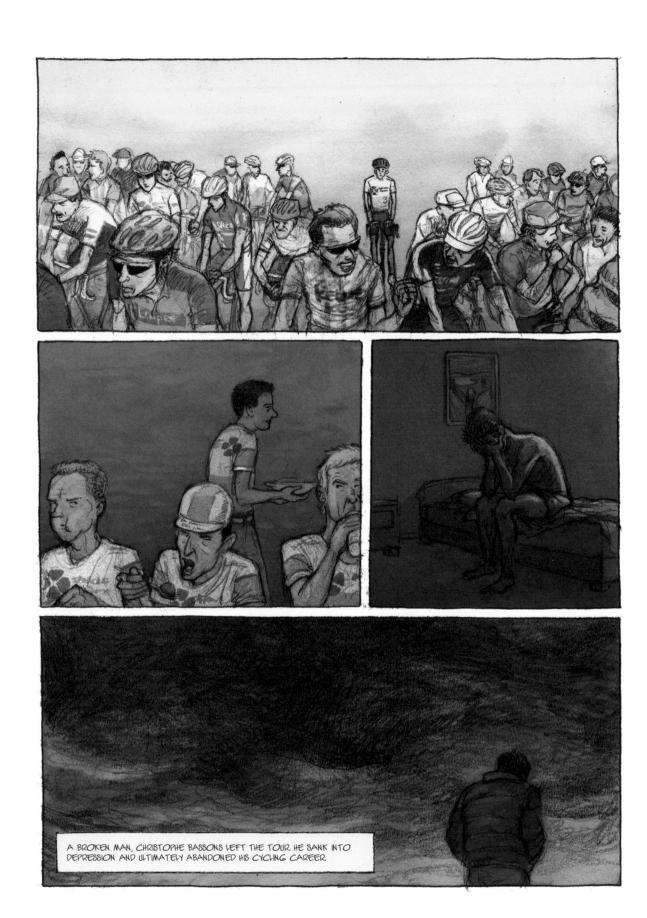

A BROKEN MAN, CHRISTOPHE BASSONS LEFT THE TOUR. HE SANK INTO DEPRESSION AND ULTIMATELY ABANDONED HIS CYCLING CAREER.

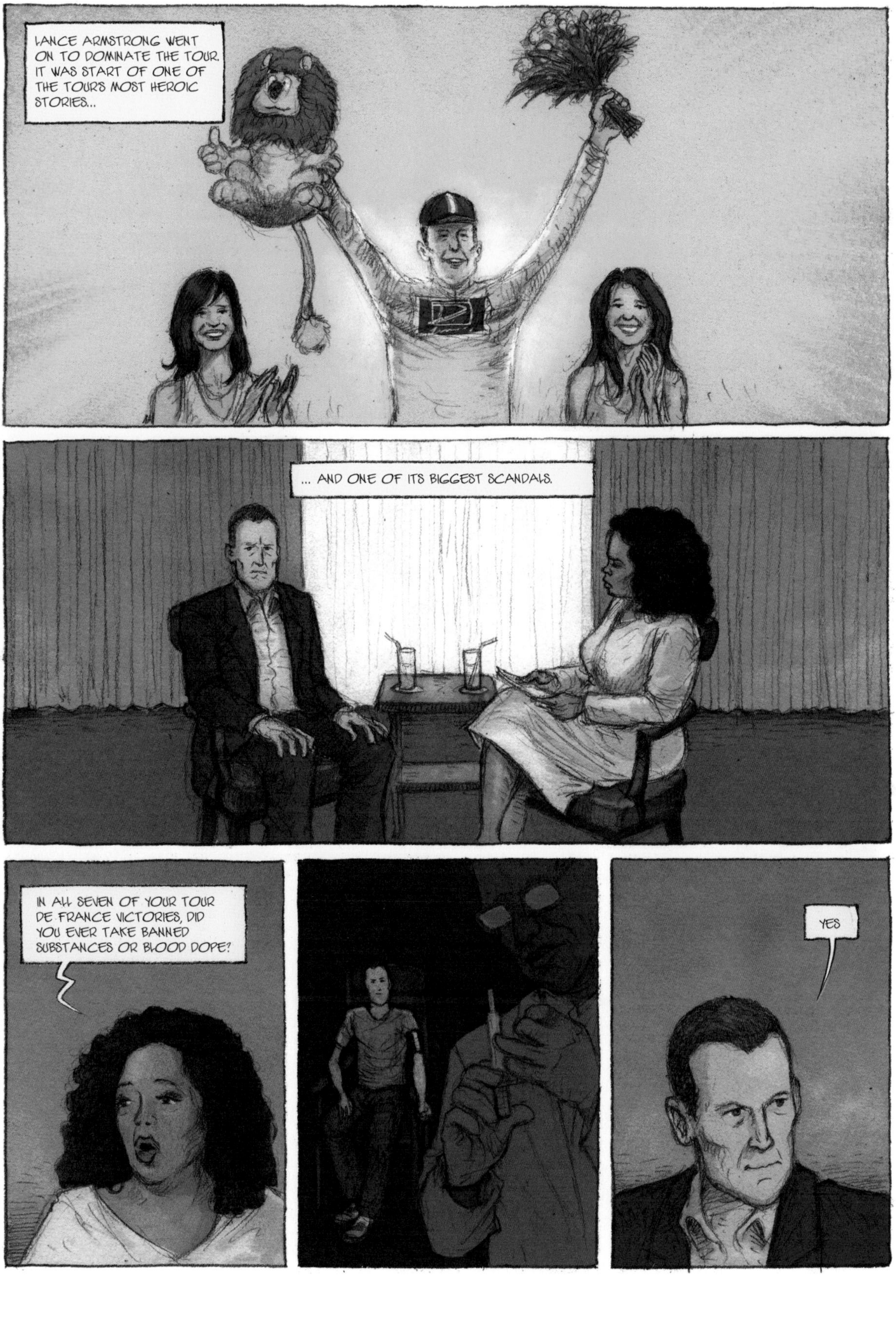
LANCE ARMSTRONG WENT ON TO DOMINATE THE TOUR. IT WAS START OF ONE OF THE TOURS MOST HEROIC STORIES...
... AND ONE OF ITS BIGGEST SCANDALS.
IN ALL SEVEN OF YOUR TOUR DE FRANCE VICTORIES, DID YOU EVER TAKE BANNED SUBSTANCES OR BLOOD DOPE?
YES

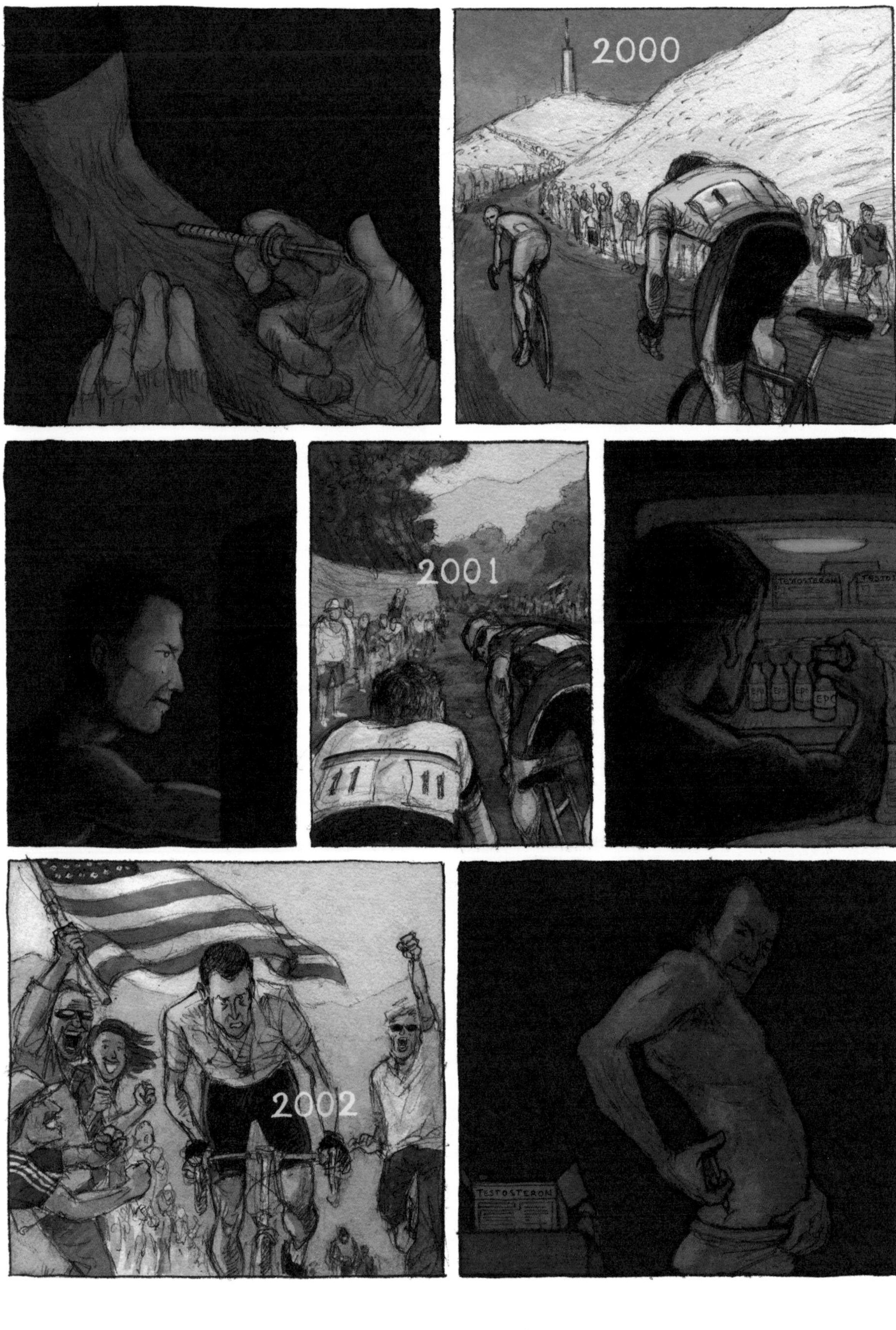
2000
2001
TESTOSTERON
EPO
2002
TESTOSTERON

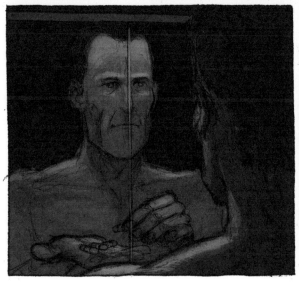

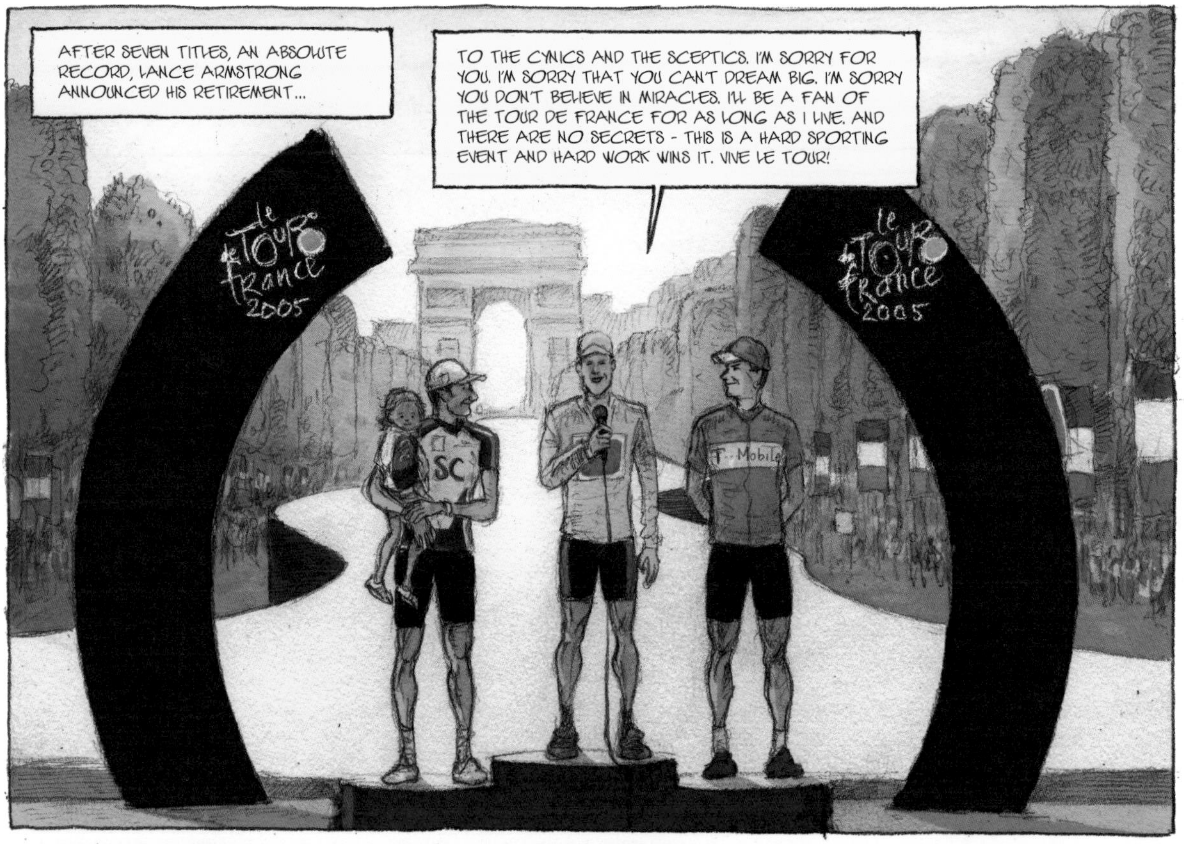
AFTER SEVEN TITLES, AN ABSOLUTE RECORD, LANCE ARMSTRONG ANNOUNCED HIS RETIREMENT...
TO THE CYNICS AND THE SCEPTICS. I'M SORRY FOR YOU. I'M SORRY THAT YOU CAN'T DREAM BIG. I'M SORRY YOU DON'T BELIEVE IN MIRACLES. I'LL BE A FAN OF THE TOUR DE FRANCE FOR AS LONG AS I LIVE. AND THERE ARE NO SECRETS - THIS IS A HARD SPORTING EVENT AND HARD WORK WINS IT. VIVE LE TOUR!
le TOUR de France 2005
le TOUR de France 2005
SC
T-Mobile

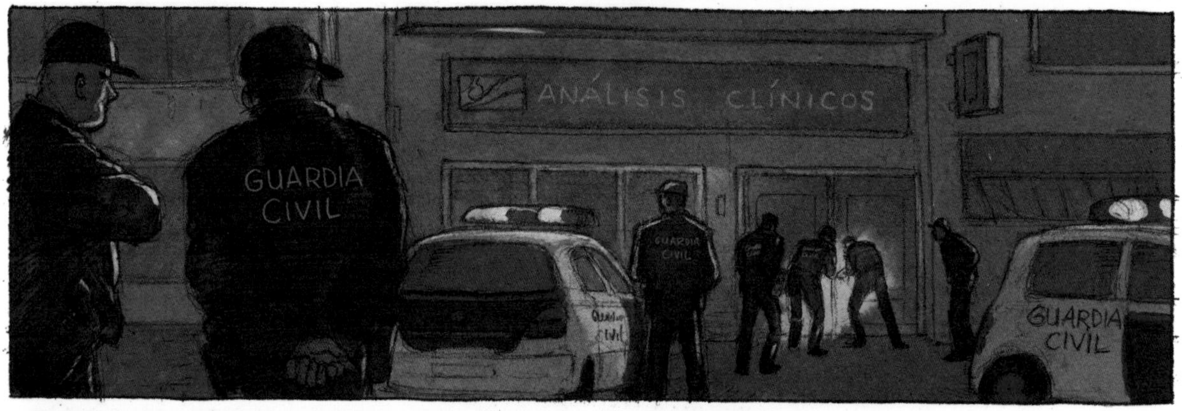
ANÁLISIS CLÍNICOS
GUARDIA CIVIL
GUARDIA CIVIL

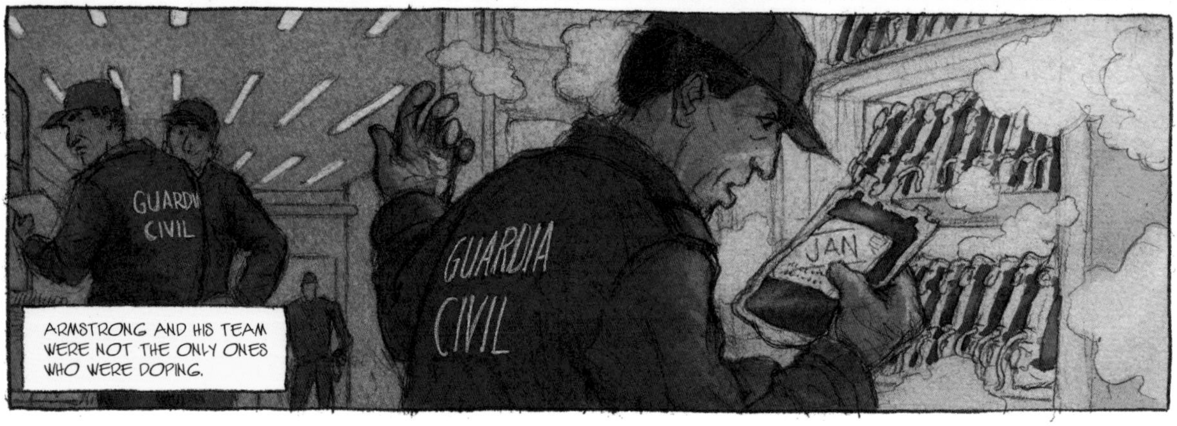
GUARDIA CIVIL
GUARDIA CIVIL
JAN
ARMSTRONG AND HIS TEAM WERE NOT THE ONLY ONES WHO WERE DOPING.

OPERACIÓN PUERTO FOCUSED ON THE DOPING DOCTOR EUFEMIANO FUENTES...

... AND THE NAMES ON HIS LIST.

José Ignacio Gutiérr
Francisco Mancebo
Constantino Zaballa
Jan Ullrich
Ivan Basso
Santiago Botero
Carlos Zárate
Óscar Sevilla
Tyler Hamilton
Jörg Jaksche
Jesús Manzano
Carlos García Quesa

IN 2006, TEAMS WITHDREW ANY FAVOURITES WHO WERE UNDER SUSPICION. BY THE START OF THE RACE, ONLY THREE REAL CONTENDERS REMAINED: SPANIARD ALEJANDRO VALVERDE AND AMERICANS LEVI LEIPHEIMER AND FLOYD LANDIS, FORMERLY ARMSTRONG'S TRUSTED LIEUTENANT, WHO NOW HAD A CHANCE TO STEP OUT OF HIS SHADOW.

WHEN VALVERDE FRACTURED HIS COLLARBONE...

... AND LEIPHEIMER BOTCHED HIS TIME TRIAL...

LEIPHEIMER 77 1:07:49
LANG 1 1:02:47

... LANDIS'S VICTORY SEEMED ASSURED.

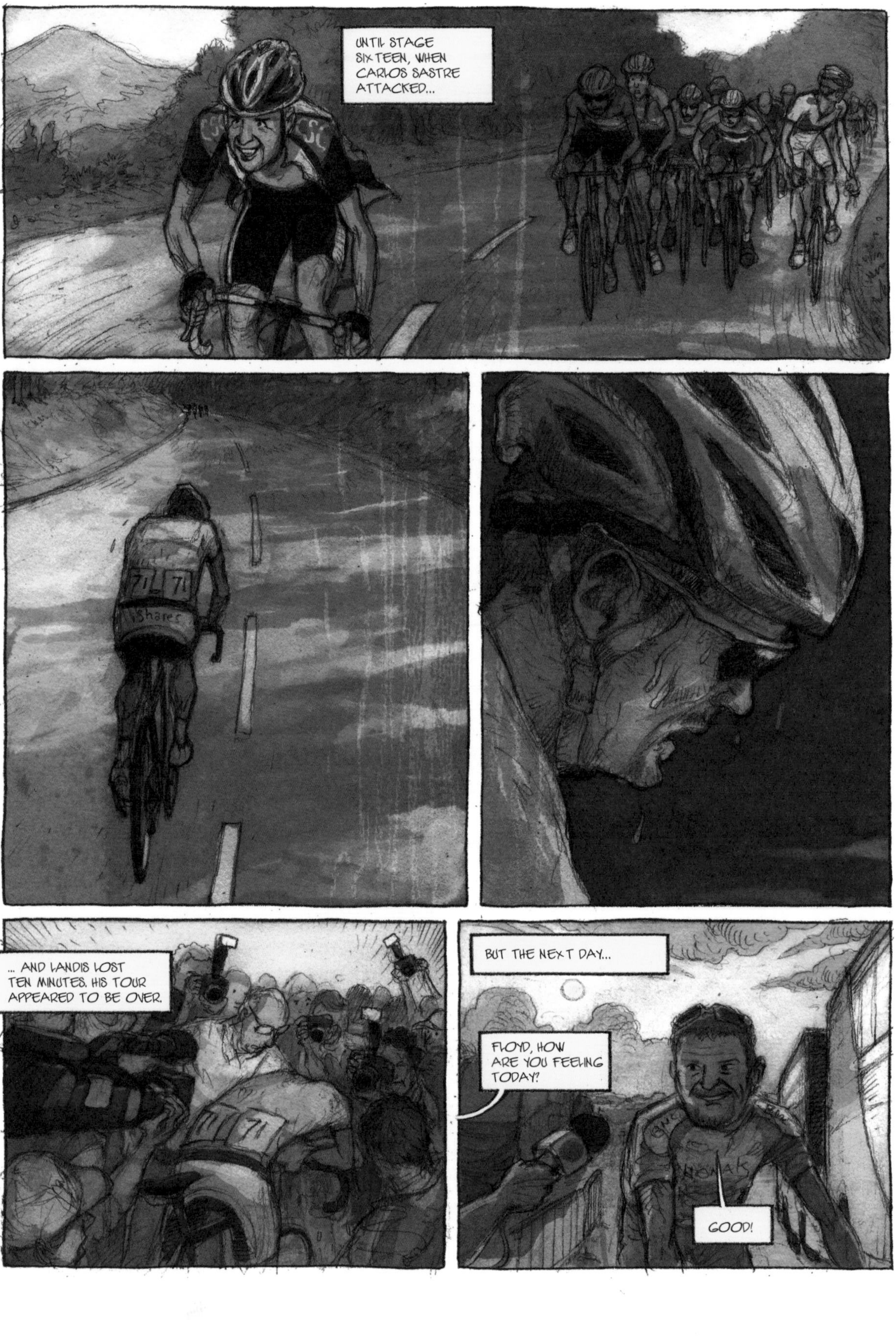
UNTIL STAGE SIXTEEN, WHEN CARLOS SASTRE ATTACKED...
CSC
71 71
iShares
... AND LANDIS LOST TEN MINUTES. HIS TOUR APPEARED TO BE OVER.
BUT THE NEXT DAY...
FLOYD, HOW ARE YOU FEELING TODAY?
GOOD!

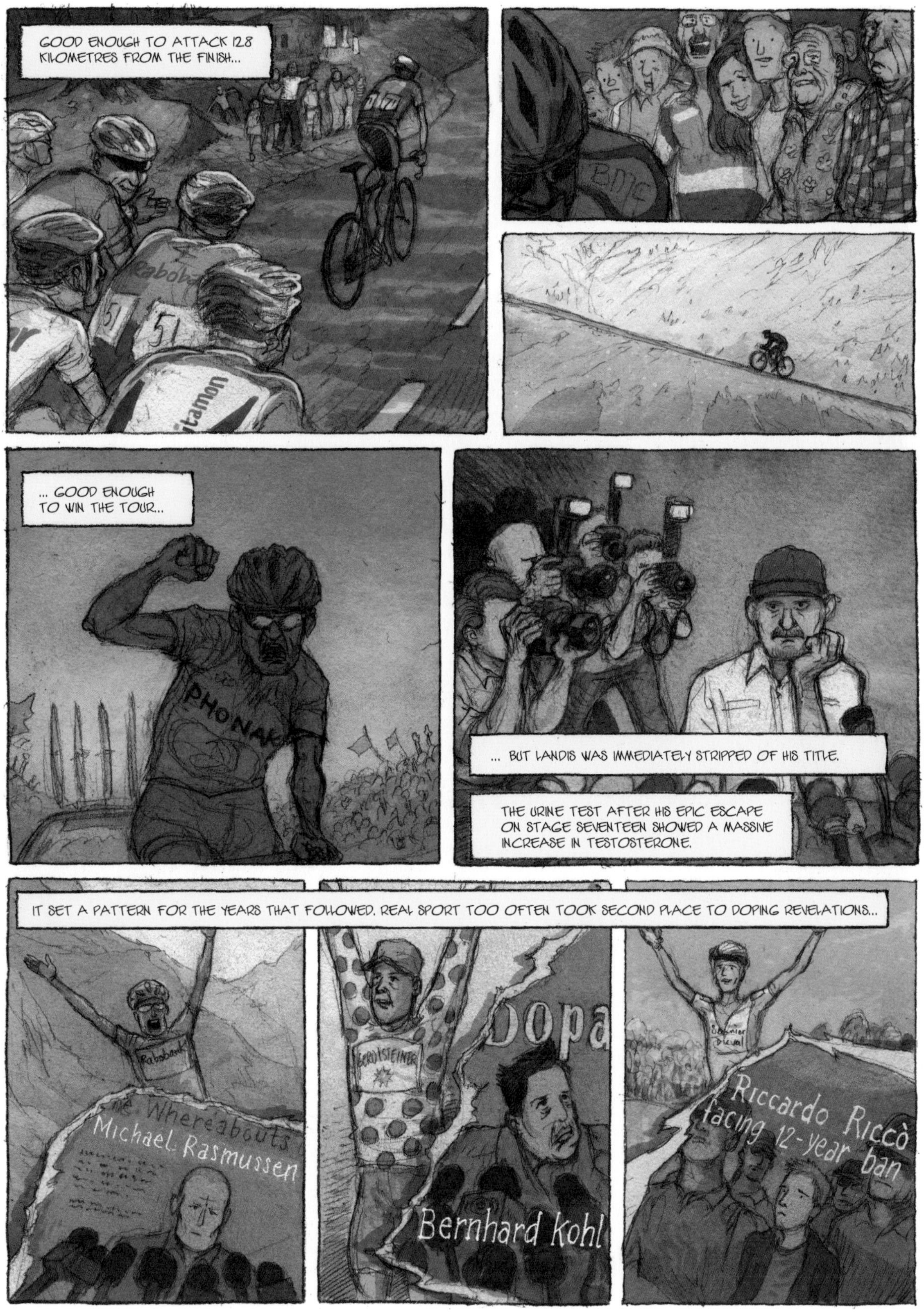
GOOD ENOUGH TO ATTACK 128 KILOMETRES FROM THE FINISH...
... GOOD ENOUGH TO WIN THE TOUR...
PHONAK
... BUT LANDIS WAS IMMEDIATELY STRIPPED OF HIS TITLE.
THE URINE TEST AFTER HIS EPIC ESCAPE ON STAGE SEVENTEEN SHOWED A MASSIVE INCREASE IN TESTOSTERONE.
IT SET A PATTERN FOR THE YEARS THAT FOLLOWED. REAL SPORT TOO OFTEN TOOK SECOND PLACE TO DOPING REVELATIONS...
Whereabouts
Michael Rasmussen
Dopa
Bernhard kohl
Riccardo Riccò facing 12-year ban

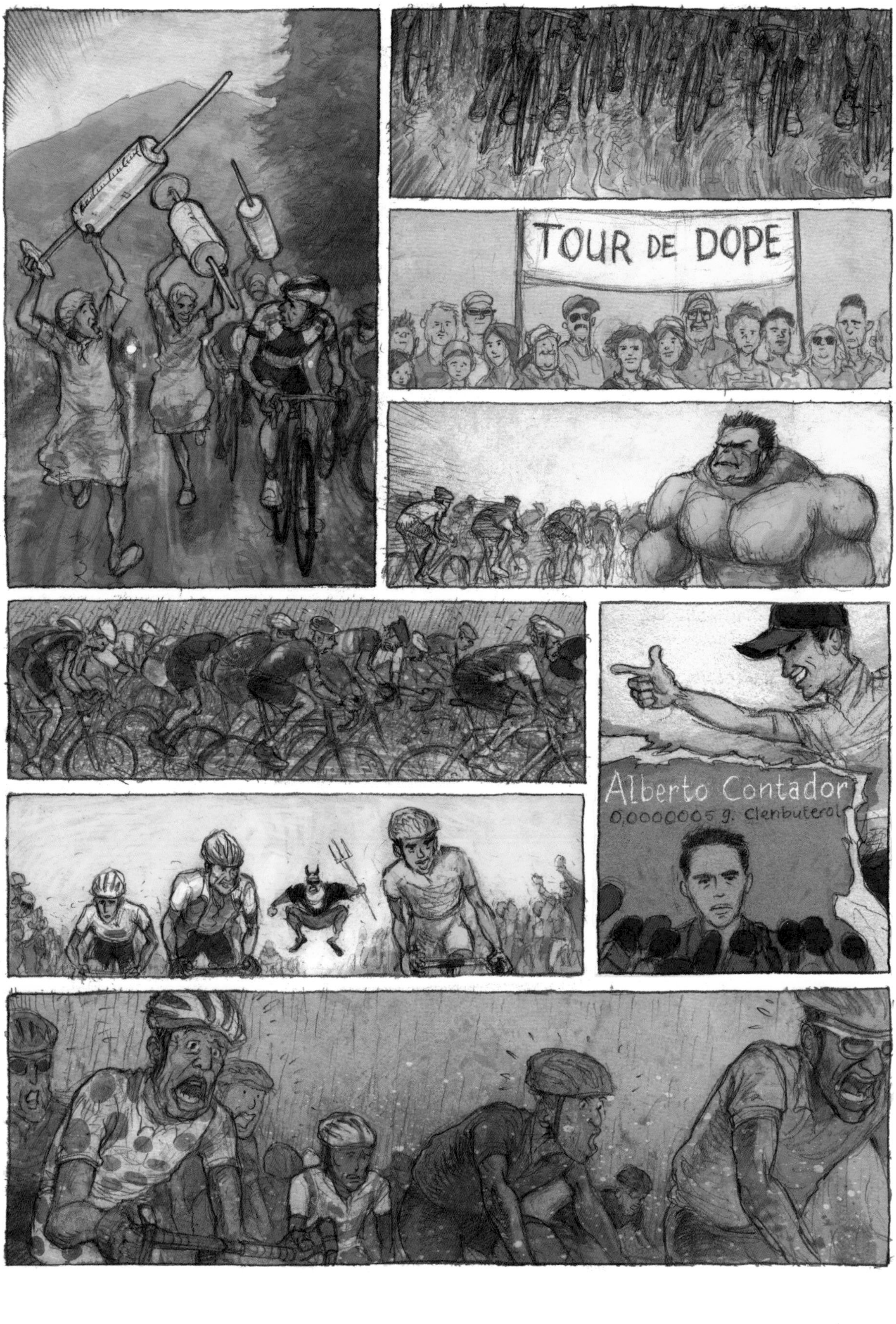
TOUR DE DOPE
Alberto Contador
0,0000005 g. Clenbuterol

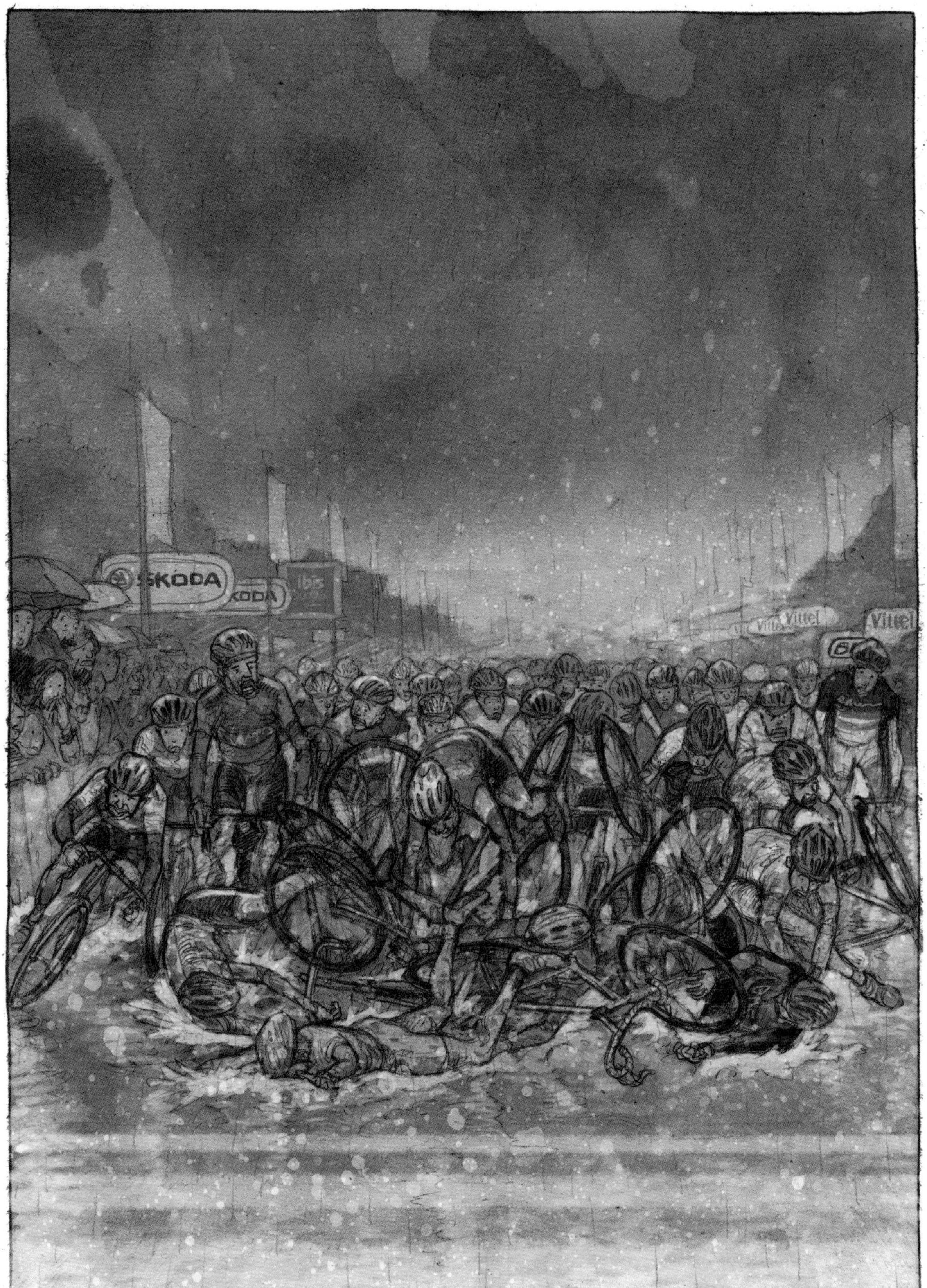
ŠKODA
KODA
ibis
Vittel
Vittel
Vittel

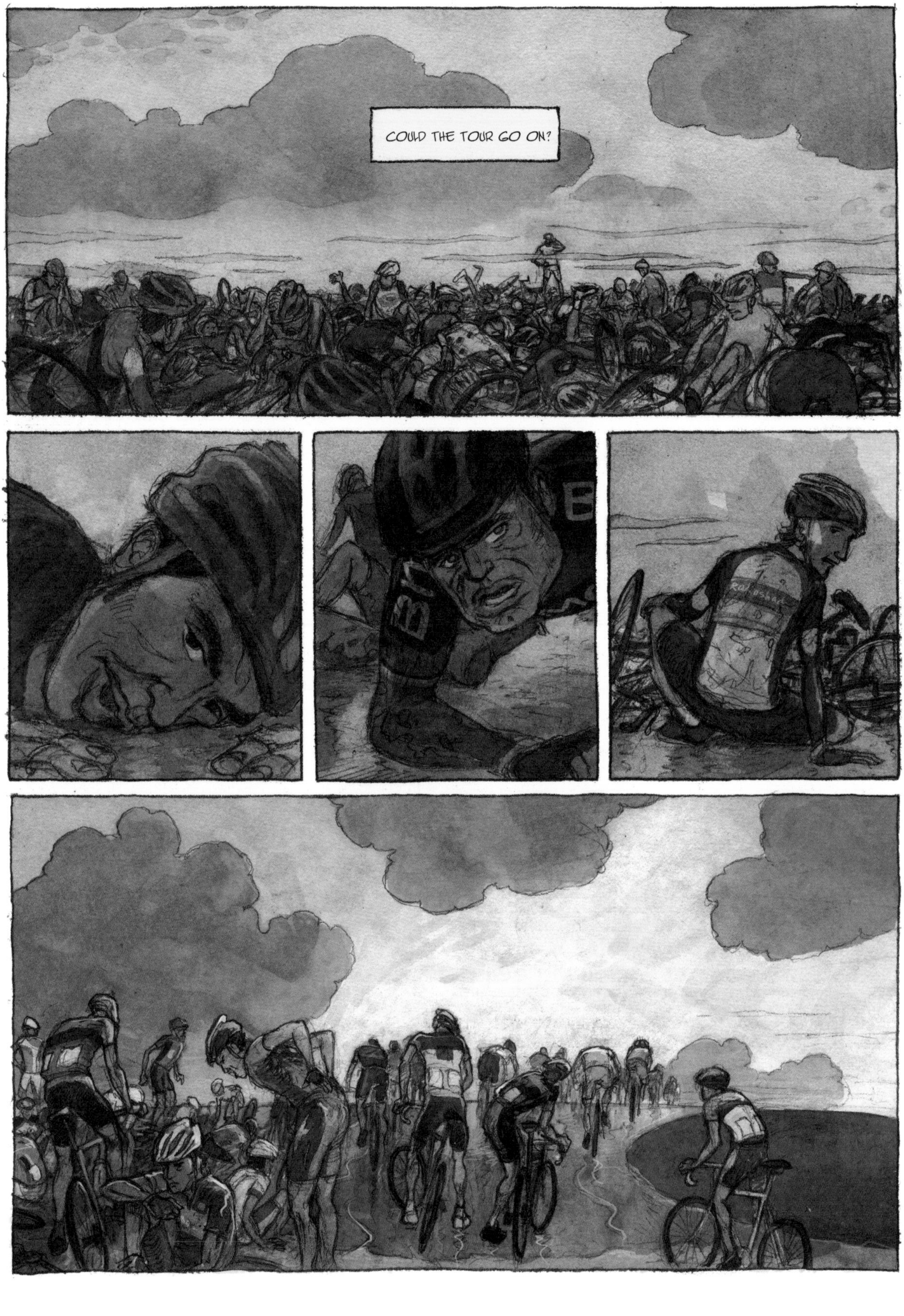
COULD THE TOUR GO ON?

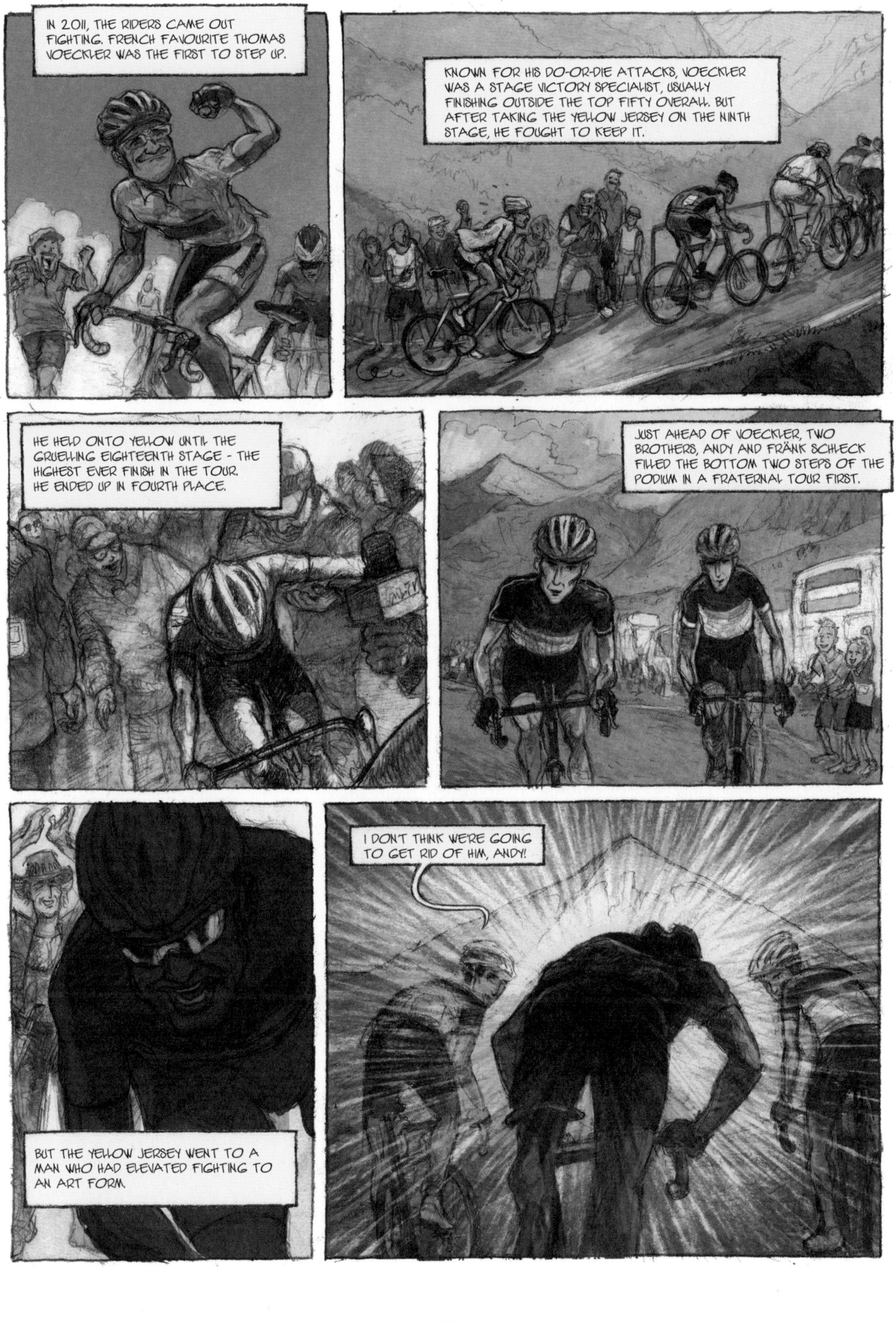

IN 2011, THE RIDERS CAME OUT FIGHTING. FRENCH FAVOURITE THOMAS VOECKLER WAS THE FIRST TO STEP UP.
KNOWN FOR HIS DO-OR-DIE ATTACKS, VOECKLER WAS A STAGE VICTORY SPECIALIST, USUALLY FINISHING OUTSIDE THE TOP FIFTY OVERALL. BUT AFTER TAKING THE YELLOW JERSEY ON THE NINTH STAGE, HE FOUGHT TO KEEP IT.
HE HELD ONTO YELLOW UNTIL THE GRUELLING EIGHTEENTH STAGE - THE HIGHEST EVER FINISH IN THE TOUR. HE ENDED UP IN FOURTH PLACE.
JUST AHEAD OF VOECKLER, TWO BROTHERS, ANDY AND FRÄNK SCHLECK FILLED THE BOTTOM TWO STEPS OF THE PODIUM IN A FRATERNAL TOUR FIRST.
BUT THE YELLOW JERSEY WENT TO A MAN WHO HAD ELEVATED FIGHTING TO AN ART FORM.
I DON'T THINK WE'RE GOING TO GET RID OF HIM, ANDY!

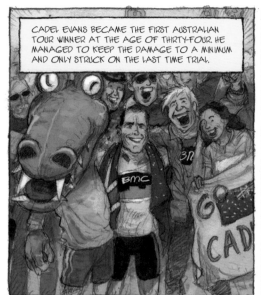

CADEL EVANS BECAME THE FIRST AUSTRALIAN TOUR WINNER AT THE AGE OF THIRTY-FOUR. HE MANAGED TO KEEP THE DAMAGE TO A MINIMUM AND ONLY STRUCK ON THE LAST TIME TRIAL.
BMC
MOST OF THE OTHER STAGES WERE WON BY BRITISH SPRINTER MARK CAVENDISH.
hTC
highroad
HIS VICTORY ON THE CHAMPS-ELYSEES WAS PARTICULARLY IMPRESSIVE.
IT EARNED HIM A PLACE ON THE AMBITIOUS AND WEALTHY TEAM SKY.
sky
SKY HOPED TO WIN THE 2011 TOUR WITH HIS COMPATRIOT BRADLEY WIGGINS.
sky
WIGGINS WAS ONE OF THE FAVOURITES BUT ON THE SEVENTH STAGE HE BROKE HIS COLLARBONE.
BUT IF YOU FALL, YOU GET BACK UP...

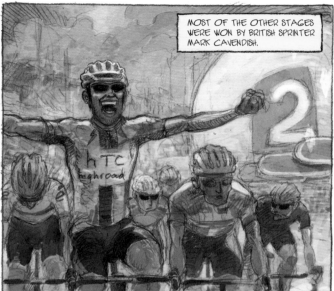

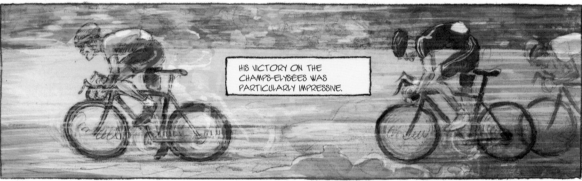

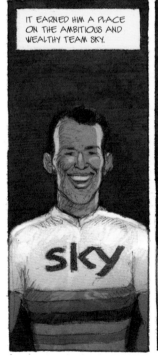

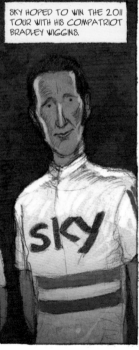

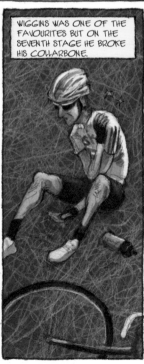

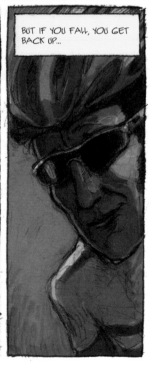

TEAM SKY REIGNED SUPREME IN 2012.

CAVENDISH CONTINUED TO WIN THE SPRINT STAGES...

... BUT THE GENERAL CLASSIFICATION WAS MORE IMPORTANT TO THE TEAM.

WIGGINS TOOK THE YELLOW JERSEY IN HIS FAVOURITE DISCIPLINE; THE INDIVIDUAL TIME TRIAL. HE WAS ASSISTED IN THE MOUNTAINS BY KENYAN-BORN CHRISTOPHER FROOME...

... WHO WAS PERHAPS TOO GOOD...

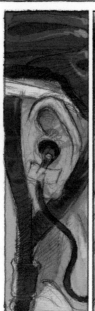

WIGGO' CONFIRMED HIS CLASS BY OBLITERATING EVERYONE IN THE SECOND INDIVIDUAL TIME TRIAL, BECOMING THE FIRST BRIT TO WIN THE TOUR.

THE HUNDREDTH TOUR MADE THE MOST OF FRANCES FINEST SCENERY.

WITH WIGGINS INJURED, FROOME WAS NOW TEAM SKYS UNDISPUTED LEADER

HE WAS ALMOST VULNERABLE ON THE FLAT, LOSING TIME WHEN SIDE-WINDS SPLIT THE PELOTON ON THE ROAD TO SAINT-AMAND-MONTROND...

... BUT AS SOON AS THE ROAD WENT UPHILL...

... ON THE ROAD TO AX 3 DOMAINES...

THOUGH THE YOUNG COLOMBIAN CLIMBER NAIRO QUINTANA PUT UP A GOOD FIGHT.

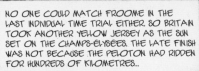

... AND ON THE SLOPES OF MONT VENTOUX, FROOME WAS IN A CLASS OF HIS OWN...

NO ONE COULD MATCH FROOME IN THE LAST INDIVIDUAL TIME TRIAL EITHER, SO BRITAIN TOOK ANOTHER YELLOW JERSEY AS THE SUN SET ON THE CHAMPS-ÉLYSÉES. THE LATE FINISH WAS NOT BECAUSE THE PELOTON HAD RIDDEN FOR HUNDREDS OF KILOMETRES...

... BUT TO MAKE THE MOST OF THE SCENERY.

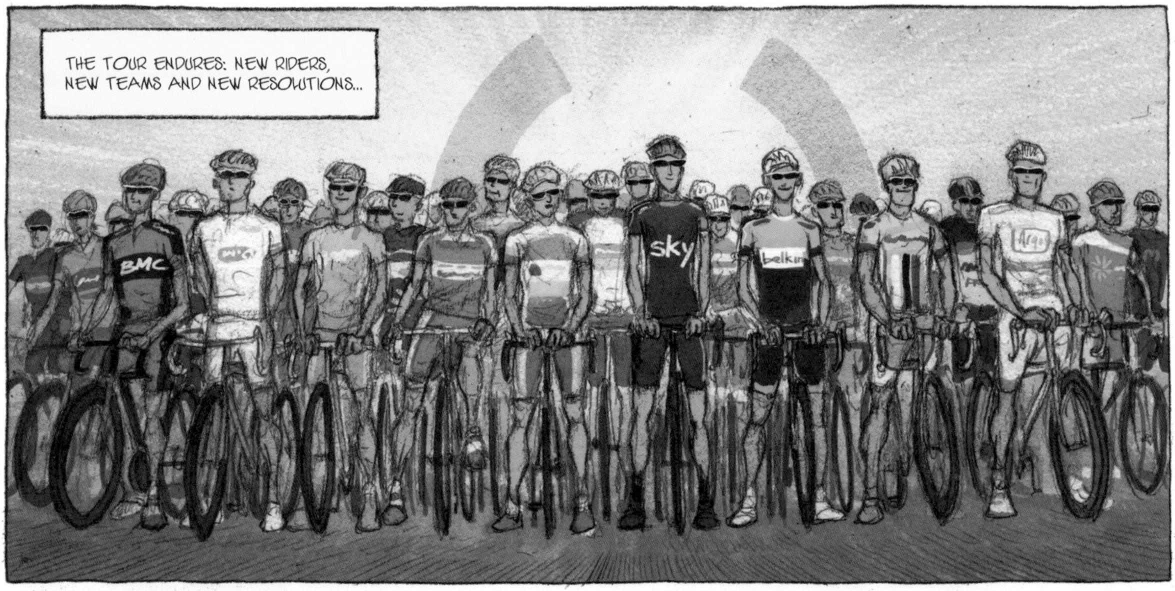
THE TOUR ENDURES: NEW RIDERS, NEW TEAMS AND NEW RESOLUTIONS...
BMC
sky
belkin

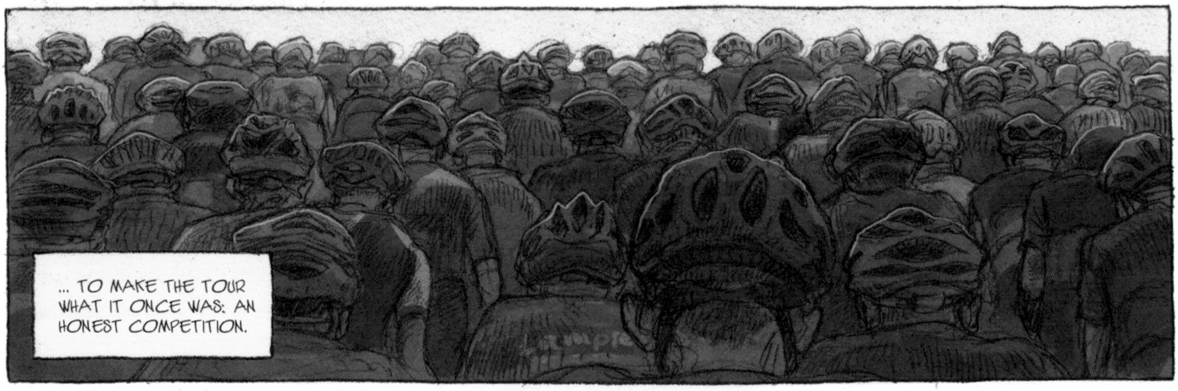
... TO MAKE THE TOUR WHAT IT ONCE WAS: AN HONEST COMPETITION.

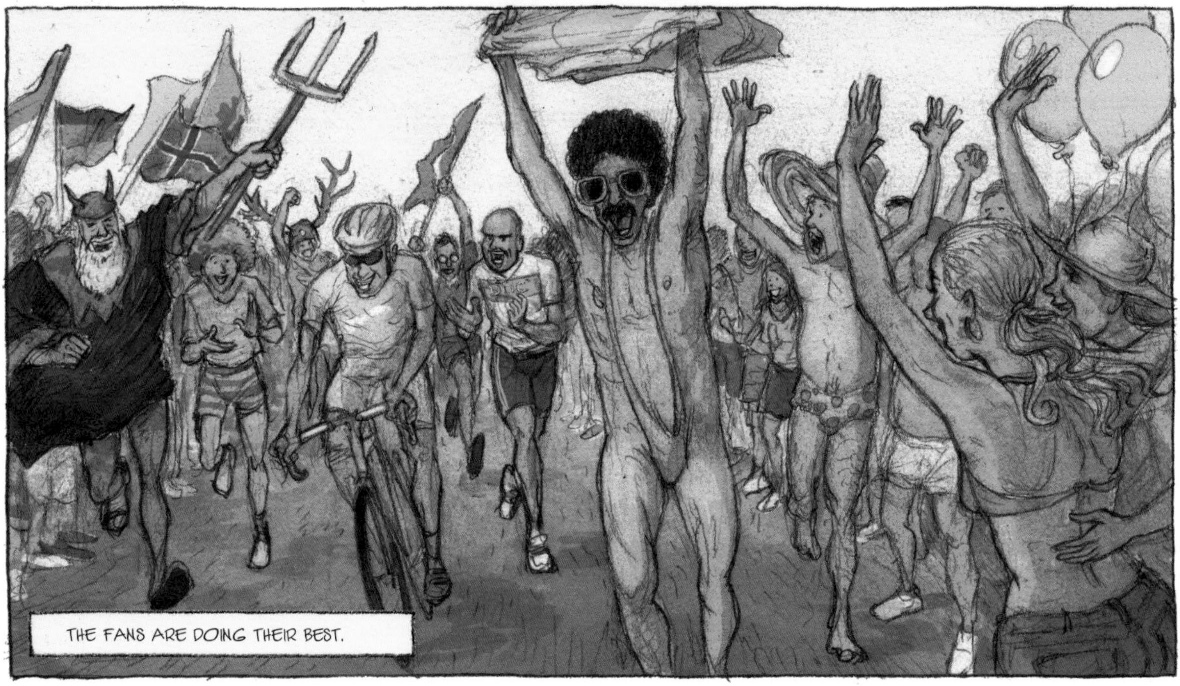
THE FANS ARE DOING THEIR BEST.

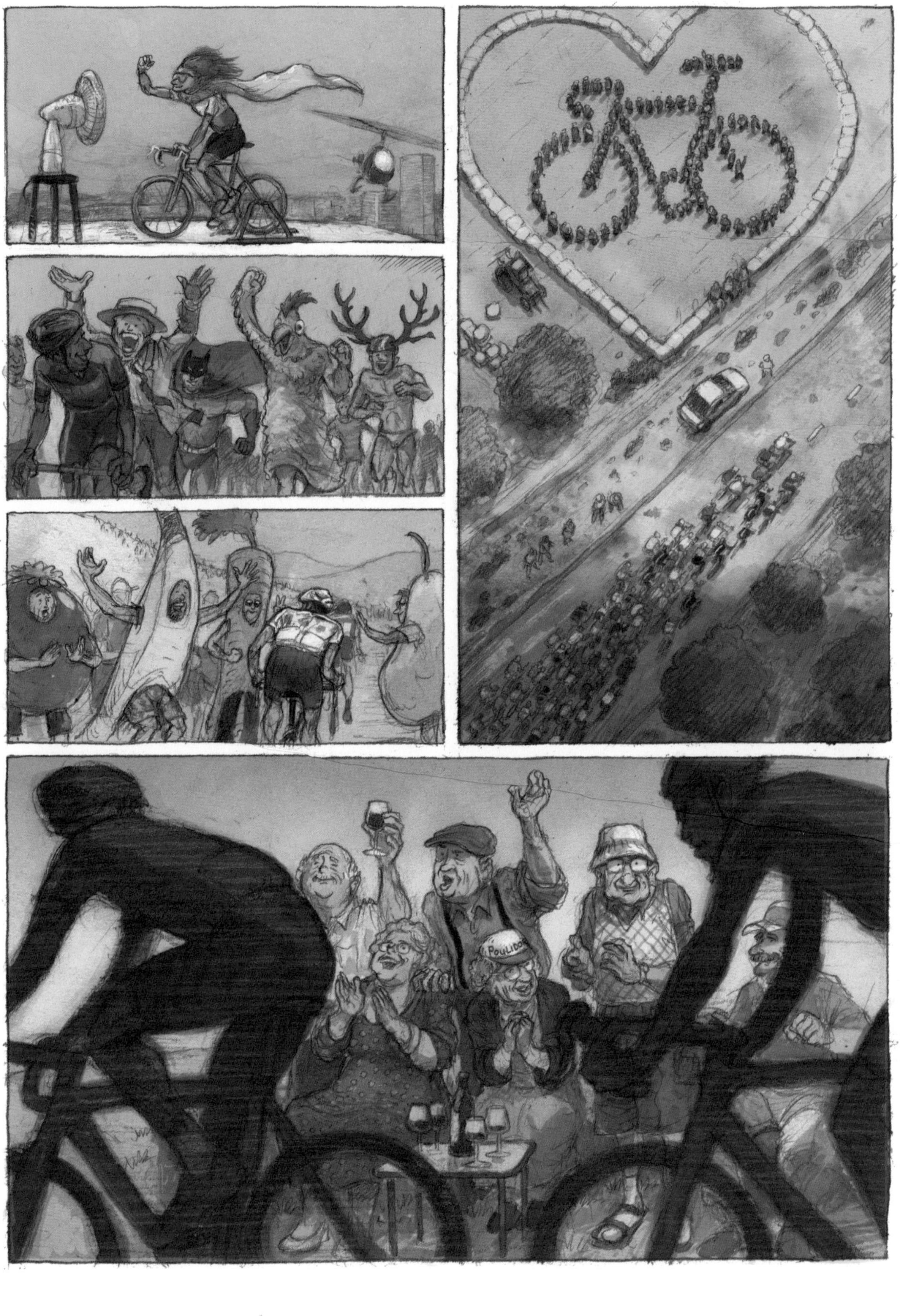

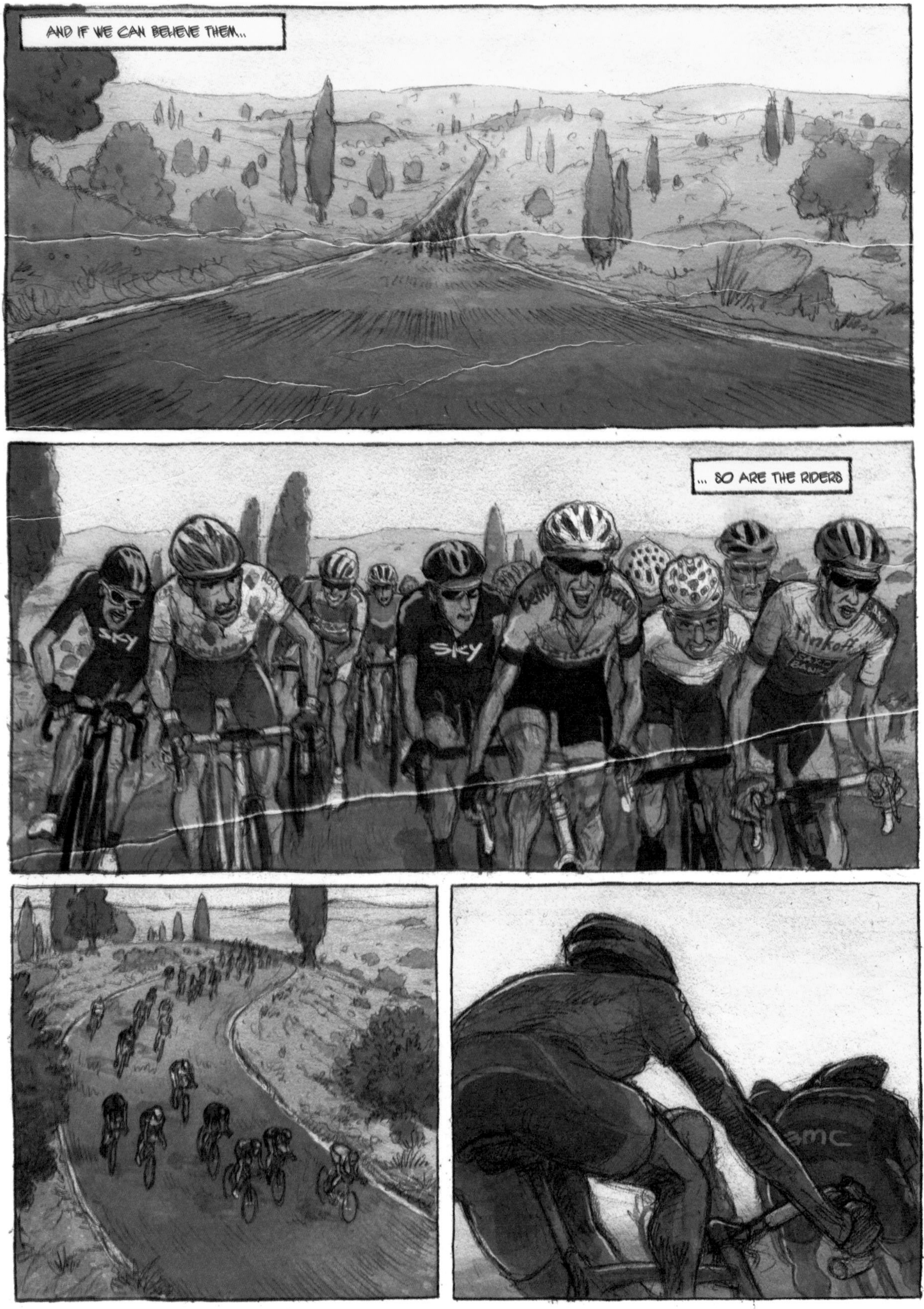
AND IF WE CAN BELIEVE THEM...
... SO ARE THE RIDERS

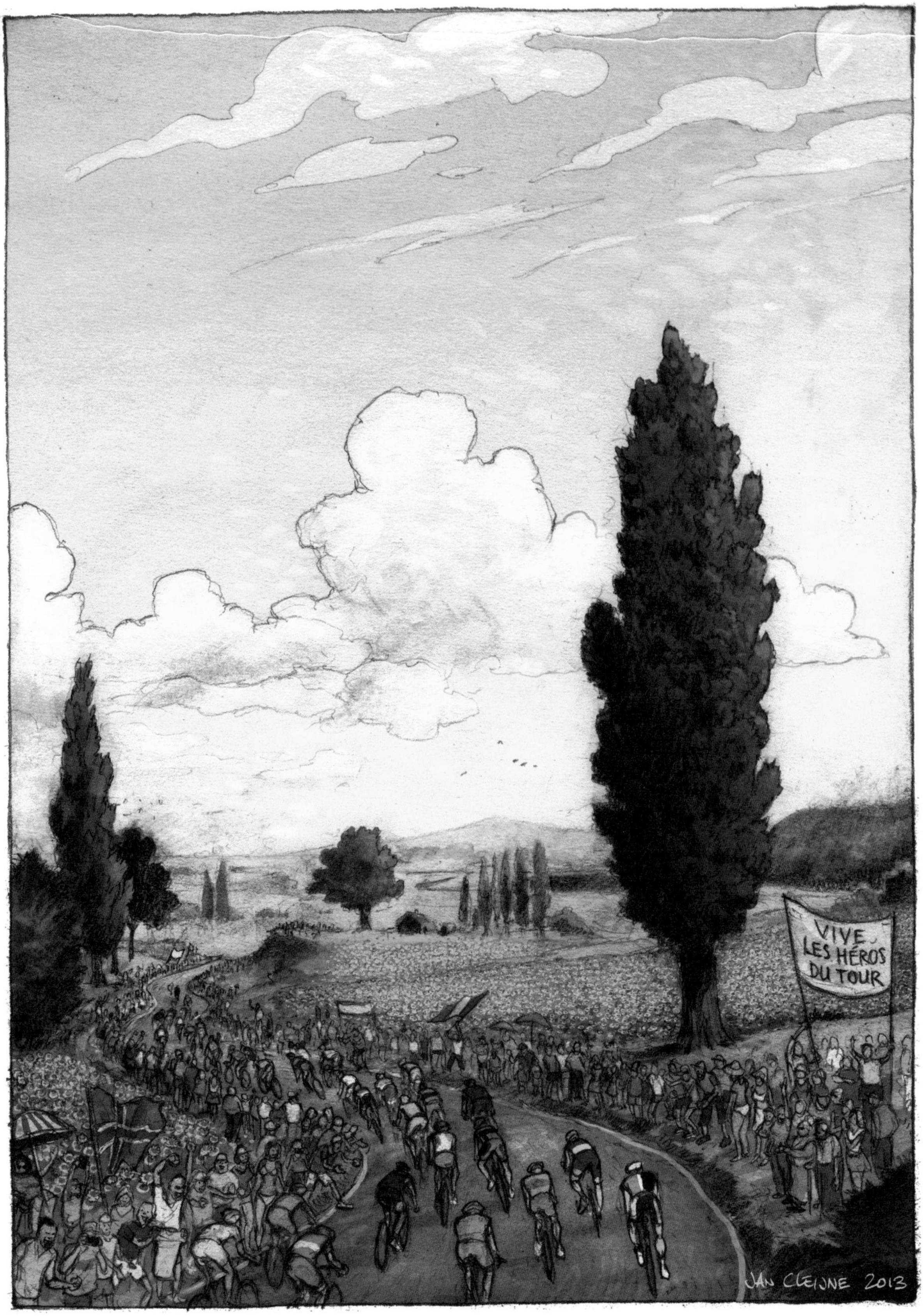
VIVE LES HÉROS DU TOUR
JAN CLEIJNE 2013

TOUR LEGENDS

THE ROLL OF HONOUR

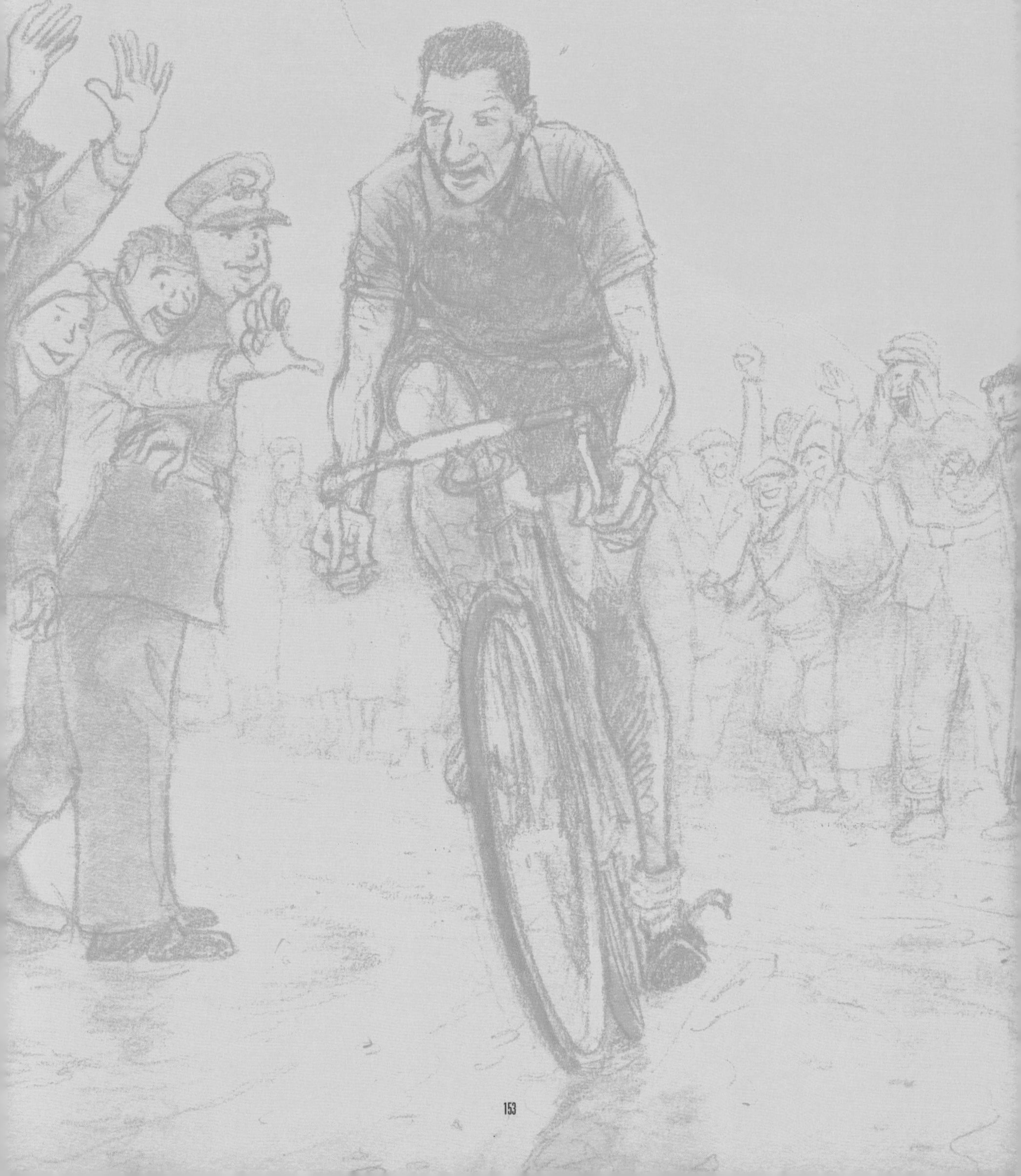

TOUR WINNERS

YEAR	RIDER	TEAM	COUNTRY	KM	TIME/POINTS	MARGIN	STAGE WINS
1903	MAURICE GARIN	LA FRANÇAISE	FRANCE	2,428	94H 33' 14"	+ 2H 59' 21"	3
1904	HENRI CORNET	CONTE	FRANCE	2,428	96H 05' 55"	+ 2H 16' 14"	1
1905	LOUIS TROUSSELIER	PEUGEOT-WOLBER	FRANCE	2,994	35	26	5
1906	RENÉ POTTIER	PEUGEOT	FRANCE	4,637	31	8	5
1907	LUCIEN PETIT-BRETON	PEUGEOT	FRANCE	4,488	47	19	2
1908	LUCIEN PETIT-BRETON	PEUGEOT	FRANCE	4,497	36	32	5
1909	FRANÇOIS FABER	ALCYON	LUXEMBOURG	4,498	37	20	6
1910	OCTAVE LAPIZE	ALCYON	FRANCE	4,734	63	4	4
1911	GUSTAVE GARRIGOU	ALCYON	FRANCE	5,343	43	18	2
1912	ODILE DEFRAYE	ALCYON	BELGIUM	5,289	49	59	3
1913	PHILIPPE THYS	PEUGEOT	BELGIUM	5,287	197H 54' 00"	+ 8' 37"	1
1914	PHILIPPE THYS	PEUGEOT	BELGIUM	5,380	200H 28' 48"	+ 1' 50"	1
1915	-NO TOUR-						
1916	-NO TOUR-						
1917	-NO TOUR-						
1918	-NO TOUR-						
1919	FIRMIN LAMBOT	LA SPORTINE	BELGIUM	5,560	231H 07' 15"	+ 1H 42' 54"	1
1920	PHILIPPE THYS	LA SPORTINE	BELGIUM	5,503	228H 36' 13"	+ 57' 21"	4
1921	LÉON SCIEUR	LA SPORTINE	BELGIUM	5,485	221H 50' 26"	+ 18' 36"	2
1922	FIRMIN LAMBOT	PEUGEOT	BELGIUM	5,375	222H 08' 06"	+ 41' 15"	0
1923	HENRI PÉLISSIER	AUTOMOTO	FRANCE	5,386	222H 15' 30"	+ 30' 41"	3
1924	OTTAVIO BOTTECCHIA	AUTOMOTO	ITALY	5,425	226H 18' 21"	+ 35' 36"	4
1925	OTTAVIO BOTTECCHIA	AUTOMOTO	ITALY	5,440	219H 10' 18"	+ 54' 20"	4
1926	LUCIEN BUYSSE	AUTOMOTO	BELGIUM	5,745	238H 44' 25"	+ 1H 22' 25"	2
1927	NICOLAS FRANTZ	ALCYON	LUXEMBOURG	5,398	198H 16' 42"	+ 1H 48' 41"	3
1928	NICOLAS FRANTZ	ALCYON	LUXEMBOURG	5,476	192H 48' 58"	+ 50' 07"	5
1929	MAURICE DE WAELE	ALCYON	BELGIUM	5,286	186H 39' 15"	+ 44' 23"	1
1930	ANDRÉ LEDUCQ	ALCYON	FRANCE	4,822	172H 12' 16"	+ 14' 13"	2
1931	ANTONIN MAGNE	FRANCE	FRANCE	5,091	177H 10' 03"	+ 12' 56"	1
1932	ANDRÉ LEDUCQ	FRANCE	FRANCE	4,479	154H 11' 49"	+ 24' 03"	6
1933	GEORGES SPEICHER	FRANCE	FRANCE	4,395	147H 51' 37"	+ 4' 01"	3
1934	ANTONIN MAGNE	FRANCE	FRANCE	4,470	147H 13' 58"	+ 27' 31"	3
1935	ROMAIN MAES	BELGIUM	BELGIUM	4,338	141H 23' 00"	+ 17' 52"	3
1936	SYLVÈRE MAES	BELGIUM	BELGIUM	4,442	142H 47' 32"	+ 26' 55"	4
1937	ROGER LAPEBIE	FRANCE	FRANCE	4,415	138H 58' 31"	+ 7' 17"	3
1938	GINO BARTALI	ITALY	ITALY	4,694	148H 29' 12"	+ 18' 27"	2
1939	SYLVÈRE MAES	BELGIUM	BELGIUM	4,224	132H 03' 17"	+ 30' 38"	2
1940	-NO TOUR-						
1941	-NO TOUR-						
1942	-NO TOUR-						
1943	-NO TOUR-						
1944	-NO TOUR-						
1945	-NO TOUR-						
1946	-NO TOUR-						
1947	JEAN ROBIC	FRANCE	FRANCE	4,642	148H 11' 25"	+ 3' 58"	3
1948	GINO BARTALI	ITALY	ITALY	4,922	147H 10' 36"	+ 26' 16"	7
1949	FAUSTO COPPI	ITALY	ITALY	4,808	149H 40' 49"	+ 10' 55"	3
1950	FERDINAND KÜBLER	SWITZERLAND	SWITZERLAND	4,773	145H 36' 56"	+ 9' 30"	3
1951	HUGO KOBLET	SWITZERLAND	SWITZERLAND	4,690	142H 20' 14"	+ 22' 00"	5
1952	FAUSTO COPPI	ITALY	ITALY	4,898	151H 57' 20"	+ 28' 17"	5
1953	LOUISON BOBET	FRANCE	FRANCE	4,476	129H 23' 25"	+ 14' 18"	2
1954	LOUISON BOBET	FRANCE	FRANCE	4,656	140H 06' 05"	+ 15' 49"	3
1955	LOUISON BOBET	FRANCE	FRANCE	4,495	130H 29' 26"	+ 4' 53"	2
1956	ROGER WALKOWIAK	FRANCE	FRANCE	4,498	124H 01' 16"	+ 1' 25"	0
1957	JACQUES ANQUETIL	FRANCE	FRANCE	4,669	135H 44' 42"	+ 14' 56"	4
1958	CHARLY GAUL	LUXEMBOURG	LUXEMBOURG	4,319	116H 59' 05"	+ 3' 10"	4

YEAR	RIDER	TEAM	COUNTRY	KM	TIME/POINTS	MARGIN	STAGE WINS
1959	FEDERICO BAHAMONTES	SPAIN	SPAIN	4,358	123H 46' 45"	+ 4' 01"	1
1960	GASTONE NENCINI	ITALY	ITALY	4,173	112H 08' 42"	+ 5' 02"	0
1961	JACQUES ANQUETIL	FRANCE	FRANCE	4,397	122H 01' 33"	+ 12' 14"	2
1962	JACQUES ANQUETIL	SAINT-RAPHAËL	FRANCE	4,274	114H 31' 54"	+ 4' 59"	2
1963	JACQUES ANQUETIL	SAINT-RAPHAËL	FRANCE	4,138	113H 30' 05"	+ 3' 35"	4
1964	JACQUES ANQUETIL	SAINT-RAPHAËL	FRANCE	4,504	127H 09' 44"	+ 55"	4
1965	FELICE GIMONDI	SALVARANI	ITALY	4,188	116H 42' 06"	+ 2' 40"	3
1966	LUCIEN AIMAR	FORD-GITANE	FRANCE	4,329	117H 34' 21"	+ 1' 07"	0
1967	ROGER PINGEON	PEUGEOT-BP-MICHELIN	FRANCE	4,779	136H 53' 50"	+ 3' 40"	1
1968	JAN JANSSEN	SAUVAGE-LEJEUNE	NETHERLANDS	4,492	133H 49' 42"	+ 38"	2
1969	EDDY MERCKX	FAEMA	BELGIUM	4,117	116H 16' 02"	+ 17' 54"	6
1970	EDDY MERCKX	FAEMA	BELGIUM	4,254	119H 31' 49"	+ 12' 41"	8
1971	EDDY MERCKX	MOLTENI	BELGIUM	3,608	96H 45' 14"	+ 9' 51"	4
1972	EDDY MERCKX	MOLTENI	BELGIUM	3,846	108H 17' 18"	+ 10' 41"	6
1973	LUIS OCANA	BIC	SPAIN	4,090	122H 25' 34"	+ 15' 51"	6
1974	EDDY MERCKX	MOLTENI	BELGIUM	4,098	116H 16' 58"	+ 8' 04"	8
1975	BERNARD THÉVENET	PEUGEOT	FRANCE	4,000	114H 35' 31"	+ 2' 47"	2
1976	LUCIEN VAN IMPE	GITANE-CAMPAGNOLO	BELGIUM	4,017	116H 22' 23"	+ 4' 14"	1
1977	BERNARD THÉVENET	PEUGEOT	FRANCE	4,096	115H 38' 30"	+ 48"	1
1978	BERNARD HINAULT	RENAULT-ELF-GITANE	FRANCE	3,908	108H 18' 00"	+ 3' 56"	3
1979	BERNARD HINAULT	RENAULT-ELF-GITANE	FRANCE	3,765	103H 06' 50"	+ 13' 07"	7
1980	JOOP ZOETEMELK	TI-RALEIGH	NETHERLANDS	3,842	109H 19' 14"	+ 6' 55"	2
1981	BERNARD HINAULT	RENAULT-ELF-GITANE	FRANCE	3,753	96H 19' 38"	+ 14' 34"	5
1982	BERNARD HINAULT	RENAULT-ELF-GITANE	FRANCE	3,507	92H 08' 46"	+ 6' 21"	4
1983	LAURENT FIGNON	RENAULT-ELF-GITANE	FRANCE	3,809	105H 07' 52"	+ 4' 04"	1
1984	LAURENT FIGNON	RENAULT-ELF-GITANE	FRANCE	4,021	112H 03' 40"	+ 10' 32"	5
1985	BERNARD HINAULT	LA VIE CLAIRE	FRANCE	4,109	113H 24' 23"	+ 1' 42"	2
1986	GREG LEMOND	LA VIE CLAIRE	UNITED STATES	4,094	110H 35' 19"	+ 3' 10"	1
1987	STEPHEN ROCHE	CARRERA JEANS	IRELAND	4,231	115H 27' 42"	+ 40"	1
1988	PEDRO DELGADO	REYNOLDS	SPAIN	3,286	84H 27' 53"	+ 7' 13"	1
1989	GREG LEMOND	ADR AGRIGEL	UNITED STATES	3,285	87H 38' 35"	+ 8"	3
1990	GREG LEMOND	Z VETEMENTS	UNITED STATES	3,504	90H 43' 20"	+ 2' 16"	0
1991	MIGUEL INDURAIN	BANESTO	SPAIN	3,914	101H 01' 20"	+ 3' 36"	2
1992	MIGUEL INDURAIN	BANESTO	SPAIN	3,983	100H 49' 30"	+ 4' 35"	3
1993	MIGUEL INDURAIN	BANESTO	SPAIN	3,714	95H 57' 09"	+ 4' 59"	2
1994	MIGUEL INDURAIN	BANESTO	SPAIN	3,978	103H 38' 38"	+ 5' 39"	1
1995	MIGUEL INDURAIN	BANESTO	SPAIN	3,635	92H 44' 59"	+ 4' 35"	2
1996	BJARNE RIIS	TEAM TELEKOM	DENMARK	3,765	95H 57' 16"	+ 1' 41"	2
1997	JAN ULLRICH	TEAM TELEKOM	GERMANY	3,950	100H 30' 35"	+ 9' 09"	2
1998	MARCO PANTANI	MERCATONE UNO	ITALY	3,875	92H 49' 46"	+ 3' 21"	2
1999	LANCE ARMSTRONG[2]	US POSTAL	UNITED STATES	3,687	91H 32' 16"	+ 7' 37"	4
2000	LANCE ARMSTRONG[2]	US POSTAL	UNITED STATES	3,662	92H 33' 08"	+ 6' 02	1
2001	LANCE ARMSTRONG[2]	US POSTAL	UNITED STATES	3,458	86H 17' 28"	+ 6' 44"	4
2002	LANCE ARMSTRONG[2]	US POSTAL	UNITED STATES	3,272	82H 05' 12"	+ 7' 17"	4
2003	LANCE ARMSTRONG[2]	US POSTAL	UNITED STATES	3,427	83H 41' 12"	+ 1' 01"	1
2004	LANCE ARMSTRONG[2]	US POSTAL	UNITED STATES	3,391	83H 36' 02"	+ 6' 19"	6
2005	LANCE ARMSTRONG[2]	US POSTAL	UNITED STATES	3,593	86H 15' 02"	+ 4' 40"	1
2006	OSCAR PEREIRO[3]	CAISSE D'EPARGNE	SPAIN	3,657	89H 40' 27"	+ 32"	0
2007	ALBERTO CONTADOR	DISCOVERY CHANNEL	SPAIN	3,570	91H 00' 26"	+ 23"	1
2008	CARLOS SASTRE	TEAM CSC	SPAIN	3,559	87H 52' 52"	+ 58"	1
2009	ALBERTO CONTADOR	ASTANA	SPAIN	3,459	85H 48' 35"	+ 4' 11"	2
2010	ANDY SCHLECK[4]	TEAM SAXO BANK	LUXEMBOURG	3,642	91H 59' 27"	+ 1' 22"	2
2011	CADEL EVANS	BMC RACING TEAM	AUSTRALIA	3,430	86H 12' 22"	+ 1' 34"	1
2012	BRADLEY WIGGINS	TEAM SKY	UNITED KINGDOM	3,496	87H 34' 47"	+ 3' 21"	2
2013	CHRIS FROOME	TEAM SKY	UNITED KINGDOM	3,404	83H 56' 20"	+ 4' 20"	3

[1] MAURICE GARIN WAS DISQUALIFIED IN DECEMBER 1904 AFTER AN INQUIRY. FOURTH PLACED HENRI CORNET WAS DECLARED THE WINNER.
[2] LANCE ARMSTRONG WAS DISQUALIFIED IN OCTOBER 2012. NO NEW WINNER HAS BEEN DECLARED.
[3] FLOYD LANDIS WAS DISQUALIFIED AND THE YELLOW JERSEY AWARDED TO SECOND PLACED OSCAR PEREIRO.
[4] ALBERTO CONTADOR WAS DISQUALIFIED AND THE YELLOW JERSEY AWARDED TO SECOND PLACE ANDY SCHLECK.

KING OF THE MOUNTAINS

FROM 1905 TO 1932 THE TOUR NAMED ONE RIDER IN EACH TOUR THE 'MEILLEUR GRIMPEUR', OR BEST CLIMBER. IN 1933 AN OFFICIAL MOUNTAINS CLASSIFICATION WAS INTRODUCED. THE DISTINCTIVE POLKA DOT JERSEY WAS NOT INTRODUCED UNTIL 1975.

YEAR	RIDER	COUNTRY	YEAR	RIDER	COUNTRY
1905	RENÉ POTTIER	FRANCE	1959	FEDERICO BAHAMONTES	SPAIN
1906	RENÉ POTTIER	FRANCE	1960	IMERIO MASSIGNAN	ITALY
1907	EMILE GEORGET	FRANCE	1961	IMERIO MASSIGNAN	ITALY
1908	GUSTAVE GARRIGOU	FRANCE	1962	FEDERICO BAHAMONTES	SPAIN
1909	FRANÇOIS FABER	LUXEMBOURG	1963	FEDERICO BAHAMONTES	SPAIN
1910	OCTAVE LAPIZE	FRANCE	1964	FEDERICO BAHAMONTES	SPAIN
1911	PAUL DUBOC	FRANCE	1965	JULIO JIMENEZ	SPAIN
1912	ODIEL DEFRAEYE	BELGIUM	1966	JULIO JIMENEZ	SPAIN
1913	PHILIPPE THYS	BELGIUM	1967	JULIO JIMENEZ	SPAIN
1914	FIRMIN LAMBOT	BELGIUM	1968	AURELIO GONZALEZ	SPAIN
1915	-NO TOUR-		1969	EDDY MERCKX	BELGIUM
1916	-NO TOUR-		1970	EDDY MERCKX	BELGIUM
1917	-NO TOUR-		1971	LUCIEN VAN IMPE	BELGIUM
1918	-NO TOUR-		1972	LUCIEN VAN IMPE	BELGIUM
1919	HONORÉ BARTHELEMY	FRANCE	1973	PEDRO TORRES	SPAIN
1920	FIRMIN LAMBOT	BELGIUM	1974	DOMINGO PERURENA	SPAIN
1921	HECTOR HEUSGHEM	BELGIUM	1975	LUCIEN VAN IMPE	BELGIUM
1922	JEAN ALAVOINE	FRANCE	1976	GIANCARLO BELLINI	ITALY
1923	HENRI PÉLISSIER	FRANCE	1977	LUCIEN VAN IMPE	BELGIUM
1924	OTTAVIO BOTTECCHIA	ITALY	1978	MARIANO MART	FRANCE
1925	OTTAVIO BOTTECCHIA	ITALY	1979	GIOVANNI BATTAGLIN	ITALY
1926	LUCIEN BUYSSE	BELGIUM	1980	RAYMOND MARTIN	FRANCE
1927	GIOVANNI-MICHELE GORDINI	ITALY	1981	LUCIEN VAN IMPE	BELGIUM
1928	VICTOR FONTAN	FRANCE	1982	BERNARD VALLET	FRANCE
1929	VICTOR FONTAN	FRANCE	1983	LUCIEN VAN IMPE	BELGIUM
1930	BENOIT FAURE	FRANCE	1984	ROBERT MILLAR	GREAT BRITAIN
1931	JOSEPH DEMUYSERE	BELGIUM	1985	LUIS HERRERA	COLUMBIA
1932	VICENTE TRUEBA	SPAIN	1986	BERNARD HINAULT	FRANCE
1933	VICENTE TRUEBA	SPAIN	1987	LUIS HERRERA	COLUMBIA
1934	RENÉ VIETTO	FRANCE	1988	STEVEN ROOKS	NETHERLANDS
1935	FÉLICIEN VERVAECKE	BELGIUM	1989	GERT-JAN THEUNISSE	NETHERLANDS
1936	JULIAN BERRENDERO	SPAIN	1990	THIERRY CLAVEYROLAT	FRANCE
1937	FÉLICIEN VERVAECKE	BELGIUM	1991	CLAUDIO CHIAPPUCCI	ITALY
1938	GINO BARTALI	ITALY	1992	CLAUDIO CHIAPPUCCI	ITALY
1939	SYLVERE MAES	BELGIUM	1993	TONY ROMINGER	SWISS
1940	-NO TOUR-		1994	RICHARD VIRENQUE	FRANCE
1941	-NO TOUR-		1995	RICHARD VIRENQUE	FRANCE
1942	-NO TOUR-		1996	RICHARD VIRENQUE	FRANCE
1943	-NO TOUR-		1997	RICHARD VIRENQUE	FRANCE
1944	-NO TOUR-		1998	CHRISTOPHE RINERO	FRANCE
1945	-NO TOUR-		1999	RICHARD VIRENQUE	FRANCE
1946	-NO TOUR-		2000	SANTIAGO BOTERO	COLUMBIA
1947	PIERRE BRAMBILLA	FRANCE	2001	LAURENT JALABERT	FRANCE
1948	GINO BARTALI	ITALY	2002	LAURENT JALABERT	FRANCE
1949	FAUSTO COPPI	ITALY	2003	RICHARD VIRENQUE	FRANCE
1950	LOUISON BOBET	FRANCE	2004	RICHARD VIRENQUE	FRANCE
1951	RAPHAEL GEMINIANI	FRANCE	2005	MICHAEL RASMUSSEN	DENMARK
1952	FAUSTO COPPI	ITALY	2006	MICHAEL RASMUSSEN	DENMARK
1953	JESUS LORONO	SPAIN	2007	MAURICIO SOLER	COLUMBIA
1954	FEDERICO BAHAMONTES	SPAIN	2008	BERNHARD KOHL	AUSTRIA
1955	CHARLY GAUL	LUXEMBOURG	2009	FRANCO PELLIZOTTI	ITALY
1956	CHARLY GAUL	LUXEMBOURG	2010	ANTHONY CHARTEAU	FRANCE
1957	GASTONE NENCINI	ITALY	2011	SAMUEL SÁNCHEZ	SPAIN
1958	FEDERICO BAHAMONTES	SPAIN	2012	THOMAS VOECKLER	FRANCE
			2013	NAIRO QUINTANA	COLUMBIA

GREEN JERSEY

BETWEEN 1905 AND 1912 THE TOUR DE FRANCE WAS DETERMINED BY A POINTS SYSTEM. THE CYCLISTS RECEIVED POINTS, EQUAL TO THEIR RANKING IN THE STAGE AND THE CYCLIST WITH THE LEAST POINTS LEAD THE RACE. IN THE 1953 TOUR DE FRANCE, TO CELEBRATE THE 50TH BIRTHDAY OF THE TOUR DE FRANCE, THE POINTS SYSTEM WAS REINTRODUCED, BUT THIS TIME AS AN ADDITIONAL CLASSIFICATION.

YEAR	WINNER	COUTRY	POINTS
1953	FRITZ SCHÄR	SWITZERLAND	271
1954	FERDI KÜBLER	SWITZERLAND	215.5
1955	STAN OCKERS	BELGIUM	322
1956	STAN OCKERS	BELGIUM	280
1957	JEAN FORESTIER	FRANCE	301
1958	JEAN GRACZYK	FRANCE	347
1959	ANDRÉ DARRIGADE	FRANCE	613
1960	JEAN GRACZYK	FRANCE	74
1961	ANDRÉ DARRIGADE	FRANCE	174
1962	RUDI ALTIG	GERMANY	173
1963	RIK VAN LOOY	BELGIUM	275
1964	JAN JANSSEN	NETHERLANDS	208
1965	JAN JANSSEN	NETHERLANDS	144
1966	WILLY PLANCKAERT	BELGIUM	211
1967	JAN JANSSEN	NETHERLANDS	154
1968	FRANCO BITOSSI	ITALY	241
1969	EDDY MERCKX	BELGIUM	244
1970	WALTER GODEFROOT	BELGIUM	212
1971	EDDY MERCKX	BELGIUM	202
1972	EDDY MERCKX	BELGIUM	196
1973	HERMAN VAN SPRINGEL	BELGIUM	187
1974	PATRICK SERCU	BELGIUM	283
1975	RIK VAN LINDEN	BELGIUM	342
1976	FREDDY MAERTENS	BELGIUM	293
1977	JACQUES ESCLASSAN	FRANCE	236
1978	FREDDY MAERTENS	BELGIUM	242
1979	BERNARD HINAULT	FRANCE	253
1980	RUDY PEVENAGE	BELGIUM	194
1981	FREDDY MAERTENS	BELGIUM	428
1982	SEAN KELLY	IRELAND	429
1983	SEAN KELLY	IRELAND	360
1984	FRANK HOSTE	BELGIUM	322
1985	SEAN KELLY	IRELAND	434
1986	ERIC VANDERAERDEN	BELGIUM	277
1987	JEAN-PAUL VAN POPPEL	NETHERLANDS	263
1988	EDDY PLANCKAERT	BELGIUM	278
1989	SEAN KELLY	IRELAND	277
1990	OLAF LUDWIG	GERMANY	256
1991	DJAMOLIDINE ABDOUJAPAROV	UZBEKISTAN	316
1992	LAURENT JALABERT	FRANCE	293
1993	DJAMOLIDINE ABDOUJAPAROV	UZBEKISTAN	298
1994	DJAMOLIDINE ABDOUJAPAROV	UZBEKISTAN	322
1995	LAURENT JALABERT	FRANCE	333
1996	ERIK ZABEL	GERMANY	335
1997	ERIK ZABEL	GERMANY	350
1998	ERIK ZABEL	GERMANY	327
1999	ERIK ZABEL	GERMANY	323
2000	ERIK ZABEL	GERMANY	321
2001	ERIK ZABEL	GERMANY	252
2002	ROBBIE MCEWEN	AUSTRALIA	280
2003	BADEN COOKE	AUSTRALIA	216
2004	ROBBIE MCEWEN	AUSTRALIA	272
2005	THOR HUSHOVD	NORWAY	194
2006	ROBBIE MCEWEN	AUSTRALIA	288
2007	TOM BOONEN	BELGIUM	256
2008	OSCAR FREIRE	SPAIN	270
2009	THOR HUSHOVD	NORWAY	280
2010	ALESSANDRO PETACCHI	ITALY	243
2011	MARK CAVENDISH	GREAT BRITAIN	334
2012	PETER SAGAN	SLOVAKIA	421
2013	PETER SAGAN	SLOVAKIA	409

MOST TOUR WINS

RANK	RIDER	COUNTRY	WINS	YEARS
1	JACQUES ANQUETIL	FRANCE	5	1957, 1961, 1962, 1963, 1964
	EDDY MERCKX	BELGIUM	5	1969, 1970, 1971, 1972, 1974
	BERNARD HINAULT	FRANCE	5	1978, 1979, 1981, 1982, 1985
	MIGUEL INDURAIN	SPAIN	5	1991, 1992, 1993, 1994, 1995
5	PHILIPPE THYS	BELGIUM	3	1913, 1914, 1920
	LOUISON BOBET	FRANCE	3	1953, 1954, 1955
	GREG LEMOND	UNITED STATES	3	1986, 1989, 1990
8	LUCIEN PETIT-BRETON	FRANCE	2	1907, 1908
	FIRMIN LAMBOT	BELGIUM	2	1919, 1922
	OTTAVIO BOTTECCHIA	ITALY	2	1924, 1925
	NICOLAS FRANTZ	LUXEMBOURG	2	1927, 1928
	ANDRÉ LEDUCQ	FRANCE	2	1930, 1932
	ANTONIN MAGNE	FRANCE	2	1931, 1934
	SYLVÈRE MAES	BELGIUM	2	1936, 1939
	GINO BARTALI	ITALY	2	1938, 1948
	FAUSTO COPPI	ITALY	2	1949, 1952
	BERNARD THÉVENET	FRANCE	2	1975, 1977
	LAURENT FIGNON	FRANCE	2	1983, 1984
	ALBERTO CONTADOR	SPAIN	2	2007, 2009

MOST STAGE WINS

RANK	NAME	COUNTRY	WINS
1	EDDY MERCKX	BELGIUM	34
2	BERNARD HINAULT	FRANCE	28
3	MARK CAVENDISH	UNITED KINGDOM	25
	ANDRÉ LEDUCQ	FRANCE	25
5	ANDRÉ DARRIGADE	FRANCE	22
6	NICOLAS FRANTZ	LUXEMBOURG	20
7	FRANÇOIS FABER	LUXEMBOURG	19
8	JEAN ALAVOINE	FRANCE	17
9	JACQUES ANQUETIL	FRANCE	16
	RENÉ LE GREVES	FRANCE	16
	CHARLES PÉLISSIER	FRANCE	16
12	FREDDY MAERTENS	BELGIUM	15
13	PHILIPPE THYS	BELGIUM	13
	LOUIS TROUSSELIER	FRANCE	13
15	GINO BARTALI	ITALY	12
	MARIO CIPOLLINI	ITALY	12
	MIGUEL INDURAIN	SPAIN	12
	ROBBIE MCEWEN	AUSTRALIA	12
	ERIK ZABEL	GERMANY	12
20	JEAN AERTS	BELGIUM	11
	LOUISON BOBET	FRANCE	11
	RAFFAELE DI PACO	ITALY	11
23	MAURICE ARCHAMBAUD	FRANCE	10
	CHARLY GAUL	LUXEMBOURG	10
	WALTER GODEFROOT	BELGIUM	10
	GERRIE KNETEMANN	NETHERLANDS	10
	ANTONIN MAGNE	FRANCE	10
	HENRI PÉLISSIER	FRANCE	10
	JAN RAAS	NETHERLANDS	10
	JOOP ZOETEMELK	NETHERLANDS	10
	THOR HUSHOVD	NORWAY	10

MOST FINISHES

NAME	COUNTRY	FINISHES		STARTS	
JOOP ZOETEMELK	NETHERLANDS	16	(1970-1973, 1975-1986)	16	(1970-1973, 1975-1986)
STUART O'GRADY	AUSTRALIA	15	(1997-1999, 2001-2006, 2008, 2009-2013)	17	(1997-2013)
LUCIEN VAN IMPE	BELGIUM	15	(1969-1981, 1983, 1985)	15	(1969-1981, 1983, 1985)
VIATCHESLAV EKIMOV	RUSSIA	15	(1990-1998, 2000-2004, 2006)	15	(1990-1998, 2000-2004, 2006)
GEORGE HINCAPIE	UNITED STATES	13	(1997-2003, 2007-2012)	17	(1996-2012)
JENS VOIGT	GERMANY	13	(1998-2002, 2004, 2006-2008, 2010-2013)	16	(1998-2013)
GUY NULENS	BELGIUM	13	(1981-1982, 1984-1994)	15	(1980-1994)
ERIK ZABEL	GERMANY	13	(1995-2004, 2006-2008)	14	(1994-2004, 2006-2008)
PHIL ANDERSON	AUSTRALIA	13	(1981-1988, 1989-1994)	13	(1981-1988, 1989-1994)
SEAN KELLY	IRELAND	12	(1978-1985, 1988-1990, 1992)	14	(1978-1985, 1987-1992)
ANDRÉ DARRIGADE	FRANCE	12	(1953-1962, 1964-1965)	14	(1953-1966)
JOAQUIM AGOSTINHO	PORTUGAL	12	(1969-1975, 1977-1980, 1983)	13	(1969-1975, 1977-1981, 1983)
CHRISTOPHE MOREAU	FRANCE	11	(1996-1997, 1999-2000, 2003-2007, 2009-2010)	15	(1996-2010)
RAYMOND POULIDOR	FRANCE	11	(1962-1965, 1967, 1969-1972, 1974-1976)	14	(1962-1976)
GERRIE KNETEMANN	NETHERLANDS	11	(1974-1975, 1977-1982, 1984, 1986-1987)	13	(1974-1982, 1984, 1986-1988)
HENK LUBBERDING	NETHERLANDS	11	(1977-1985, 1987, 1989)	13	(1977-1989)
LANCE ARMSTRONG	UNITED STATES	10	(1995, 1999-2005, 2009-2010)	13	(1993-1996, 1999-2005, 2009-2010)
JEAN DOTTO	FRANCE	10	(1951-1952, 1954, 1956-1957, 1959-1963)	13	(1951-1963)
JEAN-PIERRE GENET	FRANCE	10	(1964-1965, 1967-1971, 1973-1974, 1976)	13	(1964-1976)
GILBERT DUCLOS-LASSALLE	FRANCE	9	(1979, 1981-1983, 1985, 1987-1988, 1990-1991)	13	(1979-1983, 1985-1988, 1990-1993)
FRANÇOIS MAHÉ	FRANCE	9	(1953-1955, 1957, 1959-1960, 1962-1963, 1965)	13	(1953-1965)
MARC WAUTERS	BELGIUM	8	(1993-1994, 1996, 2000, 2002-2005)	13	(1992-1997, 1999-2005)
JULES DELOFFRE	FRANCE	7	(1908-1914, 1921)	14	(1908-1914, 1920-1928)
DIDIER ROUS	FRANCE	7	(1995, 1997, 2000-2001, 2003, 2005-2006)	13	(1994-2006)

MOST GREEN JERSEY WINS

RANK	NAME	COUNTRY	WINS	YEARS
1	ERIK ZABEL	GERMANY	6	1996, 1997, 1998, 1999, 2000, 2001
2	SEAN KELLY	IRELAND	4	1982, 1983, 1985, 1989
3	JAN JANSSEN	NETHERLANDS	3	1964, 1965, 1967
	EDDY MERCKX	BELGIUM	3	1969, 1971, 1972
	FREDDY MAERTENS	BELGIUM	3	1976, 1978, 1981
	DJAMOLIDINE ABDOUJAPAROV	UZBEKISTAN	3	1991, 1993, 1994
	ROBBIE MCEWEN	AUSTRALIA	3	2002, 2004, 2006
8	STAN OCKERS	BELGIUM	2	1955, 1956
	JEAN GRACZYK	FRANCE	2	1958, 1960
	ANDRÉ DARRIGADE	FRANCE	2	1959, 1961
	LAURENT JALABERT	FRANCE	2	1992, 1995
	THOR HUSHOVD	NORWAY	2	2005, 2009
	PETER SAGAN	SLOVAKIA	2	2012, 2013

MOST POLKA-DOT JERSEY WINS

RANK	NAME	COUNTRY	WINS	YEARS
1	RICHARD VIRENQUE	FRANCE	7	1994, 1995, 1996, 1997, 1999, 2003, 2004
2	FEDERICO BAHAMONTES	SPAIN	6	1954, 1958, 1959, 1962, 1963, 1964
	LUCIEN VAN IMPE	BELGIUM	6	1971, 1972, 1975, 1977, 1981, 1983
4	JULIO JIMÉNEZ	SPAIN	3	1965, 1966, 1967
5	FELICIEN VERVAECKE	BELGIUM	2	1935, 1937
	GINO BARTALI	ITALY	2	1938, 1948
	FAUSTO COPPI	ITALY	2	1949, 1952
	CHARLY GAUL	LUXEMBOURG	2	1955, 1956
	IMERIO MASSIGNAN	ITALY	2	1960, 1961
	EDDY MERCKX	BELGIUM	2	1969, 1970
	LUIS HERRERA	COLOMBIA	2	1985, 1987
	CLAUDIO CHIAPPUCCI	ITALY	2	1991, 1992
	LAURENT JALABERT	FRANCE	2	2001, 2002
	MICHAEL RASMUSSEN	DENMARK	2	2005, 2006

WITHOUT THESE HEROES, I COULDN'T HAVE MADE THE BOOK:

MARA JOUSTRA
HANSJE JOUSTRA
WALTER BREUKERS
PAUL DUJARDIN
AREND HOSMAN
IRENE KUNST
DENNIS DEELEN
MY MOTHER AND IN-LAWS...

... AND ESPECIALLY YVON AND LENA, MY OWN HEROES.

This edition first published by Head of Zeus in 2014

Text and illustration © Jan Cleijne, 2013, 2014
Translation © Michele Hutchison & Laura Watkinson, 2014
Originally published as *Helden van de Tour* by
Uitgeverij Oog & Blik | De Bezige Bij, Amsterdam

This book was published with the support of the Dutch Foundation for Literature.

ISBN 9781781859995

Head of Zeus,
45-47 Clerkenwell Green,
London, EC1R 0HT

www.headofzeus.com
www.jancleijne.nl